TENANT'S
SURVIVAL GUIDE

FOR ARIZONA RENTERS

By

Carlton C. Casler, Attorney at Law

CONSUMER LAW BOOKS PUBLISHING HOUSE

ACKNOWLEDGMENTS

My sincerest thanks to Bruce and Lee Fischer, of Golden West Publishers, for without their help, this book could not have become a reality.

For their assistance with editing, cite checking and a multitude of other tasks, my gratitude to:

Valerie Fasolo
Warren C. Swartz

DEDICATED to the memory of James E. Casler, Jr.

Casler, Carlton C., 1958-

Tenant's Survival Guide / by Carlton C. Casler.
p. cm.
Includes bibliographical references and index.
ISBN 1-881436-01-2

1. Landlord and tenant -- Arizona -- Popular works.   I. Title.

KFA2517.Z9C37 1994   346.791'043'4
                                        QBI93-22568

P-CIP

C. Casler, *TENANT'S SURVIVAL GUIDE (ARIZONA)* (1994)
ISBN 1-881436-01-2

CONSUMER LAW BOOKS PUBLISHING HOUSE
c/o Golden West Publishers
4113 North Longview
Phoenix, Arizona 85014

Foreword

I am a residential landlord, but I have also been a residential and a commercial tenant. Furthermore, as an attorney, I have represented many tenants (and landlords). I have heard and made arguments for both sides. I have written the *Tenant's Survival Guide* from the tenant's point of view. What this means to you is that the recommendations contained herein are intended to protect and benefit you, **the tenant**.

A thorough knowledge of the law provides a tenant with an enormous advantage, but not all tenants have the time and/or inclination to dedicate their lives to the study of landlord/tenant law. Consequently, the *Tenant's Survival Guide* was written to give you: (1) a general working knowledge of landlord/tenant law, in a short period of time; and (2) a detailed source book for the times when you need a detailed answer to a specific question. Toward that end, the entire text of the latest version of the Arizona Residential Landlord and Tenant Act and the forcible detainer statutes are reprinted in Appendix C.

Arizona law clearly favors tenants, not landlords. Nevertheless, not all tenants know the law and not all landlords follow the law (either intentionally or unintentionally). The *Tenant's Survival Guide* will tell you the law in Arizona as it applies to landlords and tenants. This book will tell you what your landlord can do under the law and, more importantly, what s/he *cannot* do under the law. The *Tenant's Survival Guide* will also tell you what **you** can and cannot do under the law. The *Tenant's Survival Guide* will explain what to do when your landlord fails to perform his contractual obligations (i.e., repair the unit, keep the premises safe, provide utilities, etc.) and will tell you what your rights and remedies are in each instance. This book will also inform you what you may (or must) do when your landlord attempts to terminate your lease or evict you.

The *Tenant's Survival Guide*, however, goes far beyond a mindless narration of Arizona law -- it will give you "real world," practical advice. Remember, I am a landlord. As a landlord, I recognize, and so should you, that being a landlord is a business. The law is only one factor that a landlord/businessman considers when making a business decision. Therefore, in addition to the law, this book will discuss some vitally important practical solutions that oftentimes yield more desirable results than the "legal" solution. For example, take the all-too-typical scenario where the tenant is two months into his one-year lease and, for whatever reason, wants to terminate the lease and move. The legal solutions are clear: (1) do not terminate until the end of the lease; or (2) terminate and face the consequences (i.e., landlord may sue you for rent due until the end of the lease or until s/he re-rents it). The practical solution is to offer the landlord some amount of money (i.e., $100, $200, $300, or more, depending on *your* facts) in exchange for a complete release of liability. This has the distinct advantage of limiting your liability (not to mention that you will not have to lose any sleep over whether or not your landlord will be "chasing you down" to garnish your bank accounts and/or wages), your credit will not be adversely affected, and, more importantly, you will probably be able to use this landlord as a reference -- many advantages for payment of a nominal sum.

The foregoing recommendation, and those that follow, cannot be found in any law book. The foregoing example, however, is typical of the practical recommendations made throughout the *Tenant's Survival Guide*. They are practical solutions -- the product of years of experience, both mine and my clients'. Prepare yourself -- you are about to discover a plethora of sensible solutions to your most common problems.

CAVEAT from the author and publisher:

The *Tenant's Survival Guide* covers a wide range of laws and rules affecting the residential landlord and tenant relationship in Arizona, but it is not an exhaustive synopsis of all laws, rules and regulations that impact upon such matters. Moreover, because many differing factual scenarios are possible for each individual tenant, the author and publisher cannot, and do not, assume any responsibility for conclusions drawn by the reader or for the conduct, acts or omissions of the reader or others taken in reliance hereon.

The author and publisher strongly recommend that you consult with your own attorney to obtain competent legal advice with regard to your own particular circumstances. In any instance where you have some doubt regarding application of the law to your specific circumstances, consult your attorney. If you don't have an attorney -- GET ONE! If you are at a loss as to how to find an attorney, call the Lawyer Referral Service at (602) 257-4434. If you cannot afford an attorney, consult Appendix D - Legal Service Organizations and Referral Services.

CONTENTS AT A GLANCE

QUICK REFERENCE SECTION (Gray edge pages)   QRS - I

CHAPTER

1. PRELIMINARY MATTERS   1

2. LEGAL ADVICE TO TENANTS   6

3. PREPARATION   14
   A. APPLICABILITY/SCOPE OF THE ARIZONA RESIDENTIAL LANDLORD AND TENANT ACT   14
   B. REVIEW YOUR RENTAL AGREEMENT   18
   C. OTHER FORMS YOU NEED TO BE FAMILIAR WITH   29

4. APPLYING TO BE A TENANT   37
   A. FINDING A SUITABLE RENTAL UNIT   37
   B. LOOK AT THE UNIT BEFORE COMPLETING AN APPLICATION   39
   C. THE APPLICATION PROCESS   39
   D. DISCRIMINATION   47
   E. TERM OF TENANCY   49
   F. READ THE RENTAL AGREEMENT   49

5. HOW TO SOLVE COMMON TENANT PROBLEMS   50
   A. PREVENT TENANT PROBLEMS   51
   B. COMMON TENANT PROBLEMS   51
   C. TENANT REMEDIES   60

6. TERMINATING TENANCY AND EVICTIONS   70
   A. HOW AND BY WHOM TENANCY MAY BE TERMINATED   71
   B. AFTER TENANCY IS TERMINATED   75
   C. EVICTIONS   76
   D. THE SPECIAL DETAINER ACTION: ANATOMY OF AN EVICTION   82

APPENDICES

   A. CHECKLISTS   102
   B. FORMS   107
   C. COMPLETE TEXT OF RELEVANT STATUTES   122
   D. LIST OF LEGAL SERVICE ORGANIZATIONS AND REFERRAL SERVICES   144

   GLOSSARY   146

   INDEX   152

TABLE OF CONTENTS

The Author   (back cover)

Foreword   i

TABLE OF CONTENTS   iii

QUICK REFERENCE SECTION (Gray edge pages)   **QRS - I**

SUMMARY OF TOPICS ADDRESSED IN THE QUICK REFERENCE SECTION
    A.   THE ARIZONA RESIDENTIAL LANDLORD AND TENANT ACT QRS-IV
    B.   THE APPLICATION   QRS-IV
    C.   FORMS   QRS-V
    D.   THE RENTAL AGREEMENT   QRS-V
    E.   DEPOSITS   QRS-VI
    F.   COMMON TENANT PROBLEMS   QRS-VII
    G.   NONPAYMENT OF RENT   QRS-VIII
    H.   EVICTION   QRS-IX

CHAPTER

  1. PRELIMINARY MATTERS   **1**
      A.   HOW TO GET THE MOST BENEFIT FROM THIS BOOK   1
      B.   WHAT THIS BOOK COVERS   2
      C.   CONVENTIONS   2
      D.   COMMENTS AND SUGGESTIONS; ERRORS   5

  2. LEGAL ADVICE TO TENANTS   **6**

<u>CHAPTER</u>

3. PREPARATION   **14**

  A. APPLICABILITY/SCOPE OF THE ARIZONA
      RESIDENTIAL LANDLORD AND TENANT ACT   14
      (1) Exclusion #5 and the Case of the On-Site Manager   17
      (2) Exclusion #7 -- Public Housing   18

  B. REVIEW YOUR RENTAL AGREEMENT   18
      (1) Rental Agreement MUST's   19
      (2) Rental Agreement CANNOT's   20
      (3) Rental Agreement SHOULD's   21
      (4) Things to LOOK OUT for in your Rental Agreement   23
      (5) Deposits   26

  C. OTHER FORMS YOU NEED TO BE FAMILIAR WITH   29

4. APPLYING TO BE A TENANT   **37**

  A. FINDING A SUITABLE RENTAL UNIT   37
      (1) Do it Yourself *OR* Real Estate Agents/Brokers,
           Locator Services   37
      (2) Curb Appeal   38
      (3) Interior Appearance   38
      (4) The Neighborhood   39

  B. LOOK AT THE UNIT BEFORE
      COMPLETING AN APPLICATION   39

  C. THE APPLICATION PROCESS   39

  D. DISCRIMINATION   47

  E. TERM OF TENANCY   49

  F. READ THE RENTAL AGREEMENT   49

CHAPTER

5. HOW TO SOLVE COMMON TENANT PROBLEMS   **50**

    A.   PREVENT TENANT PROBLEMS   51

    B.   COMMON TENANT PROBLEMS   51
        (1)   What if I Can't Pay the Rent on Time, or at All?   51
        (2)   Can the Landlord Assess and Collect a Late Fee
            when I Pay Rent Late?   52
        (3)   Under What Circumstances can the Landlord
            Terminate my Lease?   53
        (4)   Under What Circumstances Can I Terminate the Lease?   53
        (5)   Harassing/Trespassing Landlord   54
        (6)   Noisy Neighbor and Neighbor Conflicts   55
        (7)   Parking Problems   56
            (a)   Tenants/guests improperly parked   56
            (b)   Parking in areas not designated for parking   58
            (c)   Tenant taking too many spaces   59
            (d)   Parking of commercial vehicles   59
            (e)   Vehicle maintenance   59
        (8)   What If the Landlord Won't Make Repairs?   59

    C.   TENANT REMEDIES   60
        (1)   Fourteen-Day Notice of Termination of Rental Agreement
            for Material Noncompliance with Rental Agreement   60
        (2)   Ten-Day Notice of Termination of Rental Agreement
            for Noncompliance with Rental Agreement Materially
            Affecting Health and Safety   64
        (3)   Notice of Wrongful Failure to Supply Essential Services   66
        (4)   Notice of Termination or Rent Reduction Because of
            Fire or Casualty Damage   68

CHAPTER

6. TERMINATING TENANCY AND EVICTIONS   **70**
   A.   HOW AND BY WHOM TENANCY MAY BE TERMINATED   71
      (1) By Mutual Agreement   71
      (2) The Tenant Terminates Tenancy   72
      (3) The Landlord Terminates Tenancy   72
      (4) "Adequate" Notice   73

   B.   AFTER TENANCY IS TERMINATED   75
      (1) Damage to the Unit   75
      (2) Refund of Deposit(s)   76

   C.   EVICTIONS   76
      (1) "WHEN" The Landlord May Evict A Tenant   76
         (a) Material Noncompliance With Rental Agreement   77
         (b) Noncompliance with the Rental Agreement
             Materially Affecting Health and Safety   78
         (c) Material and Irreparable Noncompliance   80
         (d) Nonpayment of Rent   81

      (2) "HOW" The Landlord May Evict A Tenant   81
         (a) What the landlord CANNOT do   81
         (b) What the landlord may do   82

   D.   THE SPECIAL DETAINER ACTION: Anatomy of an EVICTION   82
      (1) EVICTION PROCESS FOR: Material Noncompliance   85
         with the Rental Agreement; Noncompliance with the
         Rental Agreement that Materially Affects Health & Safety;
         and Material and Irreparable Breach of the Rental Agreement
         (a) Final Steps   91
         (b) Inspection   91
         (c) Security Deposit   91
         (d) Lawsuit for Damages   91
         (e) Additional Important Notes   91

      (2) EVICTION PROCESS FOR: Nonpayment of Rent   94
         (a) Final Steps   100
         (b) Inspection   100
         (c) Security Deposit   100
         (d) Lawsuit for Damages   100
         (e) Additional Important Notes   100

APPENDICES

A. CHECKLISTS   102
- What to do when you have finished reading this book
  and are ready to rent a unit   103
- Review your rental agreement   104
- Deposits (everything you need to know)   105

B. FORMS   107
- Property Inspection Checklist   108
- Notice to Terminate Tenancy (by tenant)   110
- Ten-Day Notice of Termination of Rental Agreement
  for Noncompliance with Rental Agreement Materially
  Affecting Health and Safety   112
- Fourteen-Day Notice of Termination of Rental Agreement
  for Material Noncompliance with Rental Agreement   114
- Notice of Termination of Rental Agreement Because
  of Damage Due to Fire or Casualty   116
- Notice of Tenant's Intent to Effect Repairs   118
- Notice of Wrongful Failure to Provide Essential Services   120

C. COMPLETE TEXT OF RELEVANT STATUTES   122
- Arizona Residential Landlord and Tenant Act   123
- Landlord and Tenant Statutes   137
- Forcible Detainer Statutes   140

D. LIST OF LEGAL SERVICE ORGANIZATIONS
AND REFERRAL SERVICES   144

GLOSSARY   146

INDEX   152

QUICK REFERENCE SECTION

The Quick Reference Section was specifically designed to quickly answer the questions that tenants most frequently ask. This Section will give you a short, practical answer to each question and then refer you to the section of the book that discusses that particular issue or topic in depth.

The questions that are most frequently asked may be categorized into eight major areas. Listed on the next two pages are the major areas and the questions addressed within each area.

SUMMARY OF TOPICS
ADDRESSED IN THE QUICK REFERENCE SECTION

A. THE ARIZONA RESIDENTIAL LANDLORD AND TENANT ACT.

- Where does the Act apply?
- Does the Act apply to me?
- Does the Act apply to me if I am an on-site manager?

B. THE APPLICATION.

- May the landlord discriminate against certain people when evaluating whether or not to accept an applicant as a tenant?

C. FORMS.

- What are the most important forms?
- Where do I get forms?

D. THE RENTAL AGREEMENT.

- Is an oral rental agreement binding?
- Which is best: a month-to-month tenancy or a long-term lease?

E. DEPOSITS.

- What is the maximum security deposit the landlord can collect?
- Must the landlord pay me interest on my security deposit during the time that s/he holds it?
- When must the landlord refund my deposits?
- What if the landlord fails to return all or part of my deposit(s)?

F. COMMON TENANT PROBLEMS.

- How much notice must I give to terminate tenancy?
- What if the landlord fails to make required repairs?
- What if the premises are completely or partially destroyed by fire or casualty?
- Can the landlord enter my rental unit without advance notice?

G. NONPAYMENT OF RENT.

- What if I can't pay the rent on time, or at all?
- Can the landlord assess and collect a late fee?
- May the landlord shut off my utilities for non-payment of rent?
- May the landlord lock me out of my unit and/or seize my personal property for non-payment of rent?
- What do I do if I am being evicted?

H. EVICTION.

- When can the landlord serve me with a Seven-Day Notice to Pay or Quit?
- What must be contained in the Seven-Day Notice to Pay or Quit for the notice to be legally sufficient?
- What other legal grounds does the landlord have for evicting me?
- What are the steps in an eviction?
- What defenses can I raise if I am being evicted?

A. THE ARIZONA RESIDENTIAL LANDLORD AND TENANT ACT.

• Where does the Act apply?

The Act is state law and is applicable statewide. The only exceptions are instances where state law is pre-empted by federal law (i.e., on Indian reservations, Section 8 Housing).

See Chapter 3, Section A.

• Does the Act apply to me?

The Act applies to the rental of dwelling units. Therefore, generally speaking, if you rent a residential dwelling, the Act applies to you, but there are some exclusions.

See Chapter 3, Section A.

• Does the Act apply to me if I am on-site manager?

Maybe. On-site managers are specifically excluded from the scope of the Act. Nevertheless, the landlord may elect to have the Act apply to his/her on-site manager if s/he so desires. As a practical matter, most landlords have the on-site manager sign the same form of rental agreement that regular tenants sign. Most rental agreements state that the Act applies, thereby electing to have the Act apply in a case where it need not apply, which is *extremely* favorable to the on-site manager/tenant.

See Chapter 3, Section A.

B. THE APPLICATION.

• May the landlord discriminate against certain people when evaluating whether or not to accept an applicant as a tenant?

The landlord cannot discriminate against an applicant based on race, color, religion, national origin, sex, handicap or because the applicant has children. The landlord may, however, discriminate against an applicant on *any other* basis. For example, the landlord may deny to accept an applicant because s/he drives a motorcycle or because s/he is a lawyer.

See Chapter 4, Section D.

C. FORMS.

• What are the most important forms?

The rental agreement is the most important form. It is the primary source of your legal rights and remedies. As a tenant, you normally have minimal impact on the content of the rental agreement, but, at a minimum, you should read and understand the entire rental agreement before signing it. You should also have your attorney review the rental agreement.

> *See* Chapter 3, Section B.

The Tenant Application (which may include a Tenant Information Sheet) and the Property Inspection Checklist are also very important because, as a general rule, they are used whenever you rent real property.

> *See* Chapter 3, Section C and Chapter 4, Section C.

• Where do I get forms?

The landlord will normally provide you with a rental agreement form to sign; s/he may also provide you with the other forms that you will need. Other forms that you may need, as a tenant, are available from most stationery stores. You may also use the forms contained in the *Tenant's Survival Guide*.

> *See* Chapter 3, Sections B and C (discussing forms).
> *See* Appendix B (blank forms).

D. THE RENTAL AGREEMENT.

• Is an oral rental agreement binding?

Yes, but I strongly recommend against oral rental agreements.

> *See* Chapter 3, Section B.

• Which is best: a month-to-month tenancy or a long-term lease?

Both types of tenancy have advantages and disadvantages. Only you can decide which is best for you. The *Tenant's Survival Guide* discusses some specific considerations that will have an impact on your decision.

> *See* Chapter 4, Section E.

E. __DEPOSITS.__

- What is the maximum security deposit the landlord can collect?

    The landlord cannot collect a security deposit equal to more than one and one-half month's rent. A security deposit does not include cleaning or redecorating deposits. Therefore, the landlord may also require the tenant to pay a reasonable charge for cleaning or redecorating.

    See Chapter 3, Section B(2) and (5).

- Must the landlord pay me interest on my security deposit during the time that s/he holds it?

    There is no requirement in the Act for the landlord to pay interest on security deposits or any other type of deposit, but the landlord may if s/he wishes.

    See Chapter 3, Section B(5).

- When must the landlord refund my deposits?

    The landlord must refund your deposits OR provide you with an itemized list of deductions taken from your deposits along with a refund of the remaining balance of your security deposit, if any, **within fourteen days** after: (1) termination of the rental agreement, (2) transfer of possession of the premises to the landlord, and (3) demand by the tenant upon the landlord to refund his/her deposits.

    See Chapter 3, Section B(5) and Chapter 3, Section C(6).

- What if the landlord fails to return all or part of my deposit(s)?

    Your landlord is liable to you for **twice** the amount of your deposits that s/he wrongfully has withheld.

    See Chapter 3, Section B(5) and Chapter 3, Section C(6).

F. <u>COMMON TENANT PROBLEMS.</u>

Cross Reference
- Chapter 5, Section B (Common Tenant Problems).

- How much notice must I give to terminate tenancy?

  The answer may be no notice whatsoever or several months' notice, depending upon the type of tenancy that you have and the language of your rental agreement.

  See Chapter 6, Section A(4).

- What if the landlord fails to make required repairs?

  Depending on the nature of the repair, you may:

  (1) Have the work done by a licensed contractor and deduct the cost from the next month's rent, not to exceed the greater of $150.00 or one-half month's rent. You must first provide the landlord with written notice and a "reasonable" opportunity to effect repairs.

  See Chapter 5, Section C(1).

  (2) You may issue the Landlord a "Fourteen-Day Notice of Termination of Rental Agreement for Noncompliance with the Rental Agreement." If the landlord fails to effect repairs, you may terminate the rental agreement and, if applicable, sue the landlord for damages.

  See Chapter 5, Section C(1).

  (3) You may issue the Landlord a "Ten-Day Notice of Termination of Rental Agreement for Noncompliance with the Rental Agreement Materially Affecting Health and Safety." If the landlord fails to effect repairs, you may terminate the rental agreement and, if applicable, sue the landlord for damages.

  See Chapter 5, Section C(2).

  (Answer to this question continues on next page)

- What if the landlord fails to make required repairs? (Answer continued)

    (4) If the repair involves failure of the landlord to supply heat, air conditioning, cooling, water, hot water or essential services, you may: (a) obtain substitute services and deduct their cost from the rent, (b) recover damages for the diminished rental value of the premises, OR (c) obtain substitute housing for the period of the landlord's noncompliance (other limitations apply).

    See Chapter 5, Section C(3).

- What if the premises are completely or partially destroyed by fire or casualty?

    The tenant may vacate the unit or, if the unit is "liveable," the tenant may vacate the area that is unusable and deduct the diminished value of the unit from the rent.

    See Chapter 5, Section C(4).

- Can the landlord enter my rental unit without advance notice?

    No, except in cases of emergency.

    See Chapter 5, Section A(5).

G. NONPAYMENT OF RENT.

- What if I can't pay the rent on time, or at all?

    The landlord may immediately begin eviction proceedings, but if you talk to your landlord about the problem s/he *may* "work with you" and give you additional time.

    See Chapter 5, Section B(1).

- Can the landlord assess and collect a late fee?

    Only if there is a late fee provision in your written rental agreement.

    See Chapter 5, Section B(2).

- May the landlord shut off my utilities for non-payment of rent?

    Absolutely not.

    See Chapter 6, Section C(2)(a).

- May the landlord lock me out of my unit and/or seize my personal property for non-payment of rent?

    No. Distraint for rent is prohibited under the Act.

    See Chapter 6, Section C(2)(a).

- What do I do if I am being evicted?

    There is no short answer to this question: If you are being evicted for nonpayment of rent, *see* Chapter 6, Section D(2), if you are being evicted for some other type of noncompliance with the rental agreement, *see* Chapter 6, Section D(1).

H. <u>EVICTION.</u>

- What other legal grounds does the landlord have for evicting me?

    Eviction must be based on one of four categories of tenant conduct: (1) a material noncompliance with the rental agreement, (2) a noncompliance that materially affects health and safety, (3) a breach that is both material and irreparable or (4) nonpayment of rent. Do not confuse eviction with the decision not to renew tenancy. Neither the landlord nor the tenant need any reason whatsoever to not renew tenancy. Therefore, if you are on a month-to-month tenancy, which is renewed (or not) each and every month, either you or the landlord may choose to not renew tenancy for any reason whatsoever with only thirty days notice (Note: the rental agreement may require more or less than thirty days notice).

    See Chapter 6, Section A.

- When can the landlord serve a Seven-Day Notice to Pay or Quit?

    The landlord may serve you with a Seven-Day Notice on the first day after rent is due and remains unpaid. For example, if rent is due on the first day of the month, the landlord may serve the Seven-Day Notice on the second day of the month, *even though* the rental agreement provides that rent is not delinquent until the fifth day of the month.

    See Chapter 6, Section C(1)(d) and Section D(2) (Step 1).

• What must be contained in the Seven-Day Notice to Pay or Quit for the notice to be legally sufficient?

The Seven-Day Notice must inform the tenant that rent has not been paid and that the landlord intends to terminate the rental agreement if due and unpaid rent is not paid within seven days of the notice.

See Chapter 6, Section D(2) (Step 1).

• What are the steps in an eviction?

For the steps in an eviction for a material noncompliance with the rental agreement, a noncompliance that materially affects health and safety, and/or a breach that is both material and irreparable,

See Chapter 6, Sections C and D.
Flowchart 1, on page 84, graphically depicts the steps.

For the steps in an eviction for a nonpayment of rent

See Chapter 6, Sections C and D.
Flowchart 2, on page 93, graphically depicts the steps.

• What defenses can I raise if I am being evicted?

The defenses available will depend on your specific facts. Some specific examples are given in Chapter 6.

See Chapter 6, Sections D(1) (Additional Important Notes) and D(2) (Additional Important Notes).

(This page intentionally left blank)

CHAPTER 1

PRELIMINARY MATTERS

Summary of Chapter

- How to get the most benefit from this book
- What this book covers
- Conventions
- Comments and Suggestions; Errors

A. HOW TO GET THE MOST BENEFIT FROM THIS BOOK.

First, go back and briefly scan the table of contents. Get a feel for the topics covered and the general layout of the book. In the front of the book is a Quick Reference Section. This Section is specifically designed to concisely answer the questions that tenants most frequently ask. In the event the answer given in the Quick Reference Section is insufficient (i.e., not clear, not exactly applicable to your situation, etc.), the Quick Reference Section directs you to the section of the book that deals with that subject in depth. An extensive index is included in the back of the book which will refer you to both the Quick Reference Section and the section of the book that addresses, at length, the topic you are looking for. For example, if you want information regarding the Seven-Day Notice to Pay or Quit, you may look under Pay or Quit, Seven-Day Notice, 7-Day Notice, or Notice. If you run into a word or phrase that is unfamiliar, a glossary of terms is included at the back of the book. Important words are *highlighted* (like this -- bold and italics) the first time they are used and the first time the word is discussed at length. All highlighted words, plus others, are found in the glossary.

Second, read Chapters One through Six.

Third, consult Checklist Number 1 and Checklist Number 2, in Appendix A. Checklist Number 1 provides you with guidance *after* you have finished reading the *Tenant's Survival Guide*. Checklist Number 2 encourages you to review your existing rental agreement. These Checklists contain vital information -- READ THEM !

Finally, but most important, implement what you have learned and keep the *Tenant's Survival Guide* handy.

1

B. WHAT THIS BOOK COVERS.

The Table of Contents reveals the precise areas covered by the *Tenant's Survival Guide*. The main focus, however, in addition to informing you of the various laws that you should know, is to provide you with sound, *practical* suggestions. The *Tenant's Survival Guide* will tell you what provisions to look for, and "look out for," in your rental agreement; what the landlord may do under the law and what s/he cannot do; what your rights are under the Arizona Landlord and Tenant Act; and what to do if your rights are violated.

You should never lose sight of the fact that being a landlord is a business. If/when you encounter a problem with your landlord, the solution you propose to the landlord will only be accepted if it makes good business sense to him/her. Therefore, this book also covers practical solutions to common tenant problems.

C. CONVENTIONS.

The *Tenant's Survival Guide* has been divided into two main sections: (1) the **Quick Reference Section**, at the front of the book; and (2) the **main body** of the book, consisting of six Chapters. The Quick Reference Section <u>does not</u> employ any of the following conventions, except **bold** text. The main body of the book <u>does</u> employ the following conventions and type styles.

- Footnotes[1]
- Citations to statutes and cases
- **Bold lettering**
- <u>Underlined text</u>
- *Italics*
- ***Bold and italicized words***
- Indented text (indented from left and right margin)
- [bracketed text]
- Ellipses (...)

1. <u>Footnotes</u> and <u>citations to statutes and cases</u>.

Footnotes are comments made at the bottom of the page.[1] The *Tenant's Survival Guide* employs the use of footnotes to provide ***citations***. Citations direct "lawyer types" to specific statutes and cases. For example, suppose the text says:

> The landlord must give the tenant seven (7) days notice to pay or quit, prior to filing a Special Detainer action.[2]

The superscript (raised) number 2, at the end of the above printed sentence, refers to the footnote at the bottom of this page. The footnote provides the legal authority (i.e., source) for the proposition that is cited. In this instance, the

---

[1] This is a footnote.

[2] *See* ARIZ. REV. STAT. ANN. § 33-1368(B) (West Supp. 1993).

requirement that the landlord must give the tenant seven days notice to pay or quit comes from Section 33-1368, subparagraph B, of the Arizona Revised Statutes Annotated.[3]

A citation may also refer to the name of a specific case. For example, suppose the text says:

> The filing of a civil action against a tenant does not satisfy the statutory requirement that the landlord must give the tenant written notice of the amounts withheld from his security deposit within fourteen (14) days after termination of tenancy.[4]

In this instance, the requirement that the landlord must give the tenant written notice of the amounts withheld from his/her deposit within fourteen days after termination of tenancy comes from a **statute**,[5] but the principle that the filing of a civil lawsuit against the tenant does not satisfy the "written notice" requirement of the statute, comes from an actual lawsuit (or **case**) named <u>Schaefer v. Murphey</u> (the "v." stands for versus). A case is the actual written decision of a court of law about a particular lawsuit which sets forth the facts of that particular case and then (normally) gives the reasons why the judge ruled the way that s/he did. Assuming the case is well reasoned, judges hearing subsequent cases, that have similar facts, may regard the previous case as setting a **precedent** and may rule the same way. In footnote four, the numbers - 131 Ariz. 295 - are called a **cite** or **citation**. This cite tells us that the judge's written opinion of this case begins on page 295 and the quoted material appears on page 297 of volume 131, of the **Arizona Reports**. Arizona Reports is a legal publication that contains written opinions of the Arizona courts. The other cite - 640 P.2d 857 - indicates that this opinion begins on page 857 and the quoted material appears on page 859 of volume 640, of the **Pacific Reporter, Second Series**. The Pacific Reporter is a legal publication that contains written opinions of courts from Alaska, Arizona, California, Colorado, Hawaii, Idaho, Kansas, Montana, Nevada, New Mexico, Oklahoma, Oregon, Utah, Washington and Wyoming. The number in parenthesis - (1982) - denotes the year that the case was decided.

It is not necessary that you seek out and read these other publications or the cases. The citations are provided merely so that those individuals who wish additional information will know where to look.

2. **Bold lettering**, <u>underlined text</u> and *italics*.

All three of these type styles are used to emphasize a particular word, phrase or sentence.

---

[3] Arizona Revised Statutes Annotated is properly cited as: ARIZ. REV. STAT. ANN. § ##-####, where "##-####" is the specific statute title and section number, but for brevity is cited herein as **A.R.S.** § ##-#### (§ is a symbol that means Section).

[4] <u>Schaefer v. Murphey</u>, 131 Ariz. 295, 297, 640 P.2d 857, 859 (1982).

[5] *See* A.R.S. § 33-1321(C) (West 1990).

3. *Bold and italicized words*.

Words or phrases that are defined in the Glossary (in the back of this book) appear in bold and italicized print the first time they are used and the first time the word is discussed. Thereafter, they appear in normal print.

4. Indented text, [bracketed text] and ellipses (...).

Occasionally, the exact text of a statute or case will be quoted. Text indented from both the left and right margins, as seen below, alerts you that this language is reprinted <u>exactly</u> (i.e., word-for-word) as it appears in the statute or case cited. The citation for the material reprinted in this manner may be found in the footnote at the end of the quote. For example:

> **C.** Upon termination of the tenancy, property or money held by the landlord as prepaid rent and security may be applied to the payment of accrued rent and the amount of damages which the landlord has suffered by reason of the tenant's noncompliance with § 33-1341 [tenant's obligations for maintaining the dwelling unit] all as itemized by the landlord in a written notice delivered to the tenant together with the amount due within fourteen [calendar] days after termination of the tenancy and delivery of possession and demand by the tenant.

> **D.** If the landlord fails to comply with subsections B and C of this section the tenant may recover the property and money due him together with damages in an amount equal to twice the amount wrongfully withheld.

> . . . .

> **F.** The holder of the landlord's interest in the premises at the time of the termination of the tenancy is bound by this section.[6]

In the material quoted above, you will note that some text appears in brackets (i.e., [ ]). This means that the text inside the brackets <u>does not</u> actually appear in the material cited, but is included in this book for your benefit. For example, the caption for § 33-1341 is "Tenant to maintain dwelling unit." Therefore, although this information is <u>not</u> included in the text of the statute, it is included in this book in brackets so that you will have a general idea what topic § 33-1341 addresses. Similarly, the statute quoted above later states that you have fourteen days to deliver a notice to the tenant, but the statute does not specify whether this means fourteen business days or fourteen calendar days.

---

[6] A.R.S. § 33-1321(C), (D), (F) (West 1990).

4

Because this information is valuable, it is included, but is included in brackets so that you know "calendar" does not appear in the actual text of the statute.

The appearance of three periods, called an ellipsis (i.e., ...), means that some words in a sentence have been omitted. Normally this is done to make the text easier to read by filtering out portions of the sentence that do not apply. For example, if a particular discussion assumes that the landlord <u>never</u> accepts property as security, the statute (previously quoted) would then appear as:

> Upon termination of the tenancy, ... money held by the landlord ... may be applied ....[7]

This example demonstrates that an ellipsis may also indicate that the sentence continues. Similarly, the appearance of four periods, standing alone (i.e., ...), tell you that there are sentences or paragraphs to this statute that have not been reprinted here. For instance, in the example (on the prior page) § 33-1321 also contains subparagraph E, but it is not reprinted here.

D. COMMENTS AND SUGGESTIONS; ERRORS.

Every effort has been made to ensure that the *Tenant's Survival Guide* provides useful, practical and accurate information. Any comments and suggestions you would like to make to improve the usefulness of the *Tenant's Survival Guide* will be appreciated. Specific examples include:

- You have some suggestions regarding the layout or structure of the *Tenant's Survival Guide* that may be more logical and/or would make particular topics easier to find.

- The *Tenant's Survival Guide* does not include a section and/or address a particular situation that you feel would be of benefit to most readers.

In short, any comments and suggestions that you believe will improve future editions of the *Tenant's Survival Guide* will be appreciated. Likewise, in the (unlikely) event that you detect an error in the substantive law provided herein, application of the law to the facts given in one of the hypothetical situations, or even a clerical error (grammatical or typographical), please notify me directly so that I may correct the problem immediately or in the next edition, as the urgency of the correction warrants. Please send comments, suggestions and notice of error(s) to:

Carlton C. Casler
c/o Consumer Law Books Publishing House
4113 North Longview
Phoenix, Arizona 85014

[7] A.R.S. § 33-1321(C) (West 1990).

CHAPTER 2

LEGAL ADVICE
TO
TENANTS

Cross Reference
* Appendix A, Checklist 1 (What to do when you have finished reading this book)

At the beginning of this book I told you that this book does not and is not intended to take the place of individualized legal counsel with an attorney. Nevertheless, right here and right now, I am going to give you the best legal advice that you will ever receive as a tenant (or otherwise):

> *The most valuable legal advice that you will ever receive is that advice which helps you prevent and/or avoid legal problems and* **litigation** *(actual court proceedings).*

Litigation is expensive, stressful, and no one ever truly "wins." No one, except, of course, the lawyers. I know this -- I am a lawyer. I see the same scenario repeated day after day: Landlord versus Tenant or Tenant versus Landlord. The results are normally unsatisfactory for both sides. When I tell you to avoid litigation at all costs, I mean it. Granted, I may be doing a horrible disservice to my fellow members of the Bar, who may be quick to accept your retainer and champion your cause, but your fellow tenants, who have already traveled the path of litigation, will tell you that I speak the truth. Therefore, I will give you several pieces of legal advice that will help you avoid legal problems and litigation; the first three are the most important.

The first piece of legal advice is -- **Get a lawyer**. You need not retain him/her on a continual basis. Just make sure that you have someone to call when you run into trouble or, better yet, *before* you get into trouble.

The second piece of legal advice is -- **Get the right lawyer**. Make sure your lawyer is conversant with the Arizona Residential Landlord and Tenant Act.[8] The attorney who got you a zillion dollars for that personal injury lawsuit and who is otherwise a very competent attorney, may not know the first thing about land-lord/tenant law. The same goes for tax attorneys, estate planners, etc.

The third piece of legal advice is -- **Have your lawyer review your rental agreement *BEFORE* you sign it**. A few dollars spent in advance is money very well spent. A poorly drafted rental agreement or one grossly skewed in favor of the landlord can cause more problems than you can imagine. Moreover, the cost to resolve these problems may cost you many times the attorney's fee that you "saved" by *not* having your attorney review it.

You may ask, "What if I have already signed the rental agreement?" Too late. The damage is already done. You are bound by the terms of the agreement that you signed. If, however, you are on a month-to-month tenancy or your lease is coming up for renewal, now would be an excellent time to have your rental agreement reviewed and then approach the landlord about incorporating your attorney's recommendations (if any) into the new agreement.

I can hear you already, "Big deal, some legal advice, get a lawyer, hire a lawyer, pay a lawyer, etc." *You have not been listening.* The best legal advice that you will ever receive is that advice which prevents legal problems and litigation. Sound business advice and review of your rental agreement will prevent most legal problems and litigation from ever occurring -- they are worth their weight in gold. If you put this book down right now and never read another page, but adhere to these three pieces of advice, you will save yourself many times the cost of this book, not to mention the time and aggravation of defending (or prosecuting) a lawsuit.

Incidently, you may be interested to know that loan companies and mortgage companies go crazy when they discover that a lawsuit has been filed against you. Remember that "dream house" or fancy car that you have been lusting after and that you have just decided to buy? Well forget it; at least until the lawsuit against you has been finally resolved. Oh sure, you will tell the loan or mortgage company that the lawsuit filed against you is completely baseless, was filed by a vindictive landlord, that s/he has no chance of winning and that even if s/he does win it will be for a nominal amount. With regard to this lawsuit, the law may even be on your side. None of this matters. The loan or mortgage company can only see a lawsuit. And more times than not, the landlord won't even specify the exact amount for which s/he is suing you. The loan or mortgage company translates this into "unlimited" liability. Sound silly? It is silly. But that is not an argument that will

---

[8] A.R.S. §§ 33-1301 to -1381 (West 1990 & Supp. 1993).

bring the loan or mortgage company around to your point of view. The good news is that you *probably* will be able to get the loan anyway, but not without a few headaches and a mountain of additional paperwork. And it is possible that your loan will be rejected merely because of this lawsuit. This is the wrong time to realize that preventing litigation is far better than winning litigation.

The next piece of legal advice that I must give you is that you probably need an **asset protection** plan. Asset protection prevents creditors, including **judgment creditors** (a judgment creditor is someone, such as a landlord, who has taken you to court and been awarded a judgment against you by a court of law), from taking your property (i.e., real estate, bank accounts, personal property, etc.). An asset protection plan, to be effective, must be constructed <u>and</u> implemented by an attorney who is skilled in asset protection.

I do not attempt to cover asset protection in the **Tenant's Survival Guide**. Nevertheless, I would be remiss if I did not briefly discuss its significance. Do not think, however, that because I do not devote an entire chapter to this subject that it is unimportant. Nothing could be farther from the truth. I intentionally do not deal with the subject at length because asset protection must be done one-on-one between you and an attorney. Nothing I say and nothing contained in any other book or publication will apply to everyone. Therefore, the advice I wish to convey about asset protection is: (1) it is vitally important; (2) you probably need it; and (3) consult an attorney immediately so that s/he can discuss a plan that is best for you.

There are two levels of asset protection: the first you can do yourself, the second must be done by a lawyer competent in constructing an effective asset protection plan. A simple hypothetical scenario best demonstrates why I think you probably need an asset protection plan and will help to illustrate the two levels of asset protection.

Assume that someday you will be sued for "big bucks" and that you will lose. You may be asking, "How would this occur?" Several examples follow:

1. You break an expensive, long term lease (i.e., a commercial lease). You remain legally liable for the accruing rent until the expiration of the lease or until the landlord re-rents the premises.

2. You move out of a rental property. Subsequent to you moving out, but prior to the landlord receiving possession, the property is vandalized <u>extensively</u>.

3. You cause a personal injury to some person.

The first level of asset protection is insurance. <u>Now</u>, not then, would be a good time to ask yourself, "Do I have renters' insurance and do I carry enough liability insurance?"

"What if the judgment creditor gets a judgment against me in excess of my insurance coverage?" Answer - the judgment creditor now gets to satisfy the rest of his/her judgment by taking your personal assets (actually, s/he gets a Writ of Execution, whereby the sheriff seizes your assets and then sells them at a sheriff's sale; in any event, you lose your ASSets). Your next question, no doubt, is, "Will insurance guarantee that this will never happen to me?" No. Insurance will probably prevent this from happening, but there are no guarantees. Why? Because all policies of insurance have specific maximum loss limitations. If the judgment is for an amount in excess of your coverage, your personal assets are at risk.

"How much coverage should I have?" Only your insurance agent (one you can trust -- if you are that fortunate) or your attorney can adequately counsel you on the amount of insurance coverage you need. Make a phone call today, right now, to find out if you have enough coverage.

"Will a zillion dollar insurance liability policy guarantee that this will never happen to me?" No. All policies of insurance exclude certain things from coverage; insurance companies call them *exclusions*. Look at your insurance policy. It will tell you what is covered and what is excluded. You will probably be surprised by the exclusions in *your* policy.

"Are there any other risks that I should be aware of?" Yes; too many to list. For one thing, you might think you are covered for a particular event, but the insurance company may find some way to "weasel" out of covering you (insurance companies don't do that -- do they?). Or, through some incredible blunder, your insurance lapses, during which time, of course (never underestimate Murphy's law), the event occurs that is the basis for the lawsuit; a policy with no exclusions and unlimited coverage won't help you if you forget to pay the premium. Or, your premium could get lost in the mail (that never happens, does it?), or your insurance agent might abscond with your premium without issuing you a policy (actually, you might still be covered in that case, but maybe not). Get the point? Lots of things can happen that will leave you "insurance naked."

"So, what am I supposed to do?" I believe in contingency plans; so should you. Enter the second level of asset protection. The second level, to be effective, must be accomplished by an attorney. Asset protection is accomplished by structuring your business practices and personal assets in such a manner that creditors and judgment creditors (this includes your landlord with the humongous judgment against you) cannot reach all your personal assets. This is accomplished with the use of corporations, limited partnerships, trusts, etc. "Is all this really necessary?" Read on, then you tell me.

For example, suppose that you are a single person with a duplex. You live in one side (owner occupant) and that you rent out the other side. In this example, you are the landlord, rather than the tenant (to demonstrate the effect of the judgment on real property). Your only other major asset is a car and a small savings account. You might think that, under these facts, you would not need to spend much time or money on asset protection. Let's see.

Can the judgment creditor take your duplex? Probably not. In this case, the duplex is also your home and the homestead exemption will protect up to $100,000 of equity.[9] If you have more than $100,000 equity, however, s/he can force the sale of your home. Granted, you will still get the first $100,000, but you may have had some sentimental attachment to the place. In any event, you are out on the street.

Can s/he take your car? Maybe. The equity in your car is protected up to a statutory amount of $1,500.[10] If you have more equity in the car than that, s/he can force its sale. You will get the first $1,500; s/he will get the rest.

Can s/he get your bank account? Yes. The first $150 ($300 for joint accounts) of your bank account is statutorily exempted.[11] S/he gets everything over $150 (or $300). Sound grim? It gets worse.

Can s/he get to your wages? Yes. The statutes protect a portion of your wages, but s/he will get a percentage of your nonexempt wages.[12]

Can s/he get your rental income? Yes.

You are now faced with filing bankruptcy or working at your job until you pay off the judgment creditor. No doubt you are shaking your head and mumbling, "What a disaster." You are right. And remember, this is a very simple example; using a minimum of assets. Now think about your own situation. Have I scared you? I hope so. I would prefer that you send me a mountain of "hate mail" because I scared you into running down and paying your attorney to structure your holdings to provide you with maximum protection and after twenty years you never needed it, rather than have you write to me and tell me that my delivery on this point was not forceful enough, that you ignored my warnings, that you have just lost your property and may have to file bankruptcy. I also hope that this simple example illustrates just how complex the law is and why you need to consult an attorney to protect your assets.

Without question, the only way to know how to best protect your personal assets is to consult with an attorney who is competent in this field. Okay, now you tell me, "Is all this really necessary?"

The final piece of advice that I wish to impart upon you is that you will have better success as a tenant if you follow a few simple guidelines for doing business and for being a good tenant. Finding a "good landlord" is normally the product of

---

[9] *See* A.R.S. § 33-1101(A) (West 1990).

[10] A.R.S. § 33-1125(8) (West 1990).

[11] A.R.S. § 33-1126(A)(7) (West 1990).

[12] *See* A.R.S. § 33-1131 (West 1990).

being a "good tenant." Being a "good tenant" means understanding your rights and obligations under the law and your rental agreement. It also means living up to your part of the bargain. Knowing and following sound business practices will ensure that you are a "good tenant." And "good tenants" have very few, if any, problems with their landlords. The following guidelines do not apply exclusively to being a tenant. They are equally applicable to all types of businesses, including landlords, and, in fact, apply to life in general. Adherence to these guidelines will prevent most landlord/tenant problems from occurring in the first place. And remember, *preventing a problem is always better than the most clever solution to a problem.*

Be honest. It is vitally important that you impress upon your landlord that you are a person of your word. I am not cautioning you against outright falsehoods (which goes without saying). I am warning you against the hazards of "hedging." People tend to hedge when they do not know the answer or when the answer is something they do not think the listener wants to hear. Consequently, when the truth is finally revealed and it turns out to be something other than what you have stated, you lose credibility. The solution is simple. If you don't know -- say so. If you are not sure, tell the landlord that you will find out the correct answer and get back to him/her. If the answer is something you think s/he does not want to hear -- tell him/her anyway. In short, say what you mean; mean what you say.

Be businesslike. This may be the most important guideline for tenants. Tenants often forget that a landlord/tenant relationship is a **business** relationship. Conduct yourself in a businesslike manner. That means everything, and I do mean everything, should be done in writing. For example, your air conditioner is not operating properly. Notify the landlord in writing of the problem. It can be a formal letter or an informal, handwritten note, but it should be **written**. And you should keep a copy.

> Terry Tenant
> 101 N. Rental Ave.
> Phoenix, Arizona 85999
>
> [date]
>
> Dear Mr. Landlord,
>
> This shall confirm our oral agreement of [date] wherein you agreed to reduce my rent for [month] by $50.00 in exchange for [describe services].
>
> *Terry Tenant*

Second example, the landlord tells you that you can reduce this month's rent by $50.00 for something that you have done (i.e., providing the landlord with services or repairing something in the leased premises). Memorialize this seemingly casual, oral agreement by sending the landlord a brief confirming letter or note. It may be as simple as the example shown above.

Keep your landlord honest (or should I say "prevent 'clerical errors'") by insisting upon a receipt when paying your rent or pay your rent with a personal check (which you will ultimately receive back from your bank, as evidence of payment). Landlords are less apt to make "mistakes" on tenants they know keep good records. And, as a legal and practical matter, if your landlord's records are somehow lost (i.e., fire, theft, etc.), <u>you</u> will have the burden of demonstrating that you have paid rent.

Be authoritative. First, know your rights under the law. The entire Arizona Residential Landlord and Tenant Act[13] is reprinted in the back of this book at Appendix C -- READ IT. You should also be familiar with the other Landlord and Tenant statutes[14] and Forcible Entry and Detainer statutes,[15] which are also reprinted in the back of this book at Appendix C. Second, <u>subtly</u> let your landlord (or prospective landlord) know that you know the law and your rights under the Arizona Residential Landlord and Tenant Act (the "Act"). This can be done by bringing along a copy of the Act or, better yet, the *Tenant's Survival Guide,* at the time you meet with your landlord or when you are out looking for a new rental unit. Follow up by asking the landlord the following question: "Was your rental agreement form prepared by an Arizona attorney and does it comply with the Arizona Residential Landlord and Tenant Statutes?" Of course the landlord or property manager will say yes, but this question will immediately inform the landlord that you are familiar with the Act. The conduct of the landlord after making this statement is important. If, after this question, you suddenly get the feeling that the landlord is trying to "discourage" you from renting his/her units, it may be because the rental agreement <u>does not</u> comply with Arizona law or that some of the landlord's other practices are not entirely legal. Some tenant applicants interpret this conduct as a rejection and take offense. **You should interpret this conduct as a warning** and avoid this landlord/property.

Stay up-to-date. The face of the law is ever changing. You've heard it before, "Ignorance of the law is no excuse." This is quite true and may also be stated as, "Ignorance of <u>changes in the law</u> is no excuse."

The state legislature meets every year. Every year the legislature adds, changes or deletes one or more of the statutes in the Act. The changes normally become effective in the fall of each year. A copy of the Act is available free of charge from the Arizona Secretary of State (Phone Number (602) 542-4285). You should make a practice of requesting a copy of the Act each September. Make a point of keeping abreast of changes in the law that impact on you as a tenant.

Summary of General Guidelines

- Be honest.
- Be businesslike.
- Be authoritative.
- Stay up-to-date.

---

[13] A.R.S. §§ 33-1301 to -1381 (West 1990 & Supp. 1993).

[14] A.R.S. §§ 33-301 to -381 (West 1990).

[15] A.R.S. §§ 12-1171 to -1183 (West 1981 & Supp. 1990).

NOTE: The *Tenant's Survival Guide* does not take the place of individualized legal counsel. You should consult your own attorney for legal advice (*see* "Caveat from the author and publisher," on page ii). The *Tenant's Survival Guide*, however, should help you to form your questions and focus them toward specific areas, thereby cutting down on the time you need to spend with your lawyer (God knows how expensive they are). In addition, the *Tenant's Survival Guide* will help you to **avoid** legal problems, which, as stated, *is the single most valuable advice you can get anywhere, at any price*. Also, in the event legal action becomes necessary, this book will walk you through the routine procedures and steps, thereby reducing or eliminating your legal expenses. Nevertheless, you should have an attorney that you can call if you run into a problem.

Summary of Legal Advice

- Get a lawyer.

- Get the right lawyer.

- Have your lawyer review your rental agreement **before** you sign it.

- Be sure you have enough insurance.

- Discuss asset protection with your lawyer.

- Follow general guidelines for doing business and being a good tenant.

CHAPTER 3

PREPARATION

Summary of Chapter

- Applicability/Scope of the Arizona Residential
  Landlord and Tenant Act

- Review Your Rental Agreement
    - What MUST be in the rental agreement
    - What CANNOT be in the rental agreement
    - What SHOULD be in the rental agreement
    - What to LOOK OUT for in the rental agreement
    - Deposits

- Other Forms You Need to be Familiar With
    - Tenant Application
    - Tenant Information Sheet
    - Property Inspection Checklist
    - Personal Property Inspection Checklist
    - Notice to Terminate Tenancy
    - Disposition of Deposits
    - Seven-Day Notice to Pay or Quit
    - Parking Violation
    - Complaint Form
    - Miscellaneous Notices

A. APPLICABILITY/SCOPE OF THE ARIZONA RESIDENTIAL LANDLORD AND TENANT ACT.

Before you do anything else, you must first determine what law applies to your situation. Arizona law will *probably* apply, but it may not. On federal land (i.e., Indian reservations), for example, Arizona state law may be **pre-empted** by federal law. This means that where state and federal law conflict, federal law will apply. This is one of those times when, if federal law applied, you would probably know it. The bottom line, however, is that you need to know whether or not the property you are renting (or about to rent) is subject to state law or to federal law. If you don't know, ask your attorney. For the vast majority of tenants, however, federal pre-emption is not a concern, and state law will apply.

Which state law applies? Arizona has two separate sets of statutes (i.e., laws) that address landlord/tenant law. As a general rule, if you rent a residential dwelling unit, the Arizona Residential Landlord and Tenant Act (hereinafter the "Act") applies. The **Act** is contained in Chapter 10 of Title 33 of the Arizona Revised Statutes.[16] The Act has been reprinted *in its entirety* in Appendix C. If you do not fall within the scope of the Act, the second set of statutes apply. This second set of statutes is contained in Chapter 3 of Title 33 of the Arizona Revised Statutes and applies when the Act does not, which is normally (but not exclusively) in the case of commercial rental property.[17] This second set of statutes is also reprinted in Appendix C.

Where does the Act apply? The Act is state law. Thus, unless pre-empted by federal law, the Act applies to all rental agreements for dwelling unites located within Arizona.[18]

Does application of the Act vary depending on the number of units? No. When the Act does apply, it applies equally to all residential rental property, regardless of size. For example, it applies equally to a duplex and to a 400-unit apartment complex.

Does the Act apply to you? The Act applies to "the rental of dwelling units."[19] To reiterate and to clarify any misunderstanding, two separate sets of statutes address the landlord/tenant relationship in Arizona. The Act applies to almost all residential units (*see* **exclusions**, following this discussion). The second set of statutes apply <u>only</u> when the Act does not.[20] Therefore, generally speaking, if you rent a residential dwelling, the Act applies, and the second set of statutes applies to commercial rental property.[21]

"Why," you may ask, "is the issue of whether or not the Act applies important?" I'm so glad you asked. The Act gives residential tenants certain rights they would not otherwise have (i.e., limitation on the amount of security deposit that a landlord may compel a tenant to pay)[22] and takes rights away from the landlord that would otherwise be available (i.e., the Act precludes **distraint for rent**).[23] In short, the Act clearly favors tenants and, therefore, as a tenant, you *want* the Act to apply.

There is another interesting and important distinction between the two sets of statutes. The landlord may elect (by written agreement) to make the Act applicable to the rental of nonresidential (i.e., commercial) real property, which would be an enormous advantage to the tenant. The landlord <u>cannot</u>, however,

---

[16] A.R.S. §§ 33-1301 to -1381 (West 1990 & Supp. 1993).

[17] A.R.S. §§ 33-301 to -381 (West 1990).

[18] A.R.S. § 33-1307 (West 1990).

[19] A.R.S. § 33-1304 (West 1990).

[20] A.R.S. §§ 33-1303, -1304 (West 1990).

[21] *See* A.R.S. §§ 33-301 to -381 (West 1990).

[22] *See* A.R.S. § 33-1321(A) (West 1990).

[23] A.R.S. § 33-1372(B) (West 1990).

elect, by written agreement or otherwise, to make the Act not applicable to the rental of residential property.[24] This is good news for the tenant, and it makes sense. The Act is basically a set of consumer protection laws, designed to protect residential tenants.[25] The legislative intent would be easily frustrated if landlords could merely "elect" for the Act not to apply to them. <u>Bottom line</u> -- unless you fall within one of the exclusions, the Act applies. The exceptions are best repeated word-for-word from the statute:

Exclusions from application of chapter

Unless created to avoid the application of this chapter [Chapter 10, the Arizona Residential Landlord and Tenant Act], the following arrangements are not covered by this chapter:

1. Residence at an institution, public or private, if incidental to detention or the provision of medical, educational, counseling or religious services.

2. Occupancy under a contract of sale of a dwelling unit or the property of which it is a part, if the occupant is the purchaser or a person who succeeds to his interest.

3. Occupancy by a member of a fraternal or social organization in the portion of a structure operated for the benefit of the organization.

4. Transient occupancy in a hotel, motel or recreational lodging.

5. Occupancy by an employee of a landlord as a manager or custodian whose right to occupancy is conditional upon employment in and about the premises.

6. Occupancy by an owner of a condominium unit or a holder of a proprietary lease in a cooperative.

7. Occupancy in or operation of public housing as authorized, provided, or conducted under or pursuant to title 36, chapter 12, or under or pursuant to any federal law or regulation.[26]

As you can see, other than paragraphs 5 and 7 (discussed next), the exceptions have fairly narrow application.

---

[24] *See* A.R.S. § 33-1315(A)(1) (West 1990).

[25] *See, e.g.,* <u>Corrigan v. Janney</u>, 626 P.2d 838, 840 (Mont. 1981) (common law doctrine of caveat emptor (buyer beware) does not apply to rental of residence).

[26] A.R.S. § 33-1308 (West 1990) (footnote omitted).

1. <u>Exclusion #5 and the Case of the On-Site Manager</u>.

Most apartment owners and/or landlords employ an on-site manager whose tenancy in the complex is contingent upon his/her continued employment. An on-site manager, however, should not be confused with a tenant that the landlord pays (or allows to pay a reduced amount of rent) to perform various duties (i.e., maintenance). The distinction is that the on-site manager's tenancy is absolutely contingent upon his/her employment: no employment -- no apartment. Whereas, in the second case, if the tenant stops rendering services, the tenant is entitled to continue tenancy, but gives up the right to receive payment (or reduction of rent). Tenancy for the latter is subject to the Act -- the landlord **cannot** "elect" to have the Act not apply. Tenancy for the former (the on-site manager) need not be controlled by the Act. Most landlords, however, have the manager sign the same rental agreement that the other tenants sign. Typically, the rental agreement states that tenancy is controlled by the Act, thereby "electing" to have the Act apply to a landlord/tenant relationship that otherwise need not be controlled by the Act -- an incredible blunder, from the landlord's point of view, but an absolute windfall for the tenant/on-site manager. The moral: if you are going to be an on-site manager, look to see if the rental agreement states that it is controlled by the Act. If it does not, ask the landlord to add a sentence to the rental agreement that states that your tenancy is subject to the Act. Most landlords will readily comply because they are not aware that, in this situation, they have the option of having the Act <u>not</u> apply.

What if you are sure that the Act should apply to you, but the landlord has included language in the rental agreement that states the Act <u>does not</u> apply? Answer: That language is unenforceable in court. Scams engineered to circumvent application of the Act are looked upon *very* unfavorably by the courts, and the courts have the means to punish landlords for such conduct.

Prohibited provisions in rental agreements

A. A rental agreement shall not provide that the tenant does any of the following:

       1. Agrees to waive or to forego rights or remedies under this chapter.

    . . . .

      B. . . . If a landlord deliberately uses a rental agreement containing provisions known by him to be prohibited, the tenant may recover actual damages sustained by him and not more than two months' periodic rent.[27]

---

[27] A.R.S. § 33-1315 (West 1990).

2. Exclusion #7 - Public Housing.

Similarly, the Act does not apply to **public housing**,[28] as that term is defined in Chapter 12 of Title 36 of the Arizona Revised Statutes Annotated. You are probably familiar with a public housing program commonly referred to as **Section 8 Housing**. The Section 8 program is the federal housing assistance program.[29] In addition to the fact that public housing is specifically exempted from the Act,[30] the Section 8 program is federal law and, therefore, pre-empts state law. That is not to say, however, that the law applicable to public housing and the Act are *completely* different, but you should be familiar with the distinctions. In short, if you are renting property under some type of public housing program, you must comply with the rules **promulgated** by that particular agency. As a practical matter, at the time you apply to rent property under a public housing program, either the landlord or the housing agency will give you a copy of the applicable rules.

B. REVIEW YOUR RENTAL AGREEMENT.

The rental agreement form is the single, most important form to a tenant. It is the source of virtually all of your (and the landlord's) rights and remedies. I have already stated that you should have your attorney review your rental agreement form before you sign it or, in the case of an existing tenant, before you renew your rental agreement. I will say it again -- have your attorney review your rental agreement <u>before</u> you sign it. In the event you chose not to heed this recommendation, *at a very minimum*, you should take the time to <u>completely read</u> (i.e., from top to bottom, all pages) the rental agreement. The following sections will help you to assess whether the rental agreement you are about to sign (or worse, the one that you *already* signed) complies with Arizona law and/or has been written to **grossly** favor the landlord.

A properly drawn rental agreement serves two purposes. First, it prevents litigation by clearly setting forth all the terms and conditions of tenancy. Normally, when a tenant has a grievance with the landlord and the landlord sees that the rental agreement, *that both parties signed*, clearly supports the position that the tenant is taking, the landlord *should* concede. Second, in the event the landlord does not concede, a well-drafted rental agreement ensures that a court of law will support the position that the tenant has taken. **In short, a well-drafted rental agreement prevents litigation and ensures success if litigation is inevitable. What else need I say to stress how vitally important this form is to you?** CAVEAT: success in litigation will only occur if the rental agreement says what you want it to say. If the rental agreement says "no pets allowed" and you want a pet, *you will lose.*

This section provides you with a list of what **must**, by law, and what **cannot**, by law, be in the rental agreement. I will then tell you some specific items, that I

---

[28] A.R.S. §§ 36-1401 to -1501 (West 1993).

[29] *See* Tax Exemption of Obligations of Public Housing Agencies and Related Amendments, 24 C.F.R. §§ 811.101 to -.211 (1991).

[30] A.R.S. § 33-1308(7) (West 1990).

believe, **should** be in the rental agreement and some terms to *LOOK OUT* for in the rental agreement. Finally, although perhaps redundant, I have consolidated and summarized in one section everything you need to know about deposits from the various chapters.

1. Rental Agreement MUST's.

(a) Disclosure of manager and owner or owner's agent.

Oddly enough, the Act does not require that the rental agreement be written.[31] Nevertheless, even in the absence of a written rental agreement, the landlord must disclose to the tenant, in writing, at or before the commencement of the tenancy, the name and address of: (1) the property manager; and (2) the owner or the owner's agent, who must be authorized to accept notices, demands, and service of process.[32] Moreover, this information must be kept current and refurnished to the tenant upon request.[33]

(b) Deliver a signed copy of the written rental agreement.

As stated above, the Act does not require a written rental agreement, but where the rental agreement is written, the landlord must deliver a signed copy of the rental agreement to the tenant within a reasonable time after the agreement is executed.[34]

(c) The written rental agreement must be complete.

All blank spaces on a written rental agreement must be completed. Failure to complete all blank spaces is a material noncompliance by the landlord.[35] This is particularly important when your landlord uses the generic forms from the local stationery store. These forms contain a zillion blank spaces in an attempt to accommodate everyone and to suit every situation. The consequence of your landlord inadvertently leaving a space blank may be no consequence at all or may mean a completely unenforceable rental agreement, depending on the judge.[36] Bottom line - if your landlord has filed any type of lawsuit against you (i.e., forcible detainer, civil action for past due rent, etc.) look to see if all blank spaces have been filled in on the rental agreement. If not, raise this issue with the court.

(d) Nonrefundable deposits must be stated in writing.

Cleaning and redecorating deposits, if nonrefundable, must be clearly stated in writing.[37] If not so stated, then the deposit is refundable.

---

[31] *See e.g.*, A.R.S. § 33-1322(D) (West 1990).

[32] A.R.S. § 33-1322(A) (West 1990).

[33] A.R.S. § 33-1322(B) (West 1990).

[34] A.R.S. § 33-1322(D) (West 1990).

[35] A.R.S. § 33-1322(D) (West 1990).

[36] Section 33-1322(D) of the Arizona Revised Statutes Annotated provides, in part: "A written rental agreement shall have all blank spaces completed. Noncompliance with this subsection shall be deemed material noncompliance by the landlord or the tenant, as the case may be, of the rental agreement."

[37] A.R.S. § 33-1321(B) (West 1990).

(e) Rental agreements longer than one year must be written.

The Act does not require that the rental agreement be in writing.[38] Other sections of the law, however, provide that contracts that cannot be performed within one year must be in writing to be enforceable.[39] Therefore, rental agreements that provide for specific lease periods in excess of one year must be in writing. For example, a lease from January 1, 1994 to December 31, 1994 need not be in writing, but a lease from January 1, 1994, to January 1, 1995 must be in writing to be enforceable. Nevertheless, a month-to-month tenancy need not be in writing, even though the tenancy continues for more than one year. For example, suppose you rent an apartment on January 1, 1994 on a month-to-month basis. You continue to rent the apartment beyond January 1, 1995. The rental agreement need not be in writing and is enforceable. The reason is because a month-to-month tenancy terminates at the end of each month and is renewed each month, thereby complying with the requirement that the contract *may* be performed within one year.

2. Rental Agreement CANNOT's.

(a) The landlord cannot require the tenant to waive the tenant's rights, agree to pay attorneys' fees, or agree to limit the landlord's liability.

The Act specifically prohibits the landlord from including provisions in the rental agreement whereby the tenant: (1) waives the rights or remedies granted to the tenant under the Act; (2) agrees to pay the landlord's attorneys' fees (with two exceptions); and/or (3) agrees to limit the landlord's liability. Specifically, the Act provides:

Prohibited provisions in rental agreements
>   **A.** A rental agreement shall not provide that the tenant does any of the following:
>
>   1. Agrees to waive or to forego rights or remedies under this chapter [Chapter 10 -- the Act].
>
>   2. Agrees to pay the landlord's attorney's fees, except an agreement in writing may provide that attorney's fees may be awarded to the prevailing party in the event of court action and except that a prevailing party in a contested forcible detainer action is eligible to be awarded attorney fees pursuant to § 12-341.01 regardless of whether the rental agreement provides for such an award.
>
>   3. Agrees to the exculpation or limitation of any liability of the landlord arising under law or to indemnify the landlord for that liability or the costs connected therewith.

---

[38] *See, e.g.*, A.R.S. § 33-1322(D) (West 1990).

[39] A.R.S. § 44-101(5) (West Supp. 1993).

B. A provision prohibited by subsection A of this section included in a rental agreement is unenforceable. If a landlord deliberately uses a rental agreement containing provisions known by him to be prohibited, the tenant may recover actual damages sustained by him and not more than two months' periodic rent.[40]

These are the absolute taboos. The landlord <u>cannot</u> include these provisions in your rental agreement. Almost anything else, however, is permissible. So review your rental agreement very, very carefully <u>before signing it</u> to see if you are agreeing to unusual or particularly onerous terms. Your attorney will be invaluable in assessing whether a particular term is unusual or onerous.

(b) The landlord cannot collect a security deposit <u>equal to more than one and one-half month's rent</u>.

"A landlord shall not demand or receive security, however denominated, including, but not limited to, prepaid rent in an amount or value in excess of one and one-half month's rent."[41] "Security," however, does not include a "reasonable" cleaning or redecorating deposit.[42] Therefore, a landlord may require a security deposit less than or equal to one and one-half times the monthly rental amount, <u>plus</u> a "reasonable" cleaning or redecorating deposit. Cleaning and redecorating deposits that are non-refundable, **must** be so stated in writing.[43]

For example, suppose that you rent a unit for $1,000 per month. The landlord may collect a security deposit of $1,500 <u>plus</u> a "reasonable" cleaning or redecorating deposit. "Reasonable" is a subjective term that varies depending on the size and type of property. If you have looked at a few other rental units, you should already have a feel for what is "reasonable." If not, ask your attorney.

3. Rental Agreement SHOULD's.

I have already told you what **must** and **cannot**, by law, be in the rental agreement. Next I will tell you some things that **should** be done and/or should be in the rental agreement, because they are advantageous to the tenant.

(a) The rental agreement should be written.

Even if you intend to rent a piece of real estate for one week, the rental agreement should be in writing. Why? It is certainly true that an oral rental agreement is as enforceable as a written rental agreement drafted by the best attorney in the state, <u>if not challenged</u>. If challenged in a court of law, however, an oral rental agreement normally equates to no rental agreement because the

---

[40] A.R.S. § 33-1315 (West 1990). *But see* A.R.S. § 33-1314(A) (West 1990) ("The landlord and tenant may include in a rental agreement terms and conditions not prohibited by this chapter [the Act] or other rule of law including rent, term of the agreement and other provisions governing the rights and obligations of the parties.").

[41] A.R.S. § 33-1321(A) (West 1990).

[42] A.R.S. § 33-1310(13) (West 1990) ("'Security' does not include a reasonable charge for redecorating or cleaning.").

[43] A.R.S. § 33-1321(B) (West 1990).

landlord's version of "the agreement" will vary greatly from your version of the agreement. In such a case, the judge is forced to decide whether one of the parties is lying or whether both are telling the truth, which, in the latter case, means that there never really was an "agreement" (i.e., a meeting of the minds) and, therefore, the "agreement" cannot be enforced.

Nevertheless, if you insist upon having an oral agreement (an attitude you are likely to change the first time you are forced to go to court) and you and your landlord disagree about something, you do not automatically lose. If the landlord and tenant agree upon the precise language of the particular term in issue, but disagree as to the meaning of the term, then the court will decide the matter because questions regarding the interpretation of contract terms are questions of law, and courts are free to decide questions of law. For example, suppose that the landlord and the tenant agree that the landlord agreed to pay for "utilities," but disagree whether cable television is included within the definition of "utilities." This is a questions of law, which the court will decide. If, on the other hand, the landlord and tenant disagree on what a particular provision was, the judge is in the unenviable position of having to decide who is telling the truth. For example, the landlord says the agreed rent was $500, but the tenant contends the agreed rent was $400.

(b) The written rental agreement should be comprehensive.

In theory, a rental agreement should anticipate every contingency and clearly state each party's rights and remedies. This allows everyone to know in advance their rights and remedies. In practice, however, rental agreements are seldom comprehensive. Where there are "gaps" in an oral or written rental agreement, the provisions of the Act apply.[44] Because the Act favors tenants, this is good for the tenant. For example, assume that you have an oral or written agreement with your landlord specifying $500 rent, but you do not discuss when the rent is due. The Act fills in this "gap." The Act provides, "rent is payable at the beginning"[45] of the specified term, which, in the case of a month-to-month tenancy, would be at the beginning of the month. Therefore, your first choice should be a comprehensive rental agreement, so that you can assess whether the rights and remedies provided therein are acceptable before you sign it. Your second choice would be to have a very short and non-comprehensive rental agreement, because any gaps will be filled in by the Act, which favors you, the tenant.

(c) The rental agreement should provide how partial payments are applied to amounts due.

From time to time, it may be necessary to tender payment of *less than* the full amount due (otherwise, how payments are applied is not an issue). If you find yourself in this situation, the first thing to do is determine whether or not the

---

[44] *See* A.R.S. § 33-1304 (West 1990). *See, e.g.,* New Hampshire Ins. Co. v. Hewins, 6 Kan.App.2d 259, 627 P.2d 1159, 1161 (1981) (in absence of a valid rental agreement to the contrary, basic terms of landlord tenant relationship are provided by Uniform Residential Landlord and Tenant Act).
[45] A.R.S. § 33-1314(C) (West 1990).

landlord will accept a partial payment. If so, then the next point to address is **how** the partial payment will be applied to the various amounts that are due. Consequently, the rental agreement *should* provide how partial payments are to be applied. Otherwise, the landlord is likely to apply your partial payment however s/he desires (i.e., *first* to money you owe him/her for an old, personal debt, *then* to rent). If the rental agreement does not state how partial payments are to be applied, and most do not, then **you** should take the initiative to make sure your receipt reflects how the partial payment is to be applied. A simple notation is all that is required (i.e., a memo on the bottom of your check, "Partial payment of July rent," or "Payment for July late charges," etc.).

If the landlord refuses to accept a partial payment, you are out of luck. The Act requires the landlord to accept *full* payment,[46] but the Act does not require the landlord to accept partial payment (but s/he may if s/he wishes).[47] Relief from this dilemma may, however, be found in the rental agreement. Poorly drafted language in the rental agreement (frequently the product of the landlord drafting his/her own rental agreement) may actually **obligate** the landlord to accept partial payments. Check the language in *your* rental agreement. If this is the case, you can STOP eviction proceedings by offering to pay "some part" of the rent. If s/he refuses, s/he has failed to honor the terms of the rental agreement. If s/he accepts the payment, the seven-day clock (i.e., the period provided by the 7-Day Notice to Pay or Quit) will be restarted -- you win either way.

4. **Things to LOOK OUT for in your Rental Agreement.**

(a) **Providing for abandonment.**

From time to time, tenants simply disappear and abandon the rental property. A landlord will (normally) experience this *only once* before taking corrective action. When a tenant abandons rental property, the Act <u>requires</u> the landlord to store the tenant's property for at least sixty (60) days, <u>unless</u> the landlord has had the foresight to include an abandonment provision. The Act states:

> <u>If provided by a written rental agreement</u>, the landlord may destroy or otherwise dispose of some or all of the property if the landlord reasonably determines that the value of the property is so low that the cost of moving, storage and conducting a public sale exceeds the amount that would be realized from the sale.[48]

There you have it -- express permission from the Arizona legislature for the landlord to grind your abandoned property into sawdust, provided, of course, the value of said property is less than the cost to move and store it **and** the abandonment provision is included in the written rental agreement. If, however, the abandonment provision is <u>not</u> included in the written rental agreement, the landlord

---

[46] A.R.S. § 33-1368(B) (West Supp. 1993).

[47] A.R.S. § 33-1371 (West Supp. 1993).

[48] A.R.S. § 33-1370(E) (West 1990) (emphasis added).

has no alternative (i.e., <u>s/he must move and store the tenant's property</u>) no matter what the value.

There are no "magic words" that constitute an abandonment provision. An abandonment provision may simply state:

> Tenant expressly authorizes landlord to dispose of abandoned property and property left on the premises by tenant after tenancy has terminated, in any manner landlord deems fit, where the landlord reasonably determines that the value of said property is so low that the cost of moving, storing and conducting a public sale would exceed the amount that would be realized from the sale. Tenant holds landlord harmless for loss of property and/or value of said property disposed of under these circumstances.

Any similar clause that clearly conveys this message will suffice under the statute. Review your rental agreement to see if such language is present. If so, make certain that you take extra precautions to notify the landlord when you go on a trip for more than seven days.[49] The statute explicitly permits the landlord to take action after only seven days:

> In this section [§ 33-1370 -- Abandonment] "abandonment" means the absence of the tenant from the dwelling unit, without notice to the landlord for at least **seven days**, if rent for the dwelling unit is outstanding and unpaid for ten days and there is no reasonable evidence other than the presence of the tenant's personal property that the tenant is occupying the residence.[50]

As you can see, the landlord may lawfully presume you have abandoned the premises even if you have not. For this reason, and for various other reasons (i.e., insurance purposes), you should periodically photograph the furnishings, property, etc., in your rental unit. These photographs may be useful in helping you to establish the value of your property in the event something happens (i.e., the landlord mistakenly interprets your absence as an abandonment, your property is stolen or destroyed, etc.). <u>Do not</u>, however, ask the landlord to remove the abandonment clause from the rental agreement. First, there is no practical reason why s/he should remove this clause. Second, it makes the landlord wonder why you are so concerned about abandonment of the premises.

**(b)   Payment of attorneys' fees and
<u>expenses incurred to bring legal action.</u>**

The Act provides that after a Special Detainer action (commonly referred to as a forcible detainer action) has been filed, the tenants may reinstate the rental

---

[49] *See* A.R.S. § 33-1370(H) (West 1990).

[50] A.R.S. § 33-1370(H) (West 1990) (emphasis added).

agreement **only** by paying past due rent, late fees, attorneys' fees and court costs.[51] Many rental agreements contain similar language, but add language that entitles the landlord to attorneys' fees and litigation expenses <u>whether or not</u> the action is contested. The reason for this is simple -- the statute does not "guarantee" an award of expenses and attorneys' fees. First, the statute only provides for an award of attorneys' fees in a "contested action."[52] This means that if your landlord gets a judgment against you by default, a very common occurrence, s/he <u>is not</u> entitled to attorneys' fees <u>unless</u> certain language is present in the written rental agreement. Second, *even if contested*, the statute merely provides that attorneys' fees *may* be awarded to the prevailing party.[53] This means that the judge can award the landlord attorneys' fees or not, as s/he deems fit. Specific language in the rental agreement is *supposed* to make an award of attorneys' fees, expenses and costs <u>mandatory</u>. An example of such language is as follows:

> Landlord and Tenant agree that the prevailing party in any litigation, action or controversy arising from this Rental Agreement shall be entitled to an award of reasonable attorneys' fees, litigation expenses and court costs, without regard to whether or not the matter is contested.

Even the presence of this language, however, does not "guarantee" an award of expenses and attorneys' fees to the landlord. I have seen some judges (normally in justice court) refuse to award attorneys' fees regardless of the language in the rental agreement. This practice is certainly contrary to the express language of the contract (i.e., the rental agreement), but the only way for the landlord to correct this "bad decision" is to appeal the decision of the judge. For most landlords, the appeal process is normally not cost effective, in terms of time, effort and expense. Therefore, they may just let it go.

Review your rental agreement to see if this provision is present, but, again, do not waste your breath asking the landlord to remove this provision -- s/he has absolutely no reason to do so. The purpose of checking for this provision is to forewarn you about the hazards of contesting an eviction if you really don't have a defense. As stated before, judges frequently make mistakes and/or misapply the law. Therefore, if this language is present in your rental agreement and you contest an action brought by your landlord and lose, you should nevertheless ask the judge to deny the landlord's request for attorneys' fees -- what have you got to lose?

(c) Payment of "other expenses."

Look for other provisions in your rental agreement that obligate you to pay: (1) a late fee for late payment of rent (the statute requires that the late fee be "reasonable");[54] (2) a re-keying fee (normally assessed when the tenant fails to return all the keys given to him/her at the commencement of the tenancy); (3) a

---

[51] A.R.S. § 33-1368(B) (West Supp. 1993).

[52] A.R.S. § 12-341.01(A) (West 1981).

[53] A.R.S. § 12-341.01(A) (West 1981).

[54] A.R.S. § 33-1368(B) (West Supp. 1993).

garage door opener replacement fee (similar to re-keying fee); (4) notice fees (fee charged by the landlord for preparation of some type of notice, i.e., 7-Day Notice to Pay or Quit, Complaint Form, etc.); and (5) a returned check fee (fee charged for checks that are returned to landlord).

Again, the landlord is not likely to completely remove any of these provisions, but s/he may agree to modify the amount charged. Use your discretion when raising these issues. Landlords will not look favorably upon a new tenant applicant that seems "too concerned" about these types of charges (i.e., charges that are assessed when the tenant breaches the rental agreement).

5. Deposits.

Cross Reference
- Disposition of Deposit Form, Chapter 3, Section C(6)
- Appendix A, Checklist 3 (Deposits)

Everything that you need to know about *deposits* (*security deposits*, *cleaning deposits* and *redecorating deposits*) may be summarized as follows:

- The landlord cannot collect a deposit equal to more than one and one-half month's rent.[55] Example: if rent is $500 per month, s/he cannot collect a security deposit of more than $750.

- In addition to a security deposit, a "reasonable" cleaning or redecorating deposit may be collected by the landlord.[56]

- Nonrefundable cleaning and redecorating deposits must be clearly stated in writing, and a copy of the document must be given to the tenant.[57] Normally, this is addressed in the rental agreement, but if your landlord does not have a written rental agreement (shame on you for letting him/her get away with that), s/he must nevertheless have some written document that clearly states which deposits are nonrefundable. If the landlord has not disclosed in writing that a cleaning and/or redecorating deposit is nonrefundable and then fails to return said deposit to the tenant, the tenant may recover the deposit together with damages in an amount equal to **twice** the amount wrongfully withheld.[58]

- After the tenant vacates the rental unit, the landlord must either: (1) refund 100% of the tenant's deposits that s/he is holding; or (2) refund the amount due the tenant, if any, and provide a written notice that itemizes deductions from the tenant's deposits.[59] The Act

---

[55] A.R.S. § 33-1321(A) (West 1990).

[56] See A.R.S. § 33-1310(13) (West 1990) ("'Security' does not include a reasonable charge for redecorating or cleaning.").

[57] A.R.S. § 33-1321(B) (West 1990).

[58] A.R.S. § 33-1321(D) (West 1990).

[59] A.R.S. § 33-1321(C) (West 1990).

requires the landlord to do either 1 or 2, above, within fourteen (14) calendar days after: (1) termination of tenancy; (2) delivery of possession of the rental unit by the tenant to the landlord; and (3) demand for return of his/her deposit(s) by the tenant.[60] If the landlord does not comply by either failing to return the security deposit or failing to deliver a written itemization, the tenant may recover the property and money due him/her together with damages in an amount equal to **twice** the amount wrongfully withheld.[61] Consequently, whenever you vacate a rental unit, you should be in the habit of *personally* turning the keys over to the landlord and, at the same time, providing the landlord with a written demand for return of your deposits. A short, hand-written note is sufficient.

> To: Larry Landlord
>
> On [date], I, Terry Tenant, delivered possession of the rental property located at 101 N. Rental Avenue, Phoenix, Arizona, to Larry Landlord.
>
> I hereby request that my refundable deposit(s) be refunded to me.
>
> Terry Tenant   May 2, 1994

- The Act does not require landlords to pay tenants interest on their deposits.

The foregoing section summarizes virtually all that you need to know about security deposits. Nevertheless, you should read the portion of the Act that specifically addresses deposits (reprinted below).

Security deposits

      A. A landlord shall not demand or receive security, however denominated, including, but not limited to, prepaid rent in an amount or value in excess of one and one-half month's rent. This subsection does not prohibit a tenant from voluntarily paying more than one and one-half month's rent in advance.

      B. Cleaning and redecorating deposits, if nonrefundable, must be so stated in writing by the landlord.

      C. Upon termination of the tenancy, property or money held by the landlord as prepaid rent and security may

---

[60] A.R.S. § 33-1321(C) (West 1990).

[61] A.R.S. § 33-1321(D) (West 1990).

be applied to the payment of accrued rent and the amount of damages which the landlord has suffered by reason of the tenant's noncompliance with § 33-1341 [tenant's obligations for maintaining the dwelling unit] all as itemized by the landlord in a written notice delivered to the tenant together with the amount due within fourteen days after termination of the tenancy and delivery of possession and demand by the tenant.

D. If the landlord fails to comply with subsections B and C of this section the tenant may recover the property and money due him together with damages in an amount equal to twice the amount wrongfully withheld.[62]

Summary of Section B

1. MUST's:

The rental agreement **must**:
- Disclose the name of the manager and owner or owner's agent.
- Be complete (i.e., all blank spaces filled in).
- State which deposits are nonrefundable (if any).
- Be in writing, if longer than one year.

The landlord **must**:
- Deliver a signed copy of the written rental agreement to the tenant.

2. CANNOT's:

The landlord **cannot**:
- Require the tenant to:
    - waive the tenant's rights;
    - agree to pay attorneys' fees; or
    - agree to limit the landlord's liability.
- Collect a security deposit equal to more than one and one-half month's rent.

3. SHOULD's:

The rental agreement **should**:
- Be written (regardless of length of tenancy).
- Be comprehensive.
- Provide how partial payments are applied to amounts due.

4. Provisions to LOOK OUT for in your rental agreement:
- Abandonment provisions.
- Payment of attorneys' fees and legal expenses.
- Payment of "other expenses."

5. Deposits:
- Security deposit cannot exceed one and one-half times the monthly rent.
- A reasonable cleaning or redecorating deposit may be collected <u>in addition</u> to a security deposit.
- Nonrefundable deposits must be in writing.
- Landlord must refund deposit or provide written notice of deductions within 14 days.
- Landlord does not have to pay interest on deposits.

---

[62] A.R.S. § 33-1321(A)-(D) (West 1990).

C. OTHER FORMS YOU NEED TO BE FAMILIAR WITH.

A tenant completes several forms virtually every time s/he rents a unit: the Application and Tenant Information Sheet (which may be one form or two separate forms), the Rental Agreement and some type of Property Inspection Checklist (which may include a personal property checklist). In addition, as a tenant, you may encounter several other forms (below).

Tenant Application (*see* Chapter 4, Section C(1))
Tenant Information Sheet (*see* Chapter 4, Section C(3))
Property Inspection Checklist
Personal Property Inspection Checklist
Notice to Terminate Tenancy
Disposition of Deposits
Seven-Day Notice to Pay or Quit
Parking Violation
Complaint Form
Fourteen-Day Notice of Termination of Rental Agreement for Material Noncompliance with Rental Agreement
Ten-Day Notice of Termination of Rental Agreement for Noncompliance with Rental Agreement Materially Affecting Health and Safety
Notice of Immediate Termination of Rental Agreement for Material and Irreparable Breach

Each form is discussed on the following pages (the rental agreement has already been thoroughly discussed in the prior section of this chapter). A completed sample form accompanies each discussion.

1. Tenant Application.

The Tenant Application is discussed at length in Chapter 4, Section C(1).

2. Tenant Information Sheet.

Tenant Information Sheets are discussed at length in Chapter 4, Section C(3) in conjunction with Tenant Applications.

3. Property Inspection Checklist.

Next to the rental agreement, the Property Inspection Checklist is the most important form for the tenant. The purpose of the Property Inspection Checklist is to record the condition of the rental unit before you move in. The information recorded on this form is critical. Complete this form before you move in, not after or even *shortly after* you move into the premises. You should *personally* deliver a copy to the landlord and have him/her sign it and return a signed copy to you.

Why all the fuss? Here is the typical scenario: a tenant moves out; the rental unit has sustained some type of damage; the landlord alleges that the tenant has caused the damage and is responsible for repairs; the tenant asserts that the rental unit was damaged (i.e., in that condition) when s/he moved in. The typical courtroom colloquy that follows goes something like this:

Judge: "Mr. Tenant, did you cause this damage to the unit?"

Tenant: "No Judge, it was that way when I moved in."

Judge: "Mr. Tenant, do you have any evidence that demonstrates or suggests the unit was already damaged when you moved in?"

Tenant: "I saw the unit before I moved in and it was already damaged."

Judge: "Anything else, besides your word?"

Yes, I know, this dialogue is insulting because it questions the tenant's integrity. But there are unscrupulous tenants (as well as landlords) and the judge doesn't know either one of you. Enter the Property Inspection Checklist. Now, let us revisit the same scenario.

Judge: "Mr. Tenant, did you cause this damage to the unit?"

Tenant: "No Judge, it was that way when I moved in."

Judge: "Mr. Tenant, do you have any evidence that demonstrates or suggests the unit was already damaged when you moved in?"

Tenant: "Yes, your honor. Before I moved in, I filled out this Property Inspection Checklist, noting all the property defects. On line four it clearly states, "one six inch diameter, circular hole in the living room wall. Moreover, Mr. Landlord signed this form, acknowledging that it reflected the true condition of the rental unit on the date I moved in."

Judge: "What about that, Mr. Landlord?"

Landlord: "The hole was not there, judge. S/he must have written that on the form after I signed it."

Judge: "Uh huh, right. I find for Mr. Tenant and enter judgment against Mr. Landlord."

The key points to remember about a Property Inspection Checklist are:

- The form should be filled out before (or at least shortly after) you move in;

- Your copy must be signed and dated by the landlord; and

- The form must be comprehensive (i.e., very detailed).

If your landlord does not provide you with such a form, ask for one. If s/he does not have such a form, note the property deficiencies in a letter to the landlord, using the following form as a guide or use Form 1, Appendix B.

PROPERTY INSPECTION CHECKLIST

The premises located at: 111 North Maple Street, #2, Phoenix, Arizona, are clean, safe, in good repair and without defects, with only the following exceptions noted:

Exterior: Northwest bedroom window cracked; south side of building needs paint (existing paint is peeling).

(i.e., condition of the exterior structure, etc.)

Living room* : 2" circular hole in carpet (burn mark); stain on carpet, near door.

Family room* : 1" x 2" oval hole in south hall; outlet cover missing.

Kitchen: Cabinet above stove scratched; oven dented near bottom; faucet drips; one piece of floor tile broken (near refrigerator).

(i.e., appliances, cabinets, walls, floor, ceiling, etc.)

Laundry room** : None.

Hall: None.

Hall bathroom** : Towel rack bent; light cover missing; bathtub porcelain chipped (near drain).

Bedroom 1* : Door marred; 1" hole in carpet, near window; drapes torn.

Bedroom 2* : Light fixture doesn't work.

Master Bedroom** : Carpet stain near closet; hole in wall behind door.

When completed and signed, this form will be attached to your Rental Agreement. Costs to repair defects not noted on this checklist are the tenant(s)'s responsibility and will be deducted from the security deposit if not repaired prior to vacating the premises. Make a thorough inspection of the premises & note all defects!

Terry Tenant   January 1, 1994   *Larry Landlord   January 1, 1994*
    (Tenants)   (Landlord/Owner)
* i.e., floor, carpet, walls, ceilings, doors, hardware, windows.   ** i.e., fixtures, walls, ceilings, floor, outlets, door, windows.

---

4. <u>Personal Property Inspection Checklist</u>.

A Personal Property Inspection Checklist is essentially the same as the property inspection form, except that it is typically used to record the condition of personal property that a tenant may rent, in addition to the rental unit itself, as in the case of a furnished apartment. Many times, where rental of real and personal property is the norm, the landlord will combine the two forms into one form.

5. <u>Notice to Terminate Tenancy</u>.

Cross Reference
- Chapter 6, Section A (How & By Whom Tenancy May be Terminated)
- Chapter 6, Section A(4) ("Adequate" Notice)
- Appendix B, Form 2 (Notice to Terminate Tenancy)

The landlord will either furnish you with a termination form at commencement of your tenancy or make the form available upon request. Alternatively, a short note, **written** of course, is sufficient.

Dear Mr. Landlord,

    I intend to terminate tenancy on July 31, 1994.

Terry Tenant June 25, 1994

Note: Must give "adequate" notice (i.e., 30 days advance notice), as in this example. *See* Chapter 6, Section A(4), regarding "adequate notice."

Make sure that you consult your rental agreement to ensure that you are providing the landlord with ***"adequate" notice***.

6. <u>Disposition of Deposits</u>.

Cross Reference
- Chapter 3, Section B(5) (Deposits)
- Appendix A, Checklist 3 (Deposits)

As previously stated (Chapter 3, Section B(5)), within fourteen days after you move, your landlord must either: (1) refund 100% of your refundable deposits; or (2) refund the amount owed to you, if any, and provide a written notice that itemizes deductions from your deposits. Most landlords use a form similar to the one on the following page.

DISPOSITION OF DEPOSITS

In accordance with the Arizona Residential Landlord and Tenant Act, specifically, A.R.S. § 33-1321, the following discloses the disposition of your deposit(s):

DEPOSITS

Nonrefundable deposits:

Cleaning deposit (Nonrefundable)	$ 0
Redecorating deposit (Nonrefundable)	$ 100.00
Security deposit (Nonrefundable)	$ 0
Other _____	$ 0
Total:	$ 100.00
Amount refundable:	$ 0.00

Refundable deposits:

Cleaning deposit (Refundable)	$ 75.00
Redecorating deposit (Refundable)	$ 0
Security deposit (Refundable)	$ 300.00
Other _____	$ 0
Total:	$ 375.00

DEDUCTIONS

Unpaid rent	$ 0
Late charges	$ 0
Damages _Hole in Bedroom #1 Wall_	$ 65.00
Damages _Light fixture missing_	$ 40.00
Damages _____	$ 0
Other _____	$ 0
TOTAL DEDUCTIONS	$ 105.00
AMOUNT OF REFUNDABLE DEPOSITS:	$ 270.00

Refund check # _1001_ issued on September 14, 1994, for $ _270.00_

Larry Landlord

This notice delivered this date _Sept. 14, '94_ via:

☐ Certified mail
☒ Regular first class mail
☐ Hand delivered

Acknowledgment of hand delivery and receipt hereof:

N/A
_____   _____
(signature of tenant)   (date)

7. Seven Day Notice to Pay or Quit.

For residential tenants, if you fail to pay your rent, you will inevitably encounter the infamous **Seven-Day Notice to Pay or Quit**, a.k.a. the **Seven-Day Notice**. Strangely enough, the Act does not prescribe the content of the Seven-Day Notice, but the Act does provide some guidance:

> If rent is unpaid when due and the tenant fails to pay rent within seven days after written notice by the landlord of nonpayment and his intention to terminate the rental agreement if the rent is not paid within that period of time, the landlord may terminate the rental agreement by filing a special detainer action pursuant to § 33-1377.[63]

---

[63] A.R.S. § 33-1368(B) (West Supp. 1993).

There are no magic words, but the landlord must convey the appropriate message: rent is overdue and if not paid within seven days, the landlord will terminate the rental agreement. *See* sample 7-Day Notice, below.

SEVEN-DAY NOTICE TO PAY OR QUIT

Terry Tenant
101 North Rental Avenue   Date: June 10, 1994
Phoenix, Arizona 85999

Notice to Tenant,

      Pursuant to Arizona Revised Statutes, Title 33, Chapter 10, Section 33-1368(B), you are hereby tendered seven-day written notice to remit all due, but as yet unpaid, rent and other amounts owing, in the amount of: $490.00 (calculated through June 10, 1994). The stated amount is calculated as follows:

     $ 450.00   Rent from June 1 to June 30.
     $ 20.00   Late charges (calculated thru June 10, 1994)
     $ 20.00   Fee for preparing and serving Seven-Day Notice
     $ _____   Other _____
     $ _____   Other _____
     $ 490.00   Total

The stated "Total," however, is exclusive of future accruing costs. Additional charges accrue after June 10 at the daily rate of $ 2.50 .

      In the event full payment is not tendered within seven days after receipt of this notice, your Rental Agreement will terminate and you must vacate the premises on the seventh day. **THE SEVENTH DAY FALLS ON: June 18, 1994**. Vacating the premises, however, will not absolve you from liability for the outstanding balance. Alternatively, full payment within the seven-day period will reinstate the rental agreement. If you have any questions or require additional information, please feel free to contact me at 555-8888.

                           Larry Landlord
                       _____

This notice delivered this date June 10, 1994 via:
☐ Certified mail
☐ Regular first class mail
☒ Hand delivered

          Acknowledgment of hand delivery and receipt hereof:

        Terry Tenant   June 10, 1994
     _____   _____
        (signature of tenant)   (date)

      If a commercial tenant fails to pay his/her rent, the landlord can, <u>without prior notice</u>, immediately retake possession of the premises.[64] This is commonly referred to as a "lock out." If, however, the landlord chooses to file a forcible detainer action, s/he must provide the tenant with a written demand for

---

[64] A.R.S. § 33-361(A) (West 1990).

possession.[65] The amount of time that the landlord must give the tenant in the demand for possession is not set by statute, but five days is typical and is supported by case law.[66]

8. Parking Violations.

A "Parking Violation Form," threatening to tow your vehicle, may be an empty threat by the landlord or may be legitimate. How do you tell the difference? Typically, towing of vehicles that are unlawfully parked on private property is governed by local law (i.e., city or town). For more on this topic and a reprint of the Phoenix City Code addressing towing of vehicles, *see* Chapter 5, Section B(7).

9. Complaint Form.

Most commercial landlords and professional residential property managers have some type of general purpose "Complaint Form," such as the one below.

NOTICE OF ⊠ COMPLAINT ▢ VIOLATION

Terry Tenant
101 North Rental Avenue   Date: June 1, 1994
Phoenix, Arizona 85999

Notice to Tenant:

⊠　　　Complaints have been made against you for:
　　　　Excessive noise; specifically, loud music played after 10:00 p.m.
　　　　_____
　　　　_____

▢　　　You are violating the following term(s) in your Rental Agreement:
　　　　_____
　　　　_____
　　　　_____

⊠　　　Your repeated violations of the same or similar nature constitute a material noncompliance with your Rental Agreement.

　　　　You must take action to remedy this/these problems immediately ! Your Rental Agreement will be terminated and you will be evicted if you fail to comply.

　　　　　　　　　　　　　　　　　　Larry Landlord

This notice delivered this date ___June 1, 1994___ via:

▢ Certified mail
▢ Regular first class mail
⊠ Hand delivered

　　　　　　Acknowledgment of hand delivery and receipt hereof:

　*Terry Tenant*_____   *June 1, 1994*_____
　　　　(signature of tenant)　　　　　　　　　(date)

---

[65] A.R.S. §§ 12-1173, -1173.01. This requirement for written demand overrides the language of A.R.S. § 33-361(A), which provides that an action may be commenced without formal demand. *See* Alton v. Tower Capital Co., 123 Ariz. 602, 601 P.2d 602 (1979) (forcible detainer could not be brought until expiration of five-day period).
[66] *See* Alton v. Tower Capital Co., 123 Ariz. 602, 601 P.2d 602, 604 (1979).

Depending on the terms of your rental agreement, you may or may not have to pay a fee every time your landlord generates one of these forms. What does your rental agreement say?

The landlord uses this form to document the file. If the tenant demonstrates a history of "problems," and the landlord wishes to evict the tenant, copies of the previously issued Complaint Forms will go a long way toward supporting the landlord's position in a court of law. Therefore, anytime you receive a Complaint Form from the landlord you should take immediate corrective action and send a written notice to the landlord stating that you have resolved the problem.

10. Fourteen-Day Notice of Termination of Rental Agreement for Material Noncompliance with Rental Agreement.

Under appropriate circumstances, **either** the landlord or the tenant may issue this notice. For a thorough discussion of who may use this form and how/when it is used, see Chapter 5, Section C(1).

11. Ten-Day Notice of Termination of Rental Agreement for Noncompliance with Rental Agreement Materially Affecting Health and Safety.

Under appropriate circumstances, **either** the landlord or the tenant may issue this notice. For a thorough discussion of who may use this form and how/when it is used, see Chapter 5, Section C(2).

12. Notice of Immediate Termination of Rental Agreement for Material and Irreparable Breach.

The Act provides that, under certain circumstances, the landlord can **immediately** terminate your rental agreement:

> If there is a breach that is both material and irreparable, such as an illegal discharge of a weapon on the premises, infliction of serious bodily harm, threatening or intimidating as defined in § 13-1202 or assault as defined in § 13-1203 of the landlord, his agent or another tenant or involving imminent serious property damage, the landlord may deliver a written notice for immediate termination of the rental agreement and shall proceed under § 33-1377.[67]

The appearance and content of this notice is very similar to the Fourteen-Day Notice and Ten-Day Notice (discussed above). See Chapter 5, Sections C(1) and C(2) for samples of both the Fourteen-Day Notice and Ten-Day Notice.

---

[67] A.R.S. § 33-1368 (West Supp. 1993).

CHAPTER 4

APPLYING TO BE A TENANT

Summary of Chapter

FINDING A SUITABLE RENTAL UNIT
- Do it Yourself *OR* Real Estate
    Agents/Brokers, Locator Services
- Curb Appeal
- Interior Appearance
- The Neighborhood

LOOK AT THE UNIT BEFORE COMPLETING
AN APPLICATION

THE APPLICATION PROCESS
- The Written Application
- The Oral Application
- The "Second" Application

DISCRIMINATION

TERM OF TENANCY

READ THE RENTAL AGREEMENT

A. FINDING A SUITABLE RENTAL UNIT.

1. Do it Yourself *OR* Real Estate Agents/Brokers, Locator Services.

There are essentially two ways to find a rental unit: do it yourself or employ the services of some person/agency. If you do it yourself, finding a specific rental unit may be accomplished by any number of methods: classified ads, billboards, radio ads, television ads, fliers, word-of-mouth, etc. Scanning the classified advertisements may be fine, but you may also consider seeking out specialized publications (i.e., "Apartment Guide," "For Rent Magazine," etc.) that contain advertisements limited to your specific needs (i.e., available rental units).

If you employ a third party (i.e., a real estate agent/broker, a rental referral agency, rental locator services, etc.), the task may be somewhat easier, but convenience comes at a price. Naturally, the purveyors of these services will be quick to tell you that the landlord is paying their fee, but you can be sure that, one way or another, the landlord is building the fee into the rent. This is not necessarily bad. Just understand, in advance, that *you* will ultimately pay for these services.

In either case, you will eventually locate an available unit. How you hear about the particular unit is not important. What is important is what you do immediately after you see the rental unit for the first time.

2. Curb Appeal.

Curb appeal of the complex and/or the rental unit is important for two reasons. First, whether this unit is to be used as a residence or as a place of business (i.e., commercial real estate), your friends, relatives and customers (if for a business) will see this unit. You probably do not wish to live (or work) in a slum. Further, you certainly do not want others to believe that you live/work in a slum.

Second, how the landlord maintains the rental complex as a whole and/or the individual rental units is, perhaps, the best indication of how responsive the landlord will be to your wants/needs. If the roof is in serious need of repair, your chances of getting a leaky faucet fixed are probably slim. Take a good hard look at the rental unit. If the unit is a house or separate commercial building, merely look at the rental unit. If the unit is an apartment, look at the individual unit *and* the complex. In either case, you should also look at the neighborhood in general. A nicely kept unit may not be very appealing if it is located in a neighborhood of predominately run-down buildings.

If the unit is part of an organized community (i.e., a townhouse, condominium, cooperative, etc.), you should examine the governing body (i.e., the homeowners' association, etc.) to see that it is being properly run and adequately financed. You should also *insist* upon receiving a copy of the rules and regulations of the governing body. If your landlord "forgets" to mention these rules and regulations, you will nevertheless be required to abide by them.

3. Interior Appearance.

Naturally, the interior appearance must meet with your approval. If there are any deficiencies, insist that they be remedied <u>before</u> you move in. But there is an exception. From time to time, a rental unit that requires "a little repair" may become available. The landlord may intend to have this work professionally done, but if you are qualified to perform the work, you may be able to strike a "deal" with him/her, whereby you perform the work in exchange for a reduction in your move in costs. Consider asking if such a unit is available.

4. The Neighborhood.

Talk to some surrounding tenants and/or neighbors. Disgruntled tenants will be quick to tell you all of the landlord's shortcomings. If no other tenant voices complaints, you may have merely encountered a "problem tenant." If, on the other hand, all of the other tenants that you talk to echo the same shortcomings, you should act according to your needs/wants. For example, if everyone complains that the landlord has just changed the policy from allowing pets to not allowing pets and no one has voiced any other significant landlord complaints, then this is only an issue for you if you own (or want) a pet; otherwise, it is of no consequence. If, however, everyone says that it always takes the landlord five to seven days to fix the air conditioner, you may wish to pass on this unit.

B. LOOK AT THE UNIT BEFORE COMPLETING AN APPLICATION.

Look at the unit before completing an application. This is one of the most important tips. First, if you do not like the unit, you do not have to bother with an application. Second, if you do like it, you should then spend the appropriate amount of time accurately completing the application. You should not get in the habit of quickly filling in the application because you could skip significant bits of information that may "make or break" your application. Work smarter, not harder -- look at the unit first.

C. THE APPLICATION PROCESS.

1. The Written Application.

Now that you've seen the rental unit and are interested in renting it, take the time to complete the entire application form. The information that the landlord requests on the application is important to the landlord. Make sure you give the landlord complete, accurate information. When completing the application, you should try to evaluate how the information you provide will be interpreted by the landlord. Consequently, you should try to look at your application from the *landlord's* point of view. An experienced landlord looks at the application process as an applicant eliminator. As a general rule, no landlord will accept you as a tenant just by looking at your application, but may very well reject you "on the spot," without additional information or inquiry, just by looking at your application. NOTE: If the landlord rejects you immediately, you will probably not know it. Most landlords prefer to inform applicants via telephone that they have been rejected.

On the next page is a typical application. I will walk you through this *seemingly* simple application. Pay close attention -- you may be surprised. You may observe that the application does not ask for bank account numbers, a long list of prior addresses or employers, etc. This will tell you one of two things: either the landlord does not want this information (unlikely) or this application is part one of a two-part process (the "second application" is discussed in Section C(3), later in this chapter).

TENANT APPLICATION

NAME __Terry Tenant__

NAME __Tina Tenant__

ADDRESS __222 North Oak Street__

__Anytown, AZ 85111__

PHONE # __555-1111__ __555-2222__

(Day-time) (Home Phone)

CURRENT LANDLORD'S NAME __Slum Lord__

ADDRESS __112 North Oak Street__

__Anytown, AZ 85111__

PHONE # __555-3333__ PRESENT RENT $ __450.00__

HOW LONG THERE __2 years__ MAY I CALL FOR A REFERENCE ☒ Yes ☐ No

WHY ARE YOU MOVING __Job Transfer__

CURRENT EMPLOYER __OMNI Products, Inc.__

ADDRESS __505 W. Ash Street__

__Anytown, AZ 85111__

SUPERVISOR'S NAME __Sarah Supervisor__

PHONE # __555-4444__ GROSS MONTHLY INCOME $ __2,000.00__

HOW LONG THERE __5 years__ MAY I CALL FOR A REFERENCE ☒ Yes ☐ No

Taking into account all your other expenses, can you afford the rent on this unit?

HOW IS YOUR CREDIT ☐ Good ☒ Fair ☐ Ooops ☒ Yes ☐ No

WHEN DO YOU PLAN TO MOVE IN ? __30-60 days__

HOW LONG DO YOU ANTICIPATE STAYING ? __1 year__

REFERENCES: (minimum two)

NAME __Fran Friend__

Relationship (friend, boss, etc) __Friend__ PHONE __555-5555__

NAME __Barry Boss__

Relationship (friend, boss, etc) __Boss__ PHONE __555-6666__

NAME __Tom Tenant__

Relationship (friend, boss, etc) __Your tenant/a friend__ PHONE __555-7777__

HOW DID YOU HEAR ABOUT THIS RENTAL UNIT / COMPLEX?

☐ Sign ☐ Newspaper ☒ Other Tenant ☐ Friend ☐ Billboard ☐ Magazine

☐ Other _____

Home phone number. Are you a responsible person? Do you have a telephone at your home? My guess is that you answered yes to both questions. I would like to think of myself as a responsible person, and yes, I, too, have a telephone at home. Doesn't everybody? The real world answer is, "No, not everyone has a telephone at home." Who doesn't have a telephone at home and how do they live without one? Answer: deadbeats don't have a telephone at home. I don't know the answer to the second part of this question. Is it possible that someone could be responsible and make a very good tenant but not presently have a telephone at home? I suppose it is possible, but, as a landlord, I have rejected applications without further investigation simply because the applicant did not have a telephone at home. If you do not have a telephone, you should offer the landlord an explanation -- *before* the landlord asks.

<u>Present rent</u>. The purpose of this question is to determine the amount that you are accustomed to paying for rent. It also tells the landlord whether this unit will be a significant increase <u>or</u> decrease -- <u>either</u> is suspect. If the new rent will be a significant increase, you better be prepared to explain why you can now pay more for rent (i.e., you won the lottery, big promotion, etc.). Likewise, if this is a substantial decrease, you better have a very good explanation (i.e., a recent divorce, bankruptcy, etc.). "I just want to save some money" will not be enough.

<u>How long there?</u> If your answer is less than one year, you should have a plausible explanation. Landlords prefer long-term tenants.

<u>May I call for a reference?</u> This is a tricky area. If you are leaving because your present landlord is a jerk, s/he probably will not have anything good to say about anyone, much less a vacating tenant. A simple "No" on the application will be translated by the landlord into "No, because I never paid my rent on time and I certainly don't want my present landlord to tell you that." If you are in this unfortunate situation, there is only one way to answer this question: "I prefer that you do not contact my landlord." You should then explain the situation to the person taking your application.

<u>Why are you moving?</u> This seemingly simple question is critical. Landlords will accept "no fault" reasons (i.e., job transfer, change of schools, to move closer to work, etc). Fault-based reasons, however, are highly suspect. Some typical fault-based reasons follow, along with the landlord's probable interpretation/translation of them.

| Tenant: | "My landlord is/was a jerk." |
| Translation: | I was a jerk and my landlord evicted me. |

| Tenant: | "The unit was always breaking down." |
| Translation: | I broke everything in the unit and the landlord would not fix anything. |

| Tenant: | "The neighbors were jerks." |
| Translation: | I was a jerk, the neighbors reported me and I was evicted. |

And, finally,

| Tenant: | "My roommate left without paying his share of the rent, so I had to find a cheaper place." |

Translation: I was the guy who left without paying rent.

or

My roommate did leave without paying rent; therefore, I had to leave without paying rent -- my past landlord is looking for me.

Current Employer. Landlords want this information for all the usual reasons. It also allows landlords to screen applicants according to occupations. Some landlords do not like to rent to lawyers because they think they are likely to cause trouble (hard to imagine). Others like lawyers because they think they are responsible people. Who knows for sure? Yes, I hear you, "Can a landlord discriminate based on occupation?" Yes. The landlord cannot discriminate based on race, religion, national origin, sex, handicap or because the applicant has children, but discrimination based upon occupation is not against the law. *See* Chapter 4, Section D, for more about discrimination.

Gross monthly income. Naturally, the landlord will check to make sure that you can afford to pay the rent. But, the landlord will also check to see if you are making "too much" money. You probably never imagined that a landlord would reject your application because you make too much, but you are not thinking like a landlord. If a tenant makes $3,000 per month and applies to rent a $300 per month unit, there is something wrong with this picture (i.e., the tenant is either overstating his/her income or is up to his/her earlobes in debt). If your income is grossly disproportionate to the amount of rent you will be paying, you should be prepared to explain.

How long there (length of employment). The reason for this question is similar to that for "length of last tenancy." Landlords do not favor "job hoppers," for obvious reasons.

May I call for a reference? This is *seemingly* the same question that you answered with respect to your present landlord, but the answer is treated **much** differently. Your present landlord possesses very limited information. After all, how often did you see your present landlord -- once a month (to pay rent), if at all? Your supervisor, on the other hand, sees you all day long, five days a week. This person knows a great deal about you. Any competent landlord will <u>insist</u> on speaking with your supervisor. Most landlords can live with an applicant declining to allow contact with the current landlord. Most landlords, however, will look very suspiciously upon your refusal to let him/her contact your supervisor, and some landlords will immediately reject the application. The reason is simple, supervisors typically don't care if their employees move. Therefore, the landlord will likely conclude that the applicant must be hiding something.

Taking into account all your other expenses, can you afford the rent on this unit? Sounds like a foolish question, right? Don't get it wrong. The landlord wants your subjective appraisal of whether or not you can afford the rent. If you don't think so, why should the landlord?

How is your credit? You should tell the truth on this one because you know the landlord will check. Landlords can live with tenants that have bad credit, but they will not tolerate tenants that have bad credit <u>and</u> that lie on the application.

So who pays for the credit report? The answer is driven by market conditions in your geographic area. If the area that you desire to live in is in high demand, then landlords can require tenants to pay for the fee. If demand is low, landlords may be more willing to pick up the tab on this expense.

When do you plan to move in? This seemingly innocent question is very revealing. This will tell the landlord if you are leaving your prior landlord "in the lurch" (i.e., did you give adequate notice?).

How long do you anticipate staying? Unless this is transient housing (i.e., a motel), the landlord will probably reject any application that indicates less than six months.

References. This is much more important than it seems. Not all landlords call the references, but virtually all landlords insist that you *have* references. Everyone has two references. Even people in the Federal Witness Protection Program have two references. If you can't come up with two references, the landlord will assume that you are either hiding something or simply hiding.

2. The Oral Application.

Here is the scenario: thus far, you have seen the rental unit; you like it; you want it; you have diligently completed the written application. That's it, right? Wrong. Although you may think that completing the written application ends the application process, that is not the case. Any bank loan officer will tell you that the written loan application is only part of the loan application. The loan officer's oral interview with the loan applicant, more times than not, is the deciding factor in whether or not the applicant receives a loan. This is no less true in the residential landlord setting. The truth is everything you say and do is part of the application.

The second component of the tenant application, the oral application, consists of the landlord's "follow-up questions." You may not even be aware that it is occurring -- or when. The oral application may be done before, during and/or after completion of the written application. Follow-up questions fall into two categories:

- Follow-up questions prompted by responses provided on the application.

- Follow-up questions prepared in advance by the landlord.

It is impossible to anticipate all of the conceivable questions that landlords could propound, but I have listed many of the more common follow-up questions below. I have not attempted to provide you with "model" answers, however, because there are none. You should mentally prepare answers to these questions before you shop for a rental unit, and you should feel confident about your answers. Remember to try to look at your answers *from the landlord's point of view*.

- Why do you wish to live in this area/neighborhood?

- What attracted you to this unit?

- If your application is approved, do you intend to install a telephone? (*See* Chapter 4, Section C(1))

- Do you have a checking account or other bank account? (*See* Section C(3))

- Do you have a car? If so:
  - What kind?
  - How much do you owe on it?
  - What are your payments?

- What type of work do you do? (the landlord knows who your employer is, but not necessarily what you do)
  - How long have you been performing that job? (as distinguished from "How long have you worked for that employer?")
  - How many jobs have you had in the last two years?

When answering *any* question, keep in mind that *what* you say may not be as important as *how* you say it.

3. The "Second" Application.

As previously stated, some landlords use a two-step application process. Examine the form on the following page. This is the second application form that I use. I call it a "Tenant Information Sheet." Typically, each occupant and each person who will sign the rental agreement (i.e., a parent may sign the rental agreement but not occupy the unit) will complete this form. The information you put on this form will make or break your application. As with the first application, this "second" application elicits information that may eliminate you as an applicant without further inquiry. The areas of concern are denoted by the double asterisk.

Checking Account, Social Security Number and Date of Birth. Landlords view a checking account much the same way as they do a telephone -- landlords want their tenants to have a telephone and, similarly, landlords want their tenants to have a checking account. The reason is simple, most responsible people have checking accounts. In addition, if a tenant doesn't have a checking account, then that means at some point during every month s/he is walking around with lots of cash in his/her pocket. Landlords don't want to be robbed, which is much more likely if they accept cash and keep cash on the premises, and landlords don't want to hear that their tenant has been robbed.

TENANT INFORMATION SHEET

Unit # __2__

TENANT INFORMATION

Phone # 555-1111

NAME __Terry Tenant__

PLACE OF BIRTH __Tucson, AZ__ DATE OF BIRTH __June 1, 1950__

SOCIAL SECURITY # __555-11-2222__ DRIVER'S LICENSE # __558-22-9999__

EMPLOYER __OMNI Products, Inc.__

ADDRESS __101 North Central Avenue, Phoenix, Arizona__

SUPERVISOR __Sarah Supervisor__ PHONE # __555-4444__

PARENTS' NAMES __Dick & Jane Tenant__

ADDRESS __111 North Elm Street, Anytown, CA__

PERSON TO NOTIFY IN CASE OF EMERGENCY __Fran Friend__

ADDRESS __222 North 1st Avenue, Phoenix__ PHONE # __555-5555__

CHILDREN __Tanya Tenant__ AGE __2__

__Tony Tenant__ AGE __7__

Have you ever filed Bankruptcy? ☒ No ☐ Yes (when _____)

Have you ever been evicted? ☒ No ☐ Yes (when _____)

Do you wish to have pet? ☐ No ☒ Yes (type __fish__ weight __1 oz.__)

BANK INFORMATION

Where do you bank: __First Interstate Bank__ Branch: __Main__

Checking account #: __01-2222__ Savings account #: __02-1111__

Other account #: __IRA - 03-4444__ Other account #: __--__

VEHICLE INFORMATION

(list information on each vehicle):

MAKE __Nissan__ MODEL __Sentra__ YR __90__ LICENSE # __XYZ-111__

Lienholder __Valley National Bank__ Balance owed __$6,000.00__ Mo Pymt __$149.00__

MAKE __Chevrolet__ MODEL __Camaro__ YR __82__ LICENSE # __XYZ-222__

Lienholder __Clear__ Balance owed __-0-__ Mo Pymt __-0-__

__Type of car, etc.__ The type of car, the balance owed, the monthly payment and even the name of the lienholder provide the landlord with very useful information. The old adage that the type of car you drive tells a lot about your personality is true. Your car also gives people an idea of how much you spend on transportation. Landlords do not look favorably upon an applicant for a unit that rents for $300 per month who drives a Ferrari because this suggests that this applicant may have some "unreported" income from an unsavory business. It may also suggest that this tenant will not be able to pay the rent by the time s/he gets done paying the car payment, the gasoline bill and that month's accumulation of speeding tickets. On the other hand, an applicant for an exclusive, single family home who drives a Ferrari may be acceptable.

Bottom line -- the type of car you drive (or, at least, the type of car you drive when you go shopping for a rental unit) should be consistent with the price range of property that you wish to lease.

The name of the lienholder is also informative. A well-known financial institution is good. "Lurch's Pawn & Loan," however, suggests that no one else would give you a car loan. On the other hand, if your name is "Lurch," and you own an entire chain of "Lurch's Pawn & Loan" establishments, tell your landlord. This impressive information will do you no good if you don't let the landlord know.

Have you ever filed bankruptcy? Again, tell the truth on this one -- it is very easy to check. Some landlords automatically eliminate an applicant if they have filed bankruptcy; others do not. Bankruptcy is obviously not a good sign, but it is certainly not as bad as some other problems (i.e., previous eviction). If you have filed bankruptcy, be "up-front" with the landlord and stress that you are trying very hard to re-establish good credit and that you have no other bills (i.e., all your prior debts were discharged in the bankruptcy). You are probably asking, "Won't disclosing a bankruptcy (etc.) 'kill' my chances of being accepted?" Perhaps, but not necessarily. On the other hand, dishonesty on the application will certainly "kill" your chances. Significant events, such as a bankruptcy, are easily discovered by landlords. Why hide something that you know the landlord will ultimately find out?

Have you ever been evicted? Virtually all landlords view a prior eviction as being much worse than a bankruptcy. If you have previously been evicted, you should offer the landlord a well reasoned explanation.

Children. Historically, many landlords avoided renting to people with children. Today, however, landlords can no longer discriminate against applicants with children because it violates the law,[68] except where the property is subject to a valid deed restriction or where the property lies within a subdivision designed, advertised and used as an adult community (e.g., Sun City, Arizona).[69] However, don't confuse a landlord's rejection of an applicant because s/he has children with rejection of an applicant because s/he has *too many* children. A landlord may lawfully turn down an application from a couple with three children who wish to rent a two-bedroom unit. This rejection is based upon the number of occupants, not the age of the occupants.[70]

---

[68] A.R.S. § 33-1317(A) (West Supp. 1993).

[69] A.R.S. § 33-1317(B) (West Supp. 1993).

[70] A.R.S. § 33-1317(F) (West Supp. 1993).

Pets. For the most part, landlords either permit pets -- or they don't. And tenants either have (or want) pets -- or they don't. Sometimes there is a middle ground (i.e., pets under a certain number of pounds or certain types of pets are allowed). Most landlords will not change their policy on this issue because their decision does not impact solely upon you; it impacts on all their other tenants as well. Similarly, most pet owners will not give up a pet for the sake of renting a particular unit. Consequently, there normally isn't much room for negotiation in this area. This being the case, if you have (or want) a pet, one of the **FIRST** questions you should ask is whether pets are allowed. Ask this question before you fill out the application -- it may save you a lot of time. Certain landlords, however, are more likely to change their policy than others. As a practical matter, the landlord of a single-family residence is much more likely to change his/her policy if having a pet is important to you and you ask *before* you move in or, if you have already moved in, before you bring a pet onto the premises. Asking the landlord to change his/her policy *after* the landlord discovers that you have a pet on the premises normally brings unfavorable results (i.e., eviction).

D. DISCRIMINATION.

A landlord considers many factors when deciding whether or not to approve a tenant application. One factor is simply math -- can the applicant afford the unit? Another factor is common sense -- does the applicant have a steady job, good references, etc.? Much of the decision, however, is purely subjective. You may be surprised to learn just how much discretion a landlord has when deciding the criteria for measuring the acceptability of applicants. There are, however, certain limits placed on the landlord's discretion.

Under the law, a landlord cannot use the following factors in deciding whether to accept a tenant: race, color, religion, national origin, sex, handicap ("handicap" includes persons diagnosed with the HIV or AIDS virus)[71] or familial status (i.e., marital status, applicant has children).[72] But anything else is okay. Example 1: a landlord may decide that an applicant, who is an attorney, is undesirable and refuse to rent to him/her because the landlord believes (correctly or not) that the lawyer knows more about the law than s/he does and, therefore, may be likely to cause trouble. This is perfectly legal and the landlord can do it. Example 2: the landlord does not like the fact that an applicant's car is noisy because the landlord lives on the premises and s/he believes that the noise will disturb him/her every time the applicant leaves or arrives -- fine; the landlord may reject an application solely upon this basis. Example 3: a landlord would rather not rent to an applicant who rides a noisy motorcycle because it will disturb other tenants or because the landlord simply does not like "Bikers" -- no violation. Except for the factors just listed, a landlord can refuse to rent to anyone for any reason.

---

[71] 24 C.F.R. § 100.201 (prohibition against discrimination because of handicap); 54 Fed. Reg. 3245, 3288 (1989); A.R.S. § 41-1491(8) (West 1991); PHOENIX, ARIZONA, CITY CODE, Chapter 18, art. III, § 18-11 to 18-11.39 (1991).

[72] Civil Rights Act of 1866, 42 U.S.C. § 1982 (1988) (prohibits racial discrimination in sale or rental of all property); 42 U.S.C. §§ 3601-3619 (1988) (unlawful to refuse to sell or rent a dwelling to any person because of race, color, religion, sex, familial status, or national origin); A.R.S. §§ 33-1317 (West Supp. 1993), 41-1491.01 to .36 (West 1992 & Supp. 1993).

Perhaps an actual court case can best illustrate this point.[73] An unmarried black woman applied to rent an apartment in New York and was turned down. She sued the landlord, charging the landlord with discrimination on the basis of race, sex and/or her marital status. The landlord's defense was that he did not discriminate because she was black, female or unmarried (in fact, he already had several tenants who were unmarried, black and/or women). The landlord claimed that he rejected her application because she was a lawyer. The landlord stated outright that he openly discriminated against lawyers because he felt they were likely to cause trouble. The judge ruled in the landlord's favor stating that as long as the landlord was not discriminating on the basis of race, creed, color, national origin, sex, disability, or marital status, he was entitled to protect his own interests. Specifically, the court said:

> Thus, this court concludes that there is nothing illegal in a landlord discriminating against lawyers as a group, or trying to keep out of his building intelligent persons, aware of their rights, who may give him trouble in the future.[74]

Also, although a landlord may not reject an applicant because s/he has children, the landlord may reject an applicant because s/he has *too many* children.[75] A landlord may lawfully turn down an application from a couple with three children who wish to rent a two-bedroom unit. This rejection is based upon the number of occupants, not the age of the occupants.[76] To successfully defend a charge of discrimination in such a case, however, the landlord's occupancy standards (and other standards, i.e., credit, etc.) must be established in advance. The landlord's criteria may look like this:

Occupancy standard: Two person per bedroom (maximum).
Monthly Income: Four (4) times monthly rental amount.
Employment: One (1) year (or more) with same employer.
Credit: Good.   Pets: Yes (but under 10 pounds).
Smoker: Yes   Assets/Savings: Over $5,000.00.
Attitude during application: Good/pleasant/friendly. (Other Factors: phone, car, etc.)

What do you do if you know (or believe) that you have been the victim of unlawful discrimination? Answer: contact the Arizona Attorney General, who has the authority to investigate and/or bring legal action against the landlord; contact HUD (Housing and Urban Development); and/or contact your local municipality, which may also have authority to bring legal action against the landlord.[77] Do not delay; there are specific time limits for bringing these types of cases.[78]

---

[73] *See* Kramarsky v. Stahl Management, 92 Misc. 2d 1030, 401 N.Y.S.2d 943 (1977).

[74] Kramarsky v. Stahl Management, 92 Misc. 2d 1030, 401 N.Y.S.2d 943, 945 (1977).

[75] A.R.S. § 33-1317(F) (West Supp. 1993).

[76] A.R.S. § 33-1317(F) (West Supp. 1993).

[77] *See, e.g.*, PHOENIX, ARIZONA, CITY CODE, Chapter 18, art. III, § 18-11 to 18-11.39 (1991).

[78] The statute of limitations for bringing a claim under the Civil Rights Act of 1866, 42 U.S.C. § 1982, is prescribed by the state law statute of limitations for personal injury, which is two (2) years in Arizona. A.R.S. § 12-542 (West Supp. 1990). The statute of limitations for bringing a claim under the Civil Rights Act of 1968, 42 U.S.C. §§ 3601-3619, is 180 days. 42 U.S.C. § 3610(b). The statute of limitations for a private citizen to bring a claim under A.R.S. § 41-1491.31 is two years. A.R.S. § 41-1491.31(A) (West 1991). Consequently, because an action may be filed within two years (the longest applicable statute of limitations) but not actually served until some time later (plaintiff has up to one year from the date of filing of the *complaint* to serve the complaint, pursuant to 16 A.R.S. Rules of Civil Procedure, Rule

E. TERM OF TENANCY.

Okay, you have made it through the application process and the landlord has informed you that s/he will accept you as a tenant. What next? The next significant decision that you will encounter is the length of the term of tenancy. The options are fairly straightforward: either month-to-month or a specified term (i.e., six months, one year, etc.). The landlord may offer both or only one.

Naturally, this is a personal choice that you must make, but here are some considerations. A lease "locks-in" the monthly rent for the duration of the specified period. On the other hand, you are obligated to stay and pay rent for the same period. By contrast, in a month-to-month agreement, the landlord may raise the rent any time that s/he wishes, with only thirty-days advance notice. But the tenant may choose to vacate as a result thereof and/or decide to terminate tenancy for any other reason (or no reason) with only thirty-days advance notice (or the amount of notice specified in the rental agreement). The disadvantage, however, is that the landlord can refuse to renew your tenancy (which, in a month-to-month tenancy, is done automatically every month) at any time (i.e., one month after you move in), for any reason, or for no reason whatsoever.

Both types of tenancy have advantages and disadvantages. Only you can decide which is best for you.

F. READ THE RENTAL AGREEMENT.

Cross Reference
- Chapter 3, Section B (Review Your Rental Agreement)

I have said it before; I will say it again -- READ THE RENTAL AGREEMENT! And read the entire agreement, every single word. Ideally, you should have your attorney review it, also. Sign the rental agreement **only after** you have read the rental agreement, understand all your obligations thereunder and are satisfied with (or, at least, can live with) all the terms and conditions.

6(f), you should keep all applications for at least three (3) years.

CHAPTER 5

HOW TO SOLVE COMMON TENANT PROBLEMS

Summary of Chapter

PREVENT TENANT PROBLEMS

COMMON TENANT PROBLEMS
>   What if I Can't Pay the Rent on Time, or at All?
>   Can the Landlord Assess and Collect a Late Fee?
>   Under What Circumstances Can the Landlord
>   Terminate My Lease?
>   Under What Circumstances Can I Terminate The
>   Lease?
>   Harassing/Trespassing Landlord
>   Noisy Neighbor and Neighbor Conflicts
>   Parking Problems
>   What if the Landlord Won't Make Repairs?

TENANT REMEDIES
>   Fourteen-Day Notice of Termination of Rental
>   Agreement for Material Noncompliance with
>   Rental Agreement
>   Ten-Day Notice of Termination of Rental
>   Agreement for Noncompliance with Rental
>   Agreement Materially Affecting Health and
>   Safety
>   Notice of Wrongful Failure to Supply Essential
>   Services
>   Notice of Termination or Rental Reduction
>   Because of Fire or Casualty Damage

In a perfect world, this section would be unnecessary. Unfortunately, however, tenants often encounter problems with their landlord and/or other tenants. How you handle these problems will generally determine whether or not you encounter the same or similar problem in the future.

A.   PREVENT TENANT PROBLEMS.

Cross Reference
•   Chapter 2 (Legal Advice to Tenants)

Learning how to solve common tenant problems means, first, learning how to prevent problems. In the event I have not heretofore clearly stated my position on this subject, I shall do so now: preventing a problem is infinitely more desirable than any conceivable solution to a problem. And the corollary, as previously stated (*see* Chapter 2), is that preventing or avoiding litigation is always better than winning litigation. Preventing problems should be a top priority for you, too.

False expectations and a misunderstanding of important terms and conditions are the primary cause of problems between landlords and tenants. This is why reading and understanding the rental agreement and all supplementary rules and regulations issued by the landlord is **so important**. If you have a problem with a particular term or condition in the rental agreement, resolve it with the landlord **before** you sign the rental agreement. Once you sign on the "dotted line," your landlord is under no obligation to change any of the terms.

B.   COMMON TENANT PROBLEMS.

Okay, you did your best to prevent problems, but, let's face it, stuff happens and problems come up. The following pages discuss some of the most frequently encountered problems and the various solutions available to you.

1.   What if I Can't Pay the Rent on Time, or at All?

From time to time, either as a result of some colossal blunder on your part or through no fault of your own, you may be temporarily or financially "disadvantaged." I am not oblivious to the real world and, therefore, I will not merely spout "honesty is the best policy" and recommend that you *always* disclose this information to your landlord. The truth is, your landlord *may* be sympathetic to your plight or s/he may act out of self interest and do whatever is necessary to get you out as soon as possible. You are in the best position to know how your landlord will react to this type of news.

As a practical matter, most landlords will be more willing to help if you tell him/her that you "don't have the rent right now, but will pay it soon, including any late fees." On the other hand, if you cannot pay the rent at all (i.e., you lost your job and have no immediate job prospects), your landlord will be less likely to work with you. The key to resolving this problem is to work "something" out with your landlord **before** the problem becomes critical (i.e., on the day of the forcible detainer hearing). At a minimum, landlords who receive notice from a tenant that the tenant must break their lease and move out because of a financial problem are less likely to "chase you down" later for due and unpaid rent. Moreover, the more notice you give them, the better off you will be. The fact that your landlord won't sue you for the balance due on the lease may be a *very* big weight off your shoulders. Conversely, landlords truly despise tenants that disappear in the middle of the night with no advance notice whatsoever and are much more inclined to chase these tenants to "the ends of the earth" to sue them for unpaid rent. In such a case, collecting is usually not as important to the landlord as imposing additional grief upon the tenant for leaving the landlord "in the lurch." In short, honesty is *usually* the best policy, but use your discretion. Assuming that you believe your landlord will not throw you "out on your ear," you should go to your landlord and try to work something out -- the sooner the better.

So, what may the landlord do if the tenant doesn't pay the rent? Answer: The landlord may begin eviction proceedings. *See* Chapter 6, Section D(2).

2. Can the Landlord Assess and Collect a Late Fee When I Pay Rent Late?

Maybe. If there is no written rental agreement, the landlord is not legally entitled to assess and collect a late fee. If the landlord ultimately evicts you, the court will not award the landlord a money judgment for late fees without a written agreement.[79]

If you signed a rental agreement that provides for a late fee when rent is tendered late, then the landlord may assess and collect a late fee.[80] But the late fee must be "reasonable." The time to discuss whether or not the late fee is "reasonable," however, is before you sign the agreement, not after you have signed it and are late paying your rent.

Before paying the late fee, however, you may wish to ask other tenants whether or not the landlord has ever "waived" a late fee for them and, most important, why it was waived. If your landlord has a habit of "inconsistent enforcement" of policies, rules and regulations (i.e., okay for the tenant in unit one, but not okay for the tenant in unit two), then s/he may run into some trouble if this practice is revealed in court. Courts frequently declare rental provisions unenforceable, even when written in clear language, when the tenant can demonstrate that the landlord has established a habit of "selective enforcement."[81]

---

[79] A.R.S. § 33-1377(F) (West Supp. 1993).

[80] A.R.S. § 33-1377(F) (West Supp. 1993).

[81] *See, e.g.,* UNIF. RESIDENTIAL LANDLORD AND TENANT ACT § 3.102; 7B U.L.A. 475 (1985).

3.   **Under What Circumstances Can the Landlord Terminate My Lease?**

Cross Reference
- Chapter 6, Section A (How and By Whom Tenancy May Be Terminated)
- Chapter 6, Section C (Evictions)

First, do not confuse termination of your lease with the decision not to renew tenancy. Neither the landlord nor the tenant need any reason whatsoever to not renew tenancy. Tenancy is renewed (or not) each time that the agreed upon term has expired (i.e., six months, one year, etc.). Therefore, if you are on a month-to-month tenancy, which is renewed (or not) each and every month, either you or the landlord may choose to not renew tenancy for any reason whatsoever with only thirty days notice (or as much notice as is required by your rental agreement).

Termination of your rental agreement is a prelude to eviction -- if your landlord terminates your rental agreement and you do not voluntarily vacate, the only way for the landlord to remove you from the premises is by legal process (i.e., eviction). Eviction, however, must be based on one of four categories of tenant conduct: (1) a material noncompliance with the rental agreement; (2) a noncompliance that materially affects health and safety; (3) a breach that is both material and irreparable; or (4) nonpayment of rent. For more on this topic, *see* Chapter 6, Section C (Evictions).

4.   **Under What Circumstances Can I Terminate the Lease?**

Cross Reference
- For the landlord's failure to make repairs, see Chapter 5, Sections C(1) and C(2)
- For the tenant's right to make repairs and deduct the cost from next month's rent, see Chapter 5, Section C(1)
- When the rental unit is completely or partially destroyed by fire or casualty, see Chapter 5, Section C(4)

The tenant's right to terminate the rental agreement is similar to the landlord's right -- if the landlord does not comply with his/her obligations under the rental agreement and the Act, the tenant *may* be able to terminate the rental agreement. The tenant's legal basis for terminating the rental agreement are: (1) a material noncompliance with the rental agreement;[82] (2) a noncompliance that materially affects health and safety;[83] (3) failure of the landlord to supply heat, air conditioning, cooling, water, hot water or essential services;[84] (4) destruction of the leased premises by fire or casualty;[85] (5) landlord's unlawful ouster, exclusion or

---

[82] A.R.S. § 33-1361 (West 1990).

[83] A.R.S. § 33-1361 (West 1990).

[84] A.R.S. § 33-1364 (West 1990).

[85] A.R.S. § 33-1366 (West 1990).

diminution of services;[86] and (6) failure of the landlord to deliver physical possession of the rental unit to the tenant (at the beginning of the rental term).[87]

Examples of the foregoing include failure of the landlord to make required repairs, failure to provide essential services, and failure to honor certain agreements (i.e., the landlord promised to install new carpet when you moved in). The procedure to follow for each type of case is discussed in Section C -- Tenant Remedies, later in this Chapter. The forms that you will need to comply with the law are included in Appendix B.

As an alternative to terminating the rental agreement, if the landlord fails to maintain the rental unit, the tenant may sue for damages or s/he may elect to repair the condition and deduct the cost of the repairs from the rent.[88] This option is also discussed in Section C -- Tenant Remedies, later in this Chapter.

5. Harassing/Trespassing Landlord.

This is a rare problem. Nevertheless, some landlords believe that, because they own the property, they can enter whenever they feel like it. This is simply untrue. The landlord certainly has the right to inspect the property from time to time,[89] but entering without prior notice is clearly unlawful, except in emergency situations.[90] The precise language of the statute may be enlightening.

> A. The tenant shall not unreasonably withhold consent to the landlord to enter into the dwelling unit in order to inspect the premises, make necessary or agreed repairs, decorations, alterations or improvements, supply necessary or agreed services or exhibit the dwelling unit to prospective or actual purchasers, mortgagees, tenants, workmen or contractors.
>
> B. The landlord may enter the dwelling unit without consent of the tenant in case of emergency.
>
> C. The landlord shall not abuse the right to access or use it to harass the tenant. Except in case of emergency or if it is impracticable to do so, the landlord shall give the tenant at least two days' notice of his intent to enter and enter only at reasonable times.
>
> D. The landlord has no other right of access except by court order and as permitted by § 33-1369 [Failure to Maintain]

---

[86] A.R.S. § 33-1367 (West 1990).

[87] A.R.S. § 33-1362 (West 1990).

[88] *See* A.R.S. §§ 33-1324, -1361, -1363(A) (West 1990).

[89] A.R.S. § 33-1343 (West 1990).

[90] A.R.S. § 33-1343(B) (West 1990).

and § 33-1370 [Abandonment], or if the tenant has abandoned or surrendered the premises.[91]

If your landlord has violated this statute, you should notify the landlord in writing that his/her conduct constitutes a material noncompliance with the rental agreement. If the conduct continues, the tenant may terminate the rental agreement and sue for damages.[92] *See* Section C (Tenant Remedies), later in this Chapter.

6.   **Noisy Neighbor and Neighbor Conflicts.**

This section is important if: (1) you have a noisy neighbor and you want to know what you can do about it; or (2) you are the noisy neighbor and the landlord is threatening to evict you.

If you have a noisy neighbor or some other type of neighbor conflict, the solutions are simple. First, ask the offending person to stop the annoying conduct. If that does not work (and it rarely does), then, depending on the severity of the problem, you may wish to notify the landlord, notify the police, or both. Certain disturbances, such as playing loud music late at night or fighting, are violations of the law (i.e., disturbing the peace) and may warrant summoning the police.[93] Other less severe conflicts may simply warrant a complaint to the landlord if the offending party refuses to stop. In either event, depending on the nature of the conduct, said conduct may constitute a material noncompliance with the rental agreement, thereby allowing the landlord to terminate the offending party's rental agreement if the problem continues.[94] Repeated complaints about one particular tenant, especially if made by more than one tenant (or neighbor, as in the case of a single family residence), is usually enough for most landlords to take corrective action.

If, however, the landlord refuses to do anything about the situation and the problem affects your health and safety,[95] cleanliness and safety of common areas,[96] fitness and habitability of the premises,[97] unlawfully removes or excludes you from the premises,[98] or otherwise diminishes your essential services (i.e., water, heat, etc.),[99] then, after written notice to the landlord, you may be able to terminate the rental agreement and bring an action for damages against the landlord.[100] *See* Section C(2), later in this Chapter.

---

[91] A.R.S. § 33-1343 (West 1990).

[92] A.R.S. § 33-1361 (West 1990). *see also* A.R.S. § 33-1367 (West 1990).

[93] A.R.S. § 13-2904(A) (West 1990) (unreasonable noise constitutes disorderly conduct).

[94] Section 33-1341(7) provides that the tenant shall "Conduct himself and require other persons on the premises with his consent to conduct themselves in a manner that will not disturb his neighbors' peaceful enjoyment of the premises."

[95] *See* A.R.S. § 33-1324(A)(1) (West 1990).

[96] A.R.S. § 33-1324(A)(3) (West 1990).

[97] A.R.S. § 33-1324(A)(2) (West 1990).

[98] A.R.S. § 33-1367 (West 1990).

[99] A.R.S. § 33-1367 (West 1990).

[100] A.R.S. §§ 33-1361, -1367 (West 1990).

7.   Parking Problems.

Parking is such a significant source of problems that you should definitely discuss it during the application process.

You should first ask whether you will have "assigned parking" (i.e., each parking stall is numbered and reserved for exclusive use by a particular tenant), "unassigned parking" (i.e., parking stalls are not numbered and any tenant may park in any empty stall), or a combination of both (i.e., one numbered assigned parking stall for each tenant and many parking stalls that are not numbered for use by guests and tenants with more than one vehicle). There is no "right" answer, but you should understand what you are getting into before you sign the rental agreement. If you have more than one vehicle, you should also make sure that you will **truly** have enough parking spaces to accommodate your vehicles.

The following pages discuss some typical parking problems experienced by tenants and landlords, with some suggestions on how to effectively resolve each problem. Naturally, some types of parking problems are indigenous only to apartment complexes, some only to single family residential rentals and some parking problems are common to both.

- A tenant is using too many spaces because: (1) a tenant owns more vehicles than his/her allotment of parking spaces; (2) a tenant or a tenant's guest is improperly parked; (3) a tenant or a tenant's guest is parked in another tenant's assigned parking stall; (4) a tenant frequently (or infrequently) has guests over to visit him and they take several or many of the unassigned parking stalls.

- A Tenant or guest parks in an area not designated for parking.

- A tenant parks a commercial vehicle in one (or more) parking stall(s).

- A tenant leaves a disabled vehicle in one space for many days.

- A tenant frequently performs vehicle maintenance on his vehicle(s) while parked in parking stall(s).

(a)   Tenants/guests improperly parked.

There is not much to discuss if you have assigned parking and you are in the wrong parking space. The remedies are clear: if the landlord has complied with local law (i.e., city/town ordinance addressing notice and posting of tow away zones), then the landlord may have your vehicle towed if you are improperly parked. This is not surprising to most tenants. The "surprise" comes when a tenant has "a few" friends over and they improperly park. The solution is to know the landlord's policy in advance and plan accordingly. If you do not, and the landlord has complied with local law, then your guests' cars may also be towed.

You are probably asking, "When has the landlord complied with 'local law,' and when may the landlord tow my (or my guest's) vehicle?" Answer: Towing of vehicles is governed by local law (i.e., city/town). Sometimes the landlord must give written notice; sometimes signs must be posted. Given the number of cities and towns in Arizona, I have not attempted to chronicle the various laws on this utterly fascinating subject. To find out the law in your area, call your lawyer. Alternatively, call a local towing company. Because towing is their business, a towing company will probably know what the law is and what the notice requirements are in your city/town. You may also wish to check with other tenants to see if anyone has ever *really* been towed before. Or, alternatively, you could simply move your car.

For those living in Phoenix, Arizona, I have reprinted, below, the section of the Phoenix City Code that addresses parking.

Parking in driveway or private property; tow truck operators

A. No person shall park a vehicle in any private driveway or on private property or private parking areas without the express or implied consent of the owner or person in lawful possession of such property.

B. The owner or person in lawful possession of any private parking area shall be deemed to have given consent to unrestricted parking by the general public in such parking area unless such parking area is posted with signs as prescribed by this section which are clearly visible and readable from any point within the parking area and at each entrance thereto. Such signs shall contain, as a minimum, the following information:

(1) Restrictions on parking.

(2) Disposition of vehicles found in violation of parking restrictions.

(3) Maximum cost to the violator, including daily storage fees and other charges, that could result from the disposition of his unlawfully parked vehicle.

(4) Telephone number or address where the violator can locate his vehicle.

(5) Each sign shall state 'Phoenix City Code Sec. 36-144.'

C.   No tow truck operator acting under the authority of this section shall tow a vehicle from a private parking area unless the signs are posted as required by paragraph B and contain all the information specified in paragraph B, nor shall he charge fees in excess of the amounts specified on the signs.

. . . .

H.   Not withstanding any other provision of this section an abandoned vehicle may be towed from any private parking area, pursuant to a written order from the real property owner or his agent.   A tow truck operator shall not act as the agent of the real property owner.   The real property owner or his agent shall sign the towing order, which shall specify each vehicle to be towed and shall not authorize the towing of an unknown vehicle at a future date.   A tow truck operator shall not tow or transport a vehicle unless the towing order is in his possession.   For purposes of this section an "abandoned vehicle" is a vehicle left in a private parking area more than fifteen (15) days, when it has not been left under a written contract of storage and has not, during that period been removed by the person leaving it.

I.   A violation of subsection A of this section shall constitute a civil traffic violation, and the violator shall be subject to a civil sanction of not less than $50 or more than $250, provided that effective October 1, 1992, the minimum civil sanction shall be $65.   Any other violations of this section shall constitute a Class 1 misdemeanor.[101]

**(b)   Tenants/Guests Parking in areas
not designated for parking.**

Tenants parking in areas not designated for parking is a problem common to both apartment complexes (i.e., no parking zones, loading zones, driveways, etc.) and single-family residences (i.e., on the lawn, in the back yard, etc.).   If the vehicle presents an immediate problem (i.e., parked in fire lane, etc.), the landlord may have the vehicle towed, pursuant to local law.   If the vehicle is merely improperly parked (i.e., in another tenant's parking space), then the landlord may have the vehicle towed if s/he has complied with local law.   *See* Section 7(a), immediately prior hereto.   If the landlord has not complied with local law, then the landlord tows your vehicle at his/her peril.   Nevertheless, whether or not the

---

[101] PHOENIX, ARIZONA, CITY CODE, Chapter 36, art. XI, § 36-144 (1992).

landlord may or does have your vehicle towed, repeated parking violations may constitute a material noncompliance with the rental agreement and, therefore, the landlord may terminate your tenancy.

(c)   Tenant taking too many spaces.

You have a more serious problem if, after signing the rental agreement, you discover that you own more vehicles than your allotment of parking stalls. This problem also may arise when an existing tenant acquires an additional vehicle. Unfortunately, after signing the rental agreement, your options to solve this problem are few: (1) you must park on the street (assuming such parking is available and lawful); (2) you must find a tenant who is willing to give (or rent) you one of their unused parking stalls; (3) you must either dispose of one vehicle or park it somewhere else; or (4) you must move.

(d)   Parking of commercial vehicles.

Most landlords make a point of inquiring about commercial vehicles. Nevertheless, if you own a commercial vehicle, it is really your responsibility to determine the landlord's policy on this issue before you sign the rental agreement. If the rental agreement is silent on this issue and/or the landlord says, "its okay," you should still check the local (i.e., city/town) law covering parking of commercial vehicles. In some cases, the parking of certain types of vehicles (e.g., 18-wheel tractor trailer trucks) in residential neighborhoods is unlawful.[102]

(e)   Vehicle maintenance.

If you plan on doing a lot of vehicle maintenance on the premises, you should find out what the landlord's policy is on this issue very early in the applicant interview. Most landlords **do not** want you to do vehicle maintenance on their property and will not negotiate on this issue -- and justifiably so. Environmentally speaking, engine oil, anti-freeze, brake fluid and automatic transmission fluid are hazardous materials and must be disposed of "properly." Improper disposal of these substances may leave the landlord with an environmental hazard on their property. An environmental hazard brings federal and state environmental laws into play. A violation of these laws can be a landlord's worst nightmare.[103]

8.   What if the Landlord Won't Make Repairs?

The short answer is that the tenant may either terminate the rental agreement or have the repairs done and deduct the cost from the next month's rent, but the tenant must observe several **very** strict formalities. The precise procedure to follow will depend on your situation. The next Section (Section C) addresses the various remedies available to you for each type of situation.

---

[102] See, e.g., PHOENIX, ARIZ., CITY CODE, Chapter 36, art. XI, § 36-140 (1985); MESA, ARIZ., CITY CODE, title 11, Chapter 4, § 11-4-4(F) (1991).

[103] See, e.g., Comprehensive Environmental Response, Compensation, and Liability Act of 1980, 42 U.S.C. §§ 9601-9657 (1988); A.R.S. §§ 49-281 to -289 (West Supp. 1993).

C.   TENANT REMEDIES.

When the landlord fails or refuses to fulfill his/her obligations under the rental agreement and the Act, the tenant has several remedies. Sometimes the tenant may terminate the rental agreement. Sometimes the tenant may remedy the problem and deduct the cost from next month's rent. And sometimes the tenant can find substitute housing or essential services and recover the cost thereof from the landlord. In almost all cases, the tenant must first provide advance written notice. The following pages will discuss when the tenant may take certain actions. The necessary blank forms are included in Appendix B. Completed, sample forms are included and discussed in this section.

As you read through Sections C(1) - C(4), you may find that there are times when a situation will fit into more than one category (e.g., failure to provide garbage collection service is a material noncompliance, a material noncompliance affecting health and safety, and a wrongful failure to provide essential services). The amount of notice you must provide to the landlord and the procedures you must follow will depend on **your** facts, *under all the relevant circumstances*. The amount of notice you provide must comply with the applicable statute or be reasonable under the circumstances. When trying to decide how much notice is reasonable, you should imagine how you will justify your decision to the judge (which will eventually occur, if you provide *too little* notice to the landlord and the dispute ends up in court).

1.   Fourteen-Day Notice of Termination of Rental Agreement for Material Noncompliance with Rental Agreement.

Tenants frequently want to know what their rights are when the landlord has promised to do something and then fails to perform. Similarly, tenants want to know what their rights are when something, that is the landlord's responsibility to maintain (i.e., plumbing, wiring, etc.), breaks and the landlord fails or refuses to effect repairs. The Act provides tenants with various remedies, depending on the severity of the problem.

> [I]f there is a material noncompliance by the landlord with the rental agreement, the tenant may deliver a written notice to the landlord specifying the acts and omissions constituting the breach and that the rental agreement will terminate upon a date not less than fourteen days after receipt of the notice if the breach is not remedied in ten days.[104]

A "material noncompliance" by the landlord is any breach of the rental agreement that is "material" or "very important." "Material noncompliance" is best defined by example.

---

[104] A.R.S. § 33-1361(A) (West 1990).

Example 1: Before you moved in, the landlord promised to put in new carpeting before, or shortly after, you moved in because the existing carpet was bad (i.e., torn, pulled-up from the floor, excessive stains, etc.). Replacement of the carpet was a significant factor in your decision to rent this unit. Based on the landlord's representation that new carpet would be installed, you agreed to rent this unit. After you move in, the landlord informs you that s/he will not install new carpet. This is a material noncompliance. Naturally, this case will be much stronger if the agreement concerning the carpet is in writing, either on the rental agreement or in a separate agreement.

Example 2: Same as above, except that the existing carpet is not "all that bad" and installation of new carpet was not a significant factor in your decision to rent this unit. This is not a material noncompliance.

Example 3: A major plumbing fixture (i.e., tub, shower, toilet) has ceased to operate or leaks so badly that you cannot use the fixture and you did not cause the condition. The landlord's failure to effect repairs is a material noncompliance with the rental agreement.

Example 4: All the flowers in the garden have died, through no fault of yours, and the landlord refuses to plant new flowers or to allow you to pay for new flowers and deduct the cost from the rent. This is not a material noncompliance with the rental agreement, *unless* you can demonstrate to the judge that having flowers in the garden was crucial to your decision to rent this unit (an unlikely occurrence).

So what do I do if there is a material noncompliance by the landlord with the rental agreement? Answer: Send the landlord a "Fourteen-Day Notice of Termination," as provided by the Act. The Notice must specify the acts and/or omissions constituting the breach. Be specific -- "Plumbing needs repair" -- won't do. "Toilet in hall bathroom leaks, requiring it to be shut-off at the wall valve, to prevent flooding of the rental unit," is the correct way to appropriately describe the problem (*see* example on next page).

If the landlord fails to take corrective action within ten days after receipt of the Notice, you may terminate the rental agreement fourteen days (or more) after the landlord received the Notice.

Example: You hand-deliver the Notice to the landlord on January 1. Do not count the day of delivery. If the landlord has not taken corrective action by January 11 (ten days later), the rental agreement terminates on the date specified in the Notice (i.e., January 15, January 31, etc.). This date cannot be less than fourteen days after the landlord received the Notice. You must vacate the unit on or before the date of termination.

**FOURTEEN-DAY NOTICE OF
TERMINATION OF RENTAL AGREEMENT
FOR MATERIAL NONCOMPLIANCE WITH RENTAL AGREEMENT**

Larry Landlord
101 North Slum Lord Avenue   Date: September 1, 1994
Phoenix, Arizona 85999

Notice to Landlord:

You are in violation of the Rental Agreement and the Arizona Residential Landlord and Tenant Act, Article 2, Section 33-1324 (Landlord Obligations, Landlord to maintain fit premises). The specific acts constituting the violation are:

1 - Failure to repair toilet in hall bathroom; toilet leaks, requiring it to be
shut-off at the wall valve, to prevent flooding of the rental unit.
2 - Failure to repair/replace defective dead-bolt lock on rear exterior door.

You are hereby notified, pursuant to A.R.S. § 33-1361(A), that the above constitutes a material noncompliance and that the Rental Agreement will terminate upon a date not less than fourteen (14) days after receipt of this notice if this noncompliance is not remedied WITHIN TEN (10) DAYS.

The Rental Agreement will terminate on: September 15, 1994
If the noncompliance is not remedied by: September 11, 1994

Terry Tenant

This notice delivered this date Sept. 1, '94 via:
☐ Certified mail
☐ Regular first class mail
☒ Hand delivered

Acknowledgment of hand delivery and receipt hereof:

Larry Landlord   *September 1, 1994*
(signature of tenant)   (date)

Keep in mind that this is not a "one-way street." In the event that **you** commit a material noncompliance with the rental agreement, the landlord can serve you with the same type of notice, terminating your rental agreement if you fail to comply by the time specified.

**FOURTEEN-DAY NOTICE OF
TERMINATION OF RENTAL AGREEMENT
FOR MATERIAL NONCOMPLIANCE WITH RENTAL AGREEMENT**

Terry Tenant
101 North Rental Avenue   Date: September 1, 1994
Phoenix, Arizona 85999

Notice to Tenant:

You are in violation of your Rental Agreement and the Arizona Residential Landlord and Tenant Act, Article 3, Section 33-1341 (Tenant Obligations, Tenant to maintain dwelling unit). The specific acts constituting the violation are:
1 - Failure to repair damage to interior door caused by guest.
2 - Failure to comply with rules and regulations; multiple parking violations and parking commercial vehicle on premises.

You are hereby notified, pursuant to A.R.S. § 33-1368(A), that the above constitutes a material noncompliance and that your Rental Agreement will terminate upon a date not less than fourteen (14) days after receipt of this notice if this noncompliance is not remedied WITHIN TEN (10) DAYS.

Your Rental Agreement will terminate on: September 15, 1994
If the noncompliance is not remedied by: September 11, 1994

Larry Landlord

This notice delivered this date Sept. 1, '94 via:
☐ Certified mail
☐ Regular first class mail
☒ Hand delivered

Acknowledgment of hand delivery and receipt hereof:

Terry Tenant   *September 1, 1994*
(signature of tenant)   (date)

Chapter 5 - How to Solve Common Tenant Problems

What if the noncompliance is minor and you would rather make the repair yourself than move?   Naturally, you and the landlord may agree (in writing, of course) that you can do the repairs (or have the repairs done) and deduct the cost from next month's rent.   If the landlord will not agree, and the noncompliance is something the landlord is required to maintain under Section 33-1324 of the Act, then you may have the work done by a licensed contractor and deduct the cost from the rent.   A form is included in Appendix B precisely for this purpose.   The sample (below) shows how the form should be completed.

NOTICE OF TENANT'S INTENT TO EFFECT REPAIRS

Larry Landlord
101 North Slum Lord Avenue
Phoenix, Arizona 85999

Date: September 1, 1994

Notice to Landlord:

You are in violation of the Rental Agreement and the Arizona Residential Landlord and Tenant Act, Article 3, Section 33-1324 (Landlord Obligations, Landlord to maintain fit premises). The specific acts constituting the violation are:

1 - Failure to repair toilet in hall bathroom; toilet leaks, requiring it to be shut-off at the wall valve, to prevent flooding of the rental unit.
2 - Failure to repair/replace defective dead-bolt lock on rear exterior door.

You are hereby notified, pursuant to A.R.S. § 33-1363(A), if above defect(s) is not remedied by the landlord within:

☒   Ten (10) days,
☐   _____ days, because of the emergency nature of the defect,

that tenant shall cause the same to be repaired by a licensed contractor and deduct the cost thereof from next month's rent, not to exceed the greater of $150.00 or one-half month's rent. Tenant will provide landlord with a lien release from the contractor. Tenant asserts that the defect(s) was not caused by Tenant, a member of Tenant's family or Tenant's guests.

Landlord has until September 11, 1994 to take corrective action.

_____Terry Tenant_____

This notice delivered this date Sept. 1, '94 via:
☐   Certified mail
☐   Regular first class mail
☒   Hand delivered

Acknowledgment of hand delivery and receipt hereof:
_____Larry Landlord_____   _____September 1, 1994_____
(signature of landlord)   (date)

Some limitations apply, however.   The statute provides:

A.   If the landlord fails to comply with § 33-1324, and the reasonable cost of compliance is less than one hundred fifty dollars, or an amount equal to one-half of the monthly rent, whichever amount is greater, the tenant may recover damages for the breach under § 33-1361, subsection B, *OR* may notify the landlord of his intention to correct the condition at the landlord's expense. After being notified by the tenant in writing, if the landlord fails to comply within ten days or as promptly thereafter as conditions require in case of emergency, the tenant may cause the work to be done by a licensed contractor and, after submitting to the landlord an itemized statement and a waiver of lien, deduct from his rent the actual and reasonable cost of the work, not exceeding the amount specified in this subsection.

B. A tenant may not repair at the landlord's expense if the condition was caused by the deliberate or negligent act or omission of the tenant, a member of his family or other person on the premises with his consent.[105]

2. Ten-Day Notice of Termination of Rental Agreement for Noncompliance with Rental Agreement Materially Affecting Health and Safety.

Some problems are more "urgent" than others. If there is a material noncompliance with the rental agreement that affects **health and safety**, then the notice period is shortened significantly. The statute provides:

A. . . . If there is a noncompliance by the landlord with § 33-1324 materially affecting health and safety, the tenant may deliver a written notice to the landlord specifying the acts and omissions constituting the breach and that the rental agreement will terminate upon a date not less than ten days after receipt of the notice if the breach is not remedied in five days. The rental agreement shall terminate and the dwelling unit shall be vacated as provided in the notice subject to the following:

1. If the breach is remediable by repairs or the payment of damages or otherwise and the landlord adequately remedies the breach prior to the date specified in the notice, the rental agreement will not terminate.

2. The tenant may not terminate for a condition caused by the deliberate or negligent act or omission of the tenant, a member of his family or other person on the premises with his consent.

B. Except as provided in this chapter [the Act], the tenant may recover damages and obtain injunctive relief for any noncompliance by the landlord with the rental agreement or § 33-1324.

C. The remedy provided in subsection B of this section is in addition to any right of the tenant arising under subsection A of this section.

---

[105] A.R.S. § 33-1363 (West 1990) (emphasis added).

D. If the rental agreement is terminated, the landlord shall return all security recoverable by the tenant under § 33-1321.[106]

Section 33-1324 provides:

A. The landlord shall:

1. Comply with the requirements of applicable building codes materially affecting health and safety.

2. Make all repairs and do whatever is necessary to put and keep the premises in a fit and habitable condition.

3. Keep all common areas of the premises in a clean and safe condition.

4. Maintain in good and safe working order and condition all electrical, plumbing, sanitary, heating, ventilating, air-conditioning and other facilities and appliances, including elevators, supplied or required to be supplied by him.

5. Provide and maintain appropriate receptacles and conveniences for the removal of ashes, garbage, rubbish and other waste incidental to the occupancy of the dwelling unit and arrange for their removal.

6. Supply running water and reasonable amounts of hot water at all times, reasonable heat and reasonable air-conditioning or cooling where such units are installed and offered, when required by seasonal weather conditions, except where the building that includes the dwelling unit is not required by law to be equipped for that purpose or the dwelling unit is so constructed that heat, air-conditioning, cooling or hot water is generated by an installation within the exclusive control of the tenant and supplied by a direct public utility connection.[107]

Before a tenant can serve a Ten-Day Notice, there must **first** be a noncompliance with Section 33-1324 and, **second**, said noncompliance must materially affect health and safety. If both conditions are met, complete and serve a Ten-Day Notice as shown below.

---

[106] A.R.S. § 33-1361 (West 1990).

[107] A.R.S. § 33-1324 (West 1990) (paragraphs B through E not reprinted above, but may be found in Appendix C).

Again, keep in mind that this is not a "one-way street." If **you** commit a noncompliance that materially affects health and safety, the landlord can serve you with the same type of notice, terminating your rental agreement if you fail to comply by the time specified.

**TEN-DAY NOTICE OF TERMINATION OF RENTAL AGREEMENT
FOR NONCOMPLIANCE WITH RENTAL AGREEMENT
MATERIALLY AFFECTING HEALTH AND SAFETY**

Larry Landlord
101 North Slum Lord Avenue   Date: September 1, 1994
Phoenix, Arizona 85999

Notice to Landlord:

You are in violation of your Rental Agreement and the Arizona Residential Landlord and Tenant Act, Article 3, Section 33-1324 (Landlord Obligations, Landlord to maintain fit premises). The specific acts constituting the violation are:

1 - Failure to repair sliding glass door, broken by Landlord's maintenance man.
2 - Failure to have refuse removed from premises.
3 - Failure to repair unsafe wiring in kitchen.

You are hereby notified, pursuant to A.R.S. § 33-1361(A), that this noncompliance materially affects health and safety and that the Rental Agreement will terminate upon a date not less than ten (10) days after receipt of this notice if this noncompliance is not remedied within FIVE (5) DAYS.

The Rental Agreement will terminate on: September 11, 1994
If the noncompliance is not remedied by: September 6, 1994

Terry Tenant

This notice delivered this date Sept. 1, '94 via:
☐ Certified mail
☐ Regular first class mail
☒ Hand delivered

Acknowledgment of hand delivery and receipt hereof:
Larry Landlord   *September 1, 1994*
(signature of landlord)   (date)

---

3. <u>Notice of Wrongful Failure to Supply Essential Services</u>.

The Act provides for a **third** category of noncompliance: "Wrongful failure [of the landlord] to supply heat, air conditioning, cooling, water, hot water, or essential services."[108] The remedies are similar to those already discussed. The big difference is the notice requirement: "the tenant may give *reasonable notice*."[109]

> **A.** If contrary to the rental agreement or § 33-1324 the landlord deliberately or negligently fails to supply running water, hot water or heat, air-conditioning or cooling, where such units are installed and offered, or essential services, the tenant may give reasonable notice to the landlord specifying the breach and may do one of the following:

---
[108] A.R.S. § 33-1364 (West 1990).
[109] A.R.S. § 33-1364(A) (West 1990) (emphasis added).

1. Procure reasonable amounts of hot water, running water, heat and essential services during the period of the landlord's noncompliance and deduct their actual reasonable cost from the rent.

2. Recover damages based upon the diminution in the fair rental value of the dwelling unit.

3. Procure reasonable substitute housing during the period of the landlord's noncompliance, in which case the tenant is excused from paying rent for the period of the landlord's noncompliance. In the event the periodic cost of such substitute housing exceeds the amount of the periodic rent, upon delivery by tenant of proof of payment for such substitute housing, tenant may recover from landlord such excess costs up to an amount not to exceed twenty-five per cent of the periodic rent which has been excused pursuant to this paragraph.

B. In addition to the remedy provided in paragraph 3 of subsection A, in the event the landlord's noncompliance is deliberate, the tenant may recover the actual and reasonable cost of fair and reasonable value of the substitute housing not in excess of an amount equal to the periodic rent.

C. If the tenant proceeds under this section, he may not proceed under § 33-1361 or § 33-1363 as to that breach, except as to damages which occur prior to the tenant proceeding under subsection A or B of this section.

D. The rights under this section do not arise until the tenant has given notice to the landlord and such rights do not include the right to repair. Such rights do not arise if the condition was caused by the deliberate or negligent act or omission of the tenant, a member of his family or other person on the premises with his consent.[110]

What constitutes "reasonable notice" will depend on the circumstances. One day's notice to the landlord in August, in Phoenix, Arizona, to fix the air conditioner may be legally sufficient, but five days' notice may be required in October. Again, before taking action, think about whether or not you will be able to justify your notice period to the judge. (Sample form on next page).

---

[110] A.R.S. § 33-1364 (West 1990).

NOTICE OF WRONGFUL FAILURE TO PROVIDE ESSENTIAL SERVICES

Larry Landlord
101 North Slum Lord Avenue
Phoenix, Arizona 85999

Date: August 1, 1994

Notice to Landlord:

You are in violation of your Rental Agreement and the Arizona Residential Landlord and Tenant Act, Article 4, Section 33-1364 (Wrongful failure to supply heat, air conditioning, cooling, water, hot water or essential services). The specific acts constituting the violation are:

1 - Failure to supply air condition (unit ceased to function on September 1, 1994).
2 - Failure to supply water (water company employee stated you failed to pay water bill).
3 - Failure to supply essential services (garbage collection has been cancelled).

You are hereby notified, pursuant to A.R.S. § 33-1364, that if these matters are not remedied by August 2, 1994, Tenant will take the following action:

☐ Tenant shall procure reasonable amounts of water, hot water, heat and essential services during the period of landlord's noncompliance and deduct their actual reasonable cost from the rent.

☐ Tenant shall seek to recover damages based on the diminution in the fair rental value of the premises.

☒ Tenant shall procure reasonable substitute housing during the period of landlord's noncompliance and shall seek to recover the excess cost of the substitute housing, not to exceed the statutory amount. Tenant shall not pay rent during the period of noncompliance.

Terry Tenant

This notice delivered this date Aug. 1, '94 via:
☐ Certified mail
☐ Regular first class mail
☒ Hand delivered

Acknowledgment of hand delivery and receipt hereof:

Larry Landlord   *August 1, 1994*
(signature of landlord)   (date)

---

4. Notice of Termination or Rent Reduction Because of Fire or Casualty Damage.

If catastrophe strikes and your rental unit is completely, mostly or partially destroyed by fire or casualty, the tenant may **immediately** vacate the unit or, if the rental unit is "liveable," may vacate the part of the rental unit that is unusable and reduce the rent in proportion to the diminished value of the premises. Again, the precise language of the statute is informative:

> **A.** If the dwelling unit or premises are damaged or destroyed by fire or casualty to an extent that enjoyment of the dwelling unit is substantially impaired, the tenant may do either of the following:
>
> > 1. Immediately vacate the premises and notify the landlord in writing within fourteen days thereafter of his intention to terminate the rental agreement, in which case the rental

agreement terminates as of the date of vacating.

2. If continued occupancy is lawful, vacate any part of the dwelling unit rendered unusable by the fire or casualty, in which case the tenant's liability for rent is reduced in proportion to the diminution in the fair rental value of the dwelling unit.

B. If the rental agreement is terminated the landlord shall return all security recoverable under § 33-1321. Accounting for rent in the event of termination or apportionment is to occur as of the date the tenant vacates all or part of the dwelling unit.[111]

A form is included in Appendix B precisely for use under these circumstances. This sample shows how the form should be completed.

NOTICE OF TERMINATION OR RENT REDUCTION
BECAUSE OF FIRE OR CASUALTY DAMAGE

Larry Landlord
101 North Slum Lord Avenue   Date: __September 1, 1994__
Phoenix, Arizona 85999

Notice to Landlord:

You are hereby notified, pursuant to A.R.S. § 33-1366, that the leased premises have been damaged or destroyed by fire or casualty to an extent that enjoyment of the dwelling unit is substantially impaired.

☒   As a consequence thereof, I have vacated the premises on __August 20, 1994__ and, pursuant to A.R.S. § 33-1366(A)(1), the rental agreement has terminated on that date.

☐   As a consequence thereof, I have vacated the portion of the leased premises rendered unusable by the fire or casualty and have reduced my rent in proportion to the diminution in the fair rental value of the premises. Current rent is $_____ ; because of the damage, fair rental value has been reduced by ____%; therefore, rent shall be reduced to $_____ until the premises are repaired.

Terry Tenant

This notice delivered this date Sept. 1, '94 via:
☐ Certified mail
☐ Regular first class mail
☒ Hand delivered

Acknowledgment of hand delivery and receipt hereof:

_____*Larry Landlord*_____   _____*September 1, 1994*_____
(signature of tenant)   (date)

---

[111] A.R.S. § 33-1366 (West 1990).

CHAPTER 6

TERMINATING TENANCY
AND
EVICTIONS

Summary of Chapter

HOW AND BY WHOM TENANCY MAY BE TERMINATED
- By Mutual Agreement
- The Tenant Terminates Tenancy
- The Landlord Terminates Tenancy
- "Adequate" Notice

AFTER TENANCY IS TERMINATED
- Damage to the Unit
- Refund of Deposit(s)

EVICTIONS
- "When" the Landlord May Evict a Tenant
    - Material noncompliance with the rental agreement
    - Noncompliance with the rental agreement materially affecting health and safety
    - Material and irreparable breach of the rental agreement
    - Nonpayment of rent
- "How" the Landlord May Evict a Tenant
    - What the Landlord CANNOT do
    - What the Landlord MAY do

THE SPECIAL DETAINER ACTION: ANATOMY OF AN EVICTION
- Eviction Process For: (1) Material noncompliance with the rental agreement; (2) Noncompliance with the rental agreement materially affecting health and safety; and (3) Material and irreparable breach of the rental agreement
- Eviction Process For Nonpayment of Rent

A. HOW AND BY WHOM TENANCY MAY BE TERMINATED.

Tenancy is terminated in one of three ways:

- By mutual agreement.

- The tenant terminates tenancy.

- The landlord terminates tenancy.

Sounds fairly simple, right? In theory, it is. In practice, however, it can sometimes become rather complex. This chapter discusses each of these three ways to terminate tenancy, provides examples of each, discusses the various forms and procedures for each, and finally, in the event you ever need them, two eviction flowcharts are provided and discussed.

1. By Mutual Agreement.

Termination by mutual agreement occurs in five ways:

- The rental agreement provides for a specific term and notice of the tenant's intent to vacate at the end of the term is not required by the rental agreement.

In the event you are interested in the legal terminology, this type of tenancy is known as a **tenancy for years**. A tenancy for years exists whenever a rental agreement specifies a precise starting date and a precise ending date. For example, a rental agreement that specifies the term January 1, 1994 to December 31, 1994, is a tenancy for years. A rental agreement that specifies the term January 1, 1994 to June 30, 1994 (only six months in duration), is also a tenancy for years. The term "tenancy for years" is not intended to be descriptive of the duration of the term of tenancy. The term merely means that the rental agreement states a specific starting and ending date. Consequently, a rental agreement with a term of one day can be a tenancy for years, provided the start and end date are specified (i.e., January 1, 1994 to January 2, 1994).

In a tenancy for years, the tenant is not required to give notice that s/he is vacating at the end of the term because the rental agreement has already informed both parties (i.e., the landlord and the tenant) that tenancy will end on the date specified in the rental agreement and that the tenant must vacate on that day. But there is an exception to this rule. If the rental agreement requires notice that the tenant is vacating, the tenant must give the landlord the notice required by the rental agreement, in spite of the fact that this may be a tenancy for years. Otherwise, if the rental agreement says nothing about notice and a tenancy for years has been created, then no notice is required.

- Same as above, except that the rental agreement requires the tenant to give notice that s/he is vacating and the tenant does, in fact, give the required notice. This is the exception referred to in paragraph one, immediately above.

- Tenancy is month-to-month and the tenant gives the required notice.

- Tenancy is month-to-month, the landlord gives the required notice to the tenant, and the tenant voluntarily vacates the unit.

- Notice to terminate is required, either under a specified term tenancy or a month-to-month tenancy, <u>inadequate</u> notice is given (by the party giving notice), the other party nevertheless agrees to the termination, and the tenant voluntarily vacates the unit.

The key in all five instances is that the tenant voluntarily moves out.

2. <u>The Tenant Terminates Tenancy</u>.

Cross Reference
- Chapter 3, Section C(5) (Notice to Terminate Tenancy)
- Appendix B, Form 2 (Notice to Terminate Tenancy)

The tenant may terminate tenancy by:

- In the case of a tenancy for years, where no notice is required, by simply not renewing tenancy.

- In the case of a tenancy for years, where notice **is** required by the rental agreement, by giving the required notice.

- In the case of a month-to-month tenancy, by giving "adequate" notice.

- In the case of any type of tenancy, by giving <u>inadequate</u> notice. In this case, the landlord may or may not sue the tenant for damages resulting from the tenant's breach of the rental agreement.

3. <u>The Landlord Terminates Tenancy</u>.

The foregoing also applies to the landlord, except that in the latter situation (i.e., the landlord gives <u>inadequate</u> notice), the tenant will have an absolute legal defense to an action for possession brought by the landlord. In the case of a month-to-month tenancy, this may only delay the inevitable; the landlord need only serve the tenant with "adequate" notice next month. In other cases, however, the tenant may have the benefit of another term equal to the previous term, which. in the case of a one-year lease, would mean a significant extension. Whether or not your tenancy is extended for another term of equal length **will** be determined by your rental agreement. If it is not stated in the rental agreement, then tenancy converts to a month-to-month tenancy.[112]

4. "Adequate" Notice.

As discussed above, notice may (or may not) be required to terminate tenancy and/or to renew tenancy. Where notice is required, the issue becomes whether or not the notice given (by whichever party is required to give the notice) was "adequate," pursuant to the rental agreement, or, if notice is not addressed by the rental agreement, pursuant to statute.

So, what precisely is *"adequate" notice*? "Adequate" notice is defined either in the rental agreement or by statute. Normally, "adequate" notice is defined in your rental agreement. If defined in the rental agreement, the language must be clear and unambiguous.[113] What happens if the rental agreement is confusing or ambiguous? The judge will probably conclude that any "reasonable" interpretation of the language in your rental agreement constitutes "adequate notice." To reach this conclusion, the judge will probably ask how <u>you</u> interpreted the language of the rental agreement, ask the landlord how s/he interprets the same language and then decide whose interpretation is "reasonable." Who knows how that will come out? If the rental agreement does not define "adequate" notice, the following applies:

1. A residential tenant (or landlord) may terminate a month-to-month tenancy by written notice given to the other at least thirty days prior to the beginning of the next periodic period.[114]

2. A residential tenant (or landlord) may terminate a week-to-week tenancy by written notice given to the other at least ten days prior to the termination date specified in the notice.[115]

3. A commercial tenant (or landlord) may terminate a month-to-month tenancy by written notice given to the other at least ten days prior to the termination date specified in the notice.[116]

4. A commercial tenant may terminate a semi-monthly tenancy by written notice given to the other at least five days prior to the termination date specified in the notice.[117]

5. A tenant, commercial or residential, with a tenancy for a specified term (i.e., January 1, 1994 to January 1, 1998), is not required to give any type of notice, but must vacate upon expiration of the term.[118]

---

[112] A.R.S. § 33-342 (West 1990).

[113] *See, e.g.,* <u>Falcon Research & Development v. Craddock</u>, 101 N.M. 122, 679 P.2d 264 (1984) (whether lease is ambiguous is question of law).

[114] A.R.S. § 33-1375(B) (West 1990).

[115] A.R.S. § 33-1375(A) (West 1990).

[116] A.R.S. § 33-341(B) (West 1990).

[117] A.R.S. § 33-341(C) (West 1990).

[118] A.R.S. § 33-341(A) and (D) (West 1990).

You should also check your rental agreement for a provision in the rental agreement that, in the absence of a specific request by either party to renew for another period of equal or greater length, automatically: (1) extends the tenancy for a term **equal to** the original term; or (2) converts the tenancy to a month-to-month tenancy. Below is language that may be found in a typical rental agreement. This language clearly spells out the notice requirements and provides that if notice is not given, tenancy automatically converts to month-to-month. The notice provision for a month-to-month tenancy would then become effective.

> Termination. If the term of this agreement is month-to-month, either party may terminate hereunder upon thirty (30) days (or more) written notice. If the term of this agreement is for a specific term (i.e., six months or one year), either party wishing to terminate tenancy at the end of the rental term must provide forty-five (45) days written notice before the end of the rental term. Otherwise, tenancy hereunder shall thereafter convert to a month-to-month tenancy and, except for the rental term, all other provisions of this rental agreement shall continue in full force and effect. A "Notice to Terminate Tenancy" Form has been provided for this specific purpose; your signature below acknowledges receipt of this Form. The thirty (30) day written notice shall be given on or before the last day of the present rental period and tenancy shall then end on the last day of the next rental period. TENANCY CANNOT BE TERMINATED IN THE MIDDLE OF THE RENTAL PERIOD. Example: Today is April 15 and you wish to terminate tenancy. Notice must be given on the last day of the present rental period -- the present rental period is April 1 - April 30. Therefore, notice must be given on or before April 30. Tenancy will terminate on the last day of the next rental period -- the next rental period is May 1 - May 31. Therefore, tenancy will terminate on May 31.

As you can see, this notice provision gives an example which further clarifies the notice provision. In addition, this provision refers to a Termination Form, which (presumably) the tenant receives when s/he signs this rental agreement. If the notice provision of the rental agreement is repeated **word-for-word**, or does not conflict with the language used in the rental agreement, then this tenant will have an extremely difficult time claiming that s/he was unaware of the notice requirements and/or that the provision is ambiguous. You should check to see if your landlord provides termination forms. If so, check to see if the form contains language that conflicts with the notice provision in the rental agreement.

How much notice can the landlord require? There is no specific answer, but the notice required must be "reasonable." Thirty (30) days is fine. Shorter is no problem. Longer *may* be a problem, depending on *how much longer* -- six months is probably "too" long. If a judge finds the notice provision to be "too" long, s/he may find the provision to be "unconscionable," which means that the judge will disregard the provision, no matter how clear, and substitute a "reasonable" time.[119]

---

[119] *See* A.R.S. § 33-1312(A) (West 1990).

B. AFTER TENANCY IS TERMINATED.

1. Damage to the Unit.

The next issue to address is whether you have damaged the rental unit and/or failed to repair items that were your responsibility to have repaired. As a tenant, you are liable to the landlord for damages to the rental unit that are the result of your intentional or negligent conduct and that of your family and guests.[120] If the landlord is holding your security deposit, s/he may deduct the amount of damages from the security deposit held, but must provide you with an itemized list of the damages.[121] (*See* Chapter 3, Section B(5)). If the amount of damages exceeds the amount of the security deposit that the landlord is holding or if s/he is not holding a security deposit, the landlord may file a lawsuit against the tenant to recover the amounts due. Incidentally, it is also a crime (a class 2 misdemeanor) for a tenant to intentionally damage the rental unit or remove furnishings or fixtures.[122]

So what happens if the landlord charges you for damages that aren't your responsibility by deducting the cost of repairs from your deposits? Answer: The landlord is liable to you for **twice** the amount of the deposit wrongfully withheld.[123]

2. Refund of Deposit(s).

Cross Reference
• Chapter 3, Section B(5) (Deposits)

Here is the question that every tenant wants to know: "How much, if any, of the refundable deposit(s) do I get back?" The answer will depend on several factors, including, whether you gave "adequate" notice (if you are the party that terminated tenancy), whether there are any damages to the rental unit, whether you have failed to make any repairs that you were responsible for making, and whether you owe the landlord any money (i.e., unpaid rent). If there are no damages to the unit and you do not owe the landlord money for any other reason (i.e., unpaid rent), you are entitled to a refund of your security deposit. You are also entitled to your other refundable deposits (but not your nonrefundable deposits), provided you have fulfilled your obligations with respect to those deposits (e.g., a cleaning deposit may be refundable, provided that you left the premises clean). If your landlord fails or refuses to refund your deposits, the landlord may be liable to you for "twice the amount wrongfully withheld."[124]

"What if the landlord fails or refuses to give me my deposit(s)?" Answer: send a written demand for return of your deposits to your landlord (keep a copy)

---

[120] A.R.S. §§ 33-1341(6), -1368(C), -1369 (West 1990).

[121] A.R.S. § 33-1321(C) (West 1990).

[122] The statute provides, "Removal or intentional and material alteration or damage of any part of a building, the furnishings thereof, or any permanent fixture, by or at the instance of the tenant, without written permission of the landlord or his agent, is a class 2 misdemeanor." A.R.S. § 33-322 (West 1990).

[123] A.R.S. § 33-1321(D) (West 1990).

[124] A.R.S. § 33-1321(D) (West 1990).

and give the landlord a "reasonable" time to comply (i.e., seven to ten days). If the landlord still refuses to refund your deposits, file a civil lawsuit against him/her for his/her failure to comply with A.R.S. § 33-1321(D).

C. EVICTIONS.

1. "WHEN" The Landlord May Evict A Tenant.

Under the Act, a landlord may institute a "Special Detainer" action (commonly referred to as a "forcible entry and detainer" action) against a tenant when there has been a *noncompliance* with the rental agreement by the tenant.[125] A Special Detainer action is the legal process (commonly referred to as an eviction) whereby the landlord obtains a Writ of Restitution, which grants the landlord the right to possession of the leased premises and also decrees that the tenant no longer has any possessory interest in the leased premises. Ultimately, the writ is served and executed by the sheriff or constable, who forcibly removes the tenant from the leased premises.

Noncompliance falls into three categories: (a) material noncompliance; (b) noncompliance materially affecting health and safety; and (c) material and irreparable noncompliance.   Which category your situation falls into is very important because it determines whether or not your landlord must give you an opportunity to cure the noncompliance and, if so, how much time your landlord must give you to cure the noncompliance before s/he terminates the rental agreement.

Your analysis should be as follows:

Is this a material and irreparable noncompliance (i.e., discharge of weapon on premises; infliction of serious bodily harm on landlord, his/her agent, or another tenant; imminent serious property damage, etc.)?

> Yes - *see* Chapter 6, Section C(1)(c) (following).
> No - continue analysis.

Is this a noncompliance that materially affects health and safety (i.e., premises not clean, dangerous/hazardous condition, etc.)?

> Yes - *see* Chapter 6, Section C(1)(b) (following).
> No - handle as a material noncompliance (i.e., nonpayment of rent; failure to comply with other terms and conditions of rental agreement; failure to comply with rules and regulations, etc.). *See* Chapter 6, Section C(1)(a) (immediately following).

---

[125] A.R.S. §§ 33-1368(A), (B), -1377 (West Supp. 1993).

(a) Material Noncompliance With Rental Agreement.

Cross Reference
- Chapter 6, Section C(1)(b) (Noncompliance Materially Affecting Health and Safety)
- Chapter 6, Section C(1)(c) (Material and Irreparable Breach)
- Chapter 6, Section C(1)(d) (Nonpayment of Rent)

The steps for evicting a tenant for a material noncompliance (or breach) of the rental agreement are stated clearly in the statute. The statute provides:

> Except as provided in this chapter [Chapter 10 is the Residential Landlord and Tenant Act; therefore, this sentence is properly read, 'Except as provided elsewhere in the Act'], if there is a material noncompliance by the tenant with the rental agreement, the landlord may deliver a written notice to the tenant specifying the acts and omissions constituting the breach and that the rental agreement will terminate upon a date not less than fourteen [calendar] days after receipt of the notice if the breach is not remedied in ten [calendar] days . . . . However, if the breach is remediable by repair or the payment of damages or otherwise, and the tenant adequately remedies the breach prior to the date specified in the notice, the rental agreement will not terminate. If there is an additional act of these types of noncompliance of the same or similar nature within a period of six months from the previous remedy of noncompliance, the landlord may institute a special detainer action pursuant to § 33-1377 [special detainer actions] thirty days after delivery of a written notice advising the tenant that a second noncompliance of the same or similar nature has occurred.[126]

So what, precisely, is a "material noncompliance?" The "legal" answer is that a "material noncompliance" is a noncompliance that is not: (1) an irreparable noncompliance; or (2) a noncompliance materially affecting health and safety.[127] As usual, the "legal" answer is of marginal practical value.

As a practical matter, you probably have a pretty good idea what constitutes a "material noncompliance." By definition, a "material noncompliance" is a noncompliance with a particular term in the rental agreement which is "material" (i.e., an important or key element of the agreement). Keep in mind that not every noncompliance with the rental agreement is a "material noncompliance."

---

[126] A.R.S. § 33-1368(A) (West Supp. 1993).

[127] See A.R.S. § 33-1368(A) (West Supp. 1993).

Sometimes whether a noncompliance is material or not is really a "matter of degree." For example, suppose that when you leased your rental unit, the landlord was adamant that pets were not allowed and clearly stated that s/he would immediately terminate the rental agreement of any tenant who violated this term. If you get a large dog, it is fairly clear that you have committed a "material noncompliance." On the other hand, if you get one gold fish, although you have not complied with the scriptures of your rental agreement, the landlord may experience some difficulty convincing a judge (any judge) that this is a "material noncompliance" warranting termination of your rental agreement.

Some other examples of what *may* constitute a "material noncompliance" include: (1) occupants residing in the rental unit that are not listed on the rental agreement form; (2) "guests" that repeatedly stay for long periods of time; (3) parking more vehicles on the premises than the allotted spaces; (4) creating disturbances, constant noise and other conduct that disturbs the other tenants' quiet enjoyment of the premises; and (5) failing to observe the landlord's rules and regulations (if the landlord has rules and regulations). This list is not exhaustive. Moreover, even an infraction that is not a "material noncompliance" (i.e., playing loud music on one occasion) may become a "material noncompliance" if you commit repeated violations <u>after</u> the landlord has already notified you of the problem and has asked you to cure the noncompliance.

Clearly, nonpayment of rent is a material noncompliance, but the procedure the landlord must follow is different. *See* Section C(1)(d), later in this Chapter.

(b) Noncompliance with the Rental Agreement <u>Materially Affecting Health and Safety</u>.

Cross Reference
- Chapter 6, Section C(1)(a) (Material Noncompliance)
- Chapter 6, Section C(1)(c) (Material and Irreparable Breach)
- Chapter 6, Section C(1)(d) (Nonpayment of Rent)

Where the noncompliance "materially" affects "health and safety," the steps are the same, but the time limits are shorter. The statute provides:

> If there is a noncompliance by the tenant with § 33-1341 [tenant to maintain dwelling unit] materially affecting health and safety, the landlord may deliver a written notice to the tenant specifying the acts and omissions constituting the breach and that the rental agreement will terminate upon a date not less than ten [calendar] days after receipt of the notice if the breach is not remedied in five days. However, if the breach is remediable by repair or the payment of damages or otherwise, and the tenant adequately remedies the breach prior to the date specified in the notice, the

rental agreement will not terminate. If there is an additional act of these types of noncompliance of the same or similar nature within a period of six months from the previous remedy of noncompliance, the landlord may institute a special detainer action pursuant to § 33-1377 [special detainer actions] thirty days after delivery of a written notice advising the tenant that a second noncompliance of the same or similar nature has occurred.[128]

A "noncompliance materially affecting health and safety" is somewhat easier to define than a "material noncompliance." To begin with, the statute (quoted directly above) specifically states that it must first be a noncompliance with Section 33-1341. Section 33-1341 (Tenant to maintain dwelling unit) provides:

The tenant shall:

1. Comply with all obligations primarily imposed upon tenants by applicable provisions of building codes materially affecting health and safety.

2. Keep that part of the premises that he occupies and uses as clean and safe as the condition of the premises permit.

3. Dispose from his dwelling unit all ashes, rubbish, garbage and other waste in a clean and safe manner.

4. Keep all plumbing fixtures in the dwelling unit or used by the tenant as clean as their condition permits.

5. Use in a reasonable manner all electrical, plumbing, sanitary, heating, ventilating, air-conditioning and other facilities and appliances including elevators in the premises.

6. Not deliberately or negligently destroy, deface, damage, impair or remove any part of the premises or knowingly permit any person to do so.

7. Conduct himself and require other persons on the premises with his consent to conduct themselves in a manner that will not disturb his neighbors' peaceful enjoyment of the premises.[129]

_____

[128] A.R.S. § 33-1368(A) (West Supp. 1993).

[129] A.R.S. § 33-1341 (West 1990).

The statute then states that only a violation of Section 33-1341 that materially affects health and safety constitutes a "noncompliance materially affecting health and safety."[130] Consequently, a noncompliance with Section 33-1341, paragraphs 1 - 6, may constitute a "noncompliance materially affecting health and safety." Conceivably, a noncompliance with Section 33-1341, paragraph 7, could also constitute a "noncompliance materially affecting health and safety" (i.e., leaving a vehicle on "blocks" in the parking lot for several days may be a safety hazard; playing horseshoes or "yard darts" too close to buildings, property or people may be a safety hazard; etc.). The key, however, is that a noncompliance must first fall within Section 33-1341 and then must affect health and safety.

(c) Material and Irreparable Breach of the Rental Agreement.

Cross Reference
- Chapter 6, Section C(1)(a) (Material Noncompliance)
- Chapter 6, Section C(1)(b) (Noncompliance Materially Affecting Health and Safety)
- Chapter 6, Section C(1)(d) (Nonpayment of Rent)

Where the noncompliance is the result of egregious conduct or serious actual or potential harm, the Act provides for <u>immediate</u> termination of the rental agreement and an expedited issuance of the Writ of Restitution.[131] In this case, the statute even provides several examples of what constitutes a "material and irreparable" noncompliance. The statute provides:

> If there is a breach that is both material and irreparable, such as an illegal discharge of a weapon on the premises, infliction of serious bodily harm, threatening or intimidating as defined in § 13-1202 or assault as defined in § 13-1203 of the landlord, his agent or another tenant or involving imminent serious property damage, the landlord may deliver a written notice for immediate termination of the rental agreement and shall proceed under § 33-1377 [Special Detainer Actions].[132]

---

[130] *See* A.R.S. § 33-1368(A) (West Supp. 1993).

[131] A.R.S. § 33-1368(A) (West Supp. 1993).

[132] A.R.S. § 33-1368(A) (West Supp. 1992).

(d) Nonpayment of Rent.

Cross Reference
- Chapter 6, Section C(1)(a) (Material Noncompliance)
- Chapter 6, Section C(1)(b) (Noncompliance Materially Affecting Health and Safety)
- Chapter 6, Section C(1)(c) (Material and Irreparable Breach)

The procedures that the landlord and tenant must follow for nonpayment of rent are thoroughly discussed in Section D(2), later in this Chapter.

2. "HOW" The Landlord May Evict A Tenant.

(a) What the landlord CANNOT do.

If the tenant has committed any type of noncompliance (i.e., material noncompliance, material noncompliance that affects health and safety, and/or material and irreparable noncompliance), the landlord may commence legal action to have the tenant's tenancy terminated and obtain a writ of restitution to have the tenant physically removed from the rental unit (if the tenant does not voluntarily leave), but the landlord **cannot**:

(1) Refuse to supply heat, air conditioning, cooling, water, hot water or essential services.[133]

(2) Lock the tenant out of the rental unit or otherwise exclude him/her from the property.[134]

(3) Turn off the power or disconnect other utility services until the day following issuance of the Writ of Restitution. Even then, disconnection of power and/or utility services may only be performed by a person authorized by the utility to perform that function.[135]

(4) Hold or seize the tenant's personal property to pay for rent or other amounts due.[136]

(5) Raise rent, decrease available services, evict a tenant or threaten to evict a tenant in retaliation for complaints made by the tenant to the landlord or to governmental agencies (i.e., reporting a housing code violation to the appropriate authority).[137]

---

[133] A.R.S. § 33-1364 (West 1990). *See, e.g.,* State v. Main, 159 Ariz. 96, 764 P.2d 1155 (App. 1988) (landlord cannot use self-help to evict tenant; only remedy is
n).
).
upp. 1993).
).
).

(b) **What the landlord MAY do**.

Under the Act, the landlord has only two options: s/he may continue to try to work with the tenant to try to reach some mutually acceptable solution or s/he must file an action for possession of the leased premises. An action for possession under the Act is called a "Special Detainer" action (commonly referred to as a "forcible entry and detainer" action). A Special Detainer action is the legal process (the entire process is commonly referred to as an eviction) whereby the landlord obtains a Writ of Restitution, which grants the landlord the right to possession of the leased premises and also decrees that the tenant no longer has any possessory interest in the leased premises. Ultimately, the writ is served and executed by the sheriff or constable, forcibly removing the tenant from the leased premises. If the landlord files a Special Detainer action, s/he must follow the procedures set forth in Section D, the next Section of this Chapter.

D. **THE SPECIAL DETAINER ACTION: ANATOMY OF AN** *EVICTION*.

Cross Reference:
- Chapter 6, Section C(1)(a) (Material Noncompliance)
- Chapter 6, Section C(1)(b) (Noncompliance Materially Affecting Health and Safety)
- Chapter 6, Section C(1)(c) (Material and Irreparable Breach)
- Chapter 6, Section C(1)(d) (Nonpayment of Rent)

Suppose that, for whatever reason, your landlord has filed a Special Detainer action (or Forcible Detainer action, for commercial tenants and certain residential tenants). If you have never been through this process before, you should seriously consider consulting your attorney for legal advice.

If you don't have an attorney and can't afford one, call the Lawyer Referral Service. For a nominal fee (normally about $25.00), you can get one-half hour of legal consultation with an attorney, which is probably all the time you will need. In any event, whether represented by an attorney or not, you (and perhaps your attorney) will find the following flowcharts and accompanying discussions *very* useful.

Before you get to the flowcharts, however, you first need to determine if your landlord has filed the lawsuit with the correct court: justice court or superior court. First, Special Detainer actions may only be brought in justice court or superior court and cannot be brought in small claims court.[138] If your landlord has filed in superior court, s/he has filed with the correct court -- Go to Section D(1). If your landlord has filed in justice court, s/he may or may not have filed with the correct court. To file a Special Detainer action in justice court:

> (1) The damages sought (i.e., past due rent) must be $5,000.00 or less.

---

[138] A.R.S. § 22-503(B)(3) (West Supp. 1993).

and

        (2) The monthly rental amount for your rental unit must not exceed $1000.00.[139]

If your landlord meets <u>both</u> criteria, s/he may file the Special Detainer action in justice court. If the amount sought in damages is more than $5,000 <u>or</u> your monthly rental amount for your rental is more than $1000.00, then the landlord <u>must</u> file the lawsuit in superior court.[140] Superior court has concurrent jurisdiction, which means that even though the lawsuit qualifies for filing in justice court, the landlord may file his/her lawsuit in superior court, if s/he prefers,[141] but processing time is longer and court costs are higher in superior court than in justice court.

If you are **sure** that the landlord has filed in the wrong court (i.e., s/he has filed in justice court and s/he should have filed in superior court) and you would like to have "a little more time" before you are required to move, then the time to raise this defect in the landlord's lawsuit is on the day of trial. The precise language that you should use is as follows:

> "Your honor, I move that the landlord's Special Detainer [or Forcible Detainer] Complaint be dismissed for lack of subject matter jurisdiction. The monthly rental amount exceeds $1,000.00 [and/or] the total damages sought by the landlord exceeds $5,000.00 -- thereby exceeding the jurisdiction of this court, as provided by A.R.S. § 22-201(C). This case *must* be filed in superior court."

The bad news is that landlords rarely commit such a colossal blunder, but it does happen. Okay, let's assume the case was brought in the correct court (or was *refiled* in the correct court). The next question is, "What are all the significant steps in a Special Detainer action?"

The first flowchart, Chapter 6, Section D(1) (next page), shows you the significant events during the eviction process for: (1) material noncompliance with the rental agreement; (2) noncompliance with the rental agreement that materially affects health and safety; and (3) material and irreparable breach of the rental agreement (all three were thoroughly discussed in Chapter 6, Section C).

The second flowchart, Chapter 6, Section D(2) (following, on page 93), shows you the significant events during the eviction process for nonpayment of rent. You may be saying to yourself, "Isn't nonpayment of rent merely one type of material noncompliance?" You are correct. I have included a second flowchart, however, that specifically charts the steps of an eviction for nonpayment of rent because this is the most common type of eviction. Additionally, I have included a few "tips" that apply to the nonpayment of rent situation that may not apply to other situations.

---

[139] A.R.S. § 22-201(C) (West Supp. 1993).

[140] *See* A.R.S. § 22-201(C) (West Supp. 1993).

[141] *See* A.R.S. §§ 12-123(A) (West 1992), 12-1175(A) (West Supp. 1993).

EVICTION FLOWCHART

(For material noncompliance, noncompliance affecting health & safety, and material and irreparable breach)

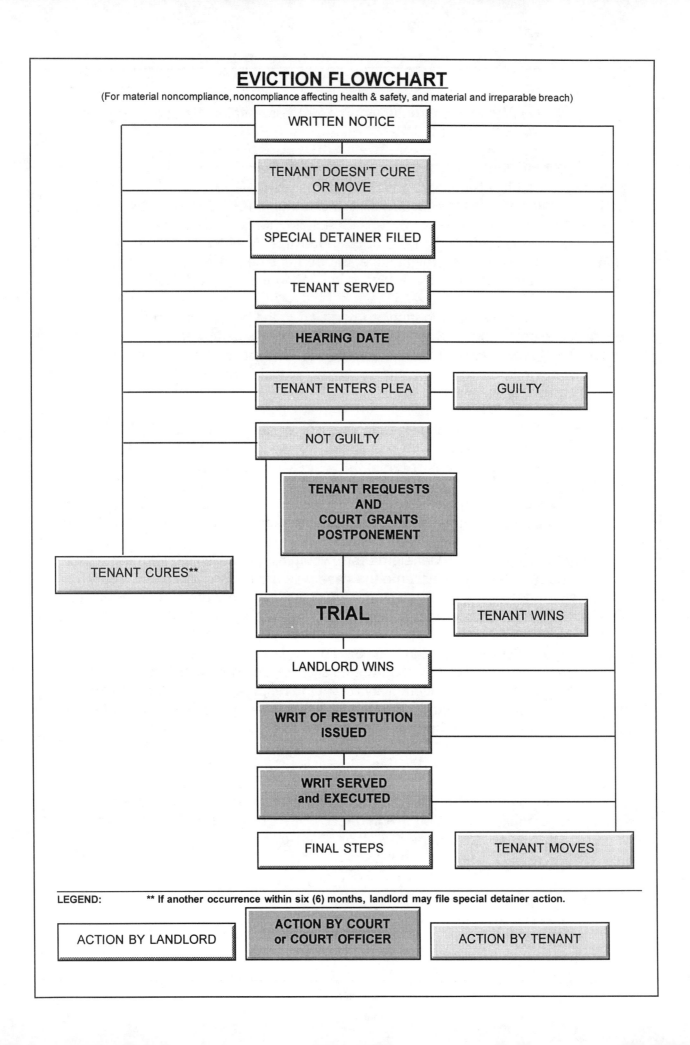

WRITTEN NOTICE

TENANT DOESN'T CURE OR MOVE

SPECIAL DETAINER FILED

TENANT SERVED

HEARING DATE

TENANT ENTERS PLEA → **GUILTY**

NOT GUILTY

TENANT REQUESTS AND COURT GRANTS POSTPONEMENT

TENANT CURES**

TRIAL → **TENANT WINS**

LANDLORD WINS

WRIT OF RESTITUTION ISSUED

WRIT SERVED and EXECUTED

FINAL STEPS → **TENANT MOVES**

LEGEND: ** If another occurrence within six (6) months, landlord may file special detainer action.

| ACTION BY LANDLORD | ACTION BY COURT or COURT OFFICER | ACTION BY TENANT |

1. **EVICTION PROCESS FOR: (1) Material Noncompliance with the Rental Agreement; (2) Noncompliance with the Rental Agreement that Materially Affects Health & Safety; and (3) Material and Irreparable Breach of the Rental Agreement.**

Cross Reference:
*   Chapter 6, Section D(2) (Nonpayment of Rent)

The boxes depicted on both flowcharts are fully discussed on the following pages and are linked to a precise or approximate time frame for when the action must or should occur.

WRITTEN NOTICE

The landlord must serve the tenant with a written notice to cure the noncompliance. For the written notice to be legally sufficient, it must specify: (1) the acts or omissions constituting the breach; and (2) the landlord's intention to terminate the rental agreement if the breach is not cured within the requisite time

```
+-------------------------------------+
|                                     |
|                                     |
|       +----------------------+      |
|       |   WRITTEN NOTICE     |      |
|       +----------------------+      |
|                                     |
|                                     |
+-------------------------------------+
```

period. In the case of a material noncompliance with the rental agreement, the written notice must state that the rental agreement will terminate not less than fourteen (14) calendar days after receipt of the written notice if the breach is not remedied within ten (10) calendar days.[142] In the case of a noncompliance with the rental agreement that materially affects health and safety, the written notice must state that the rental agreement will terminate not less than ten (10) calendar days after receipt of the written notice if the breach is not remedied within five (5) calendar days.[143] (*See* Chapter 6, Section C(1)(b)). In either case, however, the statute provides that if the noncompliance is cured before the date specified in the written notice (i.e., the fourteenth or tenth day, respectively), the rental agreement will not terminate.[144] But, if the same or a similar noncompliance occurs within six months, the landlord may institute a Special Detainer action, pursuant to A.R.S. § 33-1377.[145]

---

[142] A.R.S. § 33-1368(A) (West Supp. 1993).

[143] A.R.S. § 33-1368(A) (West Supp. 1993).

[144] A.R.S. § 33-1368(A) (West Supp. 1993).

[145] A.R.S. § 33-1368(A) (West Supp. 1993).

TENANT CURES

If the noncompliance is remediable by repair, payment of damages or otherwise, the tenant can stop the eviction process by taking the remedial action stated in the written notice prior to the date specified. But the tenant <u>cannot</u> stop the eviction process for a material and irreparable breach.[146] A key point to

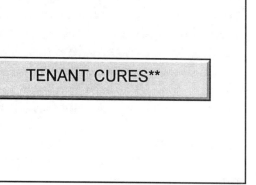

TENANT CURES**

remember is that if the noncompliance is curable and the tenant cures the noncompliance, a similar noncompliance by the tenant within six months may be a sufficient basis to evict the tenant and/or to refuse to renew the tenant's lease.[147]

TENANT MOVES

Naturally, anytime prior to actual "forcible" eviction by the sheriff, the tenant may elect to voluntarily move. When this happens, the landlord may still have a legal cause of action against the tenant for past due rent, money damages for breach of lease, damages to the rental unit, etc. As a practical

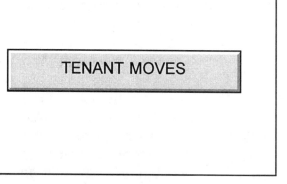

TENANT MOVES

matter, however, if the amount that the tenant owes is small, most landlords will not go to the time and trouble of chasing a tenant down and filing a lawsuit to collect a nominal sum.

IMPORTANT NOTE: You should also be aware of the distinction between: (1) a tenant voluntarily moving out; and (2) a tenant offering to surrender possession <u>and</u> the landlord accepting surrender of possession of the premises. The tenant's conduct of voluntarily moving out <u>does not</u> automatically equate to an acceptance of surrender of possession of the premises by the landlord. Why is this important? A Special Detainer action is a lawsuit to recover possession of rental property. As long as the landlord does not have possession, the Special Detainer action may go forward. But if the tenant voluntarily surrenders possession of the rental unit <u>and</u> <u>the landlord accepts</u> the surrender of possession before the hearing date, the court will dismiss the Special Detainer action. Why is that important? Because the landlord loses the opportunity to get a judgment against you for past rent. Moreover, acceptance of surrender by the landlord may be (and usually is) deemed a waiver of the landlord's right to pursue the tenant for <u>all</u> damages (i.e., past due

---

[146] *See* A.R.S. § 33-1368(A) (West Supp. 1993) (if a breach is both material and irreparable, the landlord may deliver to the tenant a written notice for immediate termination of the rental agreement).

[147] A.R.S. § 33-1368(A) (West Supp. 1993).

rent, damages to the unit, etc.). If you are being <u>lawfully</u> evicted (i.e., <u>you</u> breached the rental agreement), it is **very important** that you try to get the landlord to accept surrender of the premises. This may significantly reduce, or completely eliminate, your liability to the landlord. Naturally, you may voluntarily move out anytime you wish, but the landlord is not required to accept surrender of possession of the premises. "Acceptance" of surrender turns on the <u>landlord's</u> intent. For example, a tenant may abandon the premises and deposit the keys in the landlord's mail slot, but this conduct does not "force" the landlord to accept surrender of the premises.

LANDLORD FILES SPECIAL DETAINER ACTION

The day after the date specified in the written notice, the landlord may file the Special Detainer action. When calculating the fourteen or ten days, do not count the day that the written notice was served. Example: suppose that on the first day of the

SPECIAL DETAINER FILED

month, the landlord issues a written notice for a material noncompliance, specifying that the breach must be cured within ten calendar days or the rental agreement will terminate on the <u>fourteenth</u> calendar day. The earliest date that the Special Detainer action may be filed is the sixteenth (not the fifteenth) day of the month.

TENANT MUST BE SERVED

The *summons* and *complaint* must be served on the tenant. The complaint is the legal document that the landlord must file with the court to institute the Special Detainer action. Service of the summons and complaint is known as *service of process*. Service of process must be

TENANT SERVED

made by a person authorized by law to deliver legal papers. Typically, this is the sheriff or a private *process server*. Service must be completed at least two business days (not calendar days) before the entry of the tenant's plea on the hearing date/trial date. The plea and/or trial date is entered on the summons by the clerk of the court at the time the complaint is filed and the summons issued.

HEARING DATE

HEARING DATE

This date is entered on the summons by the clerk of the court at the time the complaint is filed and the summons issued. This date cannot be less than three (3) business days nor more than six (6) business days from the date the summons was issued (i.e., the date the landlord filed the Special Detainer action).[148]

TENANT ENTERS PLEA

TENANT ENTERS PLEA

Entry of the tenant's plea occurs on the hearing date. Tenant enters his/her plea -- guilty or not guilty.

TENANT REQUESTS AND COURT GRANTS POSTPONEMENT

TENANT REQUESTS AND COURT GRANTS POSTPONEMENT

A tenant may request a postponement of the trial, but s/he must show "good cause" for the postponement. If the court grants the postponement, the postponement may be no longer than three (3) business days in justice court or five (5) business days in superior court.[149] If the tenant does not request a postponement or if the court denies the request, trial of the case may immediately follow entry of the tenant's plea, which is the normal practice in justice court, or may be scheduled for a few days later, which is the normal practice in superior court.

---

[148] A.R.S. § 33-1377(B) (West Supp. 1993).

[149] A.R.S. § 33-1377(C) (West Supp. 1993).

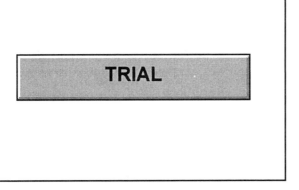

TRIAL

The only issue the court will examine in a Special Detainer action is which party is entitled to immediate possession of the premises. Essentially, this boils down to a question of whether the rental agreement was properly terminated (i.e., was there a material noncompliance, a noncompliance that materially affects health and safety, or a material and irreparable noncompliance?). Unfortunately, there are very few defenses available to the tenant (i.e., improper notice, breach by landlord, etc). *See* Note 2, at the end of this Flowchart.

Judgment is typically entered for the prevailing party at the conclusion of the trial. If the tenant wins (i.e., s/he shows that there was "just cause" for the noncompliance, that the breach was curable and s/he cured the breach, etc.), the court will enter judgment in the tenant's favor, the tenant will be entitled to retain possession of the unit and the tenant will be entitled to judgment against the landlord for his/her attorneys' fees and costs. If the landlord wins, the court will enter judgment in the landlord's favor, including attorneys' fees and costs, and the judgment will restore the landlord's legal right of possession to the rental unit.

If the landlord fails to appear at the trial, the judge will dismiss the Special Detainer action. If the tenant fails to appear at the trial, the landlord must still prove to the judge that s/he is entitled to judgment in his/her favor. If the landlord presents sufficient evidence to prove his/her case, the judge will enter judgment in the landlord's favor. This process is known as obtaining a judgment by default (i.e., in the tenant's absence). If judgment is obtained by default and the tenant was personally served with the summons and complaint (as opposed to service by *posting*),[150] the judgment <u>may</u> also include a specific monetary amount, representing past due rent (but not including damages to the unit, which must be pursued in a separate action). Actual eviction, however, may not be initiated until a *Writ of Restitution* is issued by the court.

---

[150] The Justice Court Administrator for Maricopa County has issued instructions to the justice courts that money judgments against tenants may not be granted unless the tenant is personally served -- posting service of process on the door and mailing the tenant a copy of the forcible detainer complaint is sufficient to obtain a determination of possession only – posting and mailing is not sufficient to obtain a money judgment. *See* Letter from Peter M. Gorski, Justice Court Administrator for Maricopa County, to Litigants and Process Servers, dated July 11, 1991 (on file with author).

WRIT OF RESTITUTION ISSUED

WRIT OF RESTITUTION ISSUED

The Writ of Restitution will not issue until five business days (not calendar days) after entry of judgment. Issuance of the writ is not automatic; the landlord must request the court to issue the Writ of Restitution. Upon receiving the writ, the landlord takes the writ to the sheriff or constable, who will then serve the writ.

WRIT SERVED and EXECUTED

WRIT SERVED and EXECUTED

Service and execution of the writ may be a two-step process. The precise time of service/execution will depend on the present backlog -- it may be one day or it may be three weeks. Actual eviction must be conducted by the sheriff or constable (not the landlord; not a process server). Eviction may not be initiated until a Writ of Restitution is issued by the court and delivered to the sheriff or constable (the sheriff serves and executes the writ in superior court cases; the constable serves and executes the writ in justice court cases) along with a payment of the fee. The sheriff/constable has the legal authority to forcibly remove the tenant, but the responsibility for removing the tenant's personal property falls on the landlord. Typically, the procedure is as follows: the sheriff/constable goes to the tenant's home, tells the tenant that s/he must get out within twenty-four (24) hours or the sheriff/constable will forcibly remove the tenant and his/her belongings. If the tenant does not move out within the time specified, the sheriff/constable will forcibly remove the tenant. The landlord is responsible for moving and storage of the tenant's personal property. To reclaim the personal property, the tenant must pay the charge for moving and storage of the property, but not any other amounts that are due.[151] If the tenant does not claim the property within sixty (60) days, the property may be sold at public auction.[152] Once the tenant and his/her property is removed and the premises re-keyed, the landlord is lawfully in possession of the premises. If the tenant subsequently attempts to reenter the premises, the tenant has committed criminal trespass upon the landlord's property. If the tenant does, in fact, reenter the rental unit, the tenant has committed criminal trespass, breaking and entering, criminal damage and burglary.

---

[151] A.R.S. § 33-1368(E) (West Supp. 1993).

[152] A.R.S. § 33-1368(E) (West Supp. 1993).

FINAL STEPS

These steps do not appear individually on the flowchart, but they are critical.

Inspection. Just prior to vacating the unit, the tenant should conduct an inspection of the rental unit. The tenant should use the same property inspection form that s/he completed when s/he moved in. The tenant should take copious notes and photographs, if necessary. This evidence may be crucial if the landlord attempts to pursue the tenant for damage to the rental unit that s/he did not cause.

Security deposit. Within fourteen (14) calendar days, the landlord must send the tenant a statement disclosing the disposition of their deposit (*see* Chapter 3, Section B(5)). Although the tenant has been evicted, s/he may still be entitled to a refund of "some portion" of the security deposit. Therefore, the tenant should provide the landlord with an address where the funds may be sent. Otherwise, the landlord may be justified in holding the tenant's funds for longer than the statutory fourteen days. The address can be any address that the tenant would like the refund check sent to.

Lawsuit for damages. After eviction, the landlord may file a lawsuit against the tenant for: (1) past due rent (if personal service was not obtained in the Special Detainer action), (2) rent that accrued after entry of the Special Detainer judgment through the last date that s/he occupied the rental unit, (3) damages to the rental unit, and (4) any other amounts to which the landlord is entitled under the law.

ADDITIONAL IMPORTANT NOTES.

1. Assuming that the tenant does not voluntarily vacate during the eviction process, the entire process, from the date the Written Notice is served until the date the tenant is "forcibly evicted" by the sheriff or constable, cannot take less than twenty-five (25) days and could take as long as sixty days, depending on how tenacious the landlord is.

2. The tenant has very few defenses available in a Special Detainer action. Most defenses are procedural. The tenant may raise the following defenses:

   a. The Written Notice was improperly served or the notice itself was defective (i.e., lacks required information).

b. The Special Detainer complaint was filed before the fourteen day period (for a material noncompliance) or ten-day period (for a material noncompliance that materially affects health and safety) expired.

c. The Special Detainer action was filed in the wrong court. *See* Chapter 6, Section D.

d. The summons and complaint were improperly served.

e. You no longer live in the rental unit and the landlord has accepted surrender of possession.

f. The Special Detainer action is an unlawful retaliation against the tenant (i.e., retaliation for reporting building code violations, etc.).

g. Noncompliance was justified because of some type of breach of the rental agreement by the landlord (i.e., failure to repair, failure to provide heat/cooling, etc.).

h. The landlord failed to give "adequate" notice. The tenant may wish to argue that the notice provision of the rental agreement is unclear or ambiguous. Any conflicting language on other forms used by the landlord may support this argument. *See* Chapter 6, Section A(4).

i. The landlord inconsistently enforces the terms in the rental agreement (i.e., s/he allows some tenants to violate certain rules, but not others). If the tenant can prove to the court that s/he is the victim of "selective enforcement," the landlord's action may be dismissed.[153]

3. Depending on the situation, if the tenant has breached the agreement, s/he may wish to consider offering the landlord some amount of money (e.g., $100, $200, $300, or more, depending on the particular facts) in exchange for a complete release of liability. This has the distinct advantage of limiting the tenant's liability (not to mention that s/he will not have to lose any sleep over whether or not the landlord will be "chasing him/her down" to garnish his/her bank accounts and/or wages). In addition, the tenant's credit will not be adversely affected. And most importantly, the tenant may be able to use this landlord as a reference. Thus, there are many advantages for payment of this nominal sum.

4. The "Eviction Flowchart" and the foregoing discussion are intended to illustrate the critical stages of a Special Detainer action brought by a landlord against a tenant, however, these steps are not exhaustive. You should consult with your attorney before appearing in court to defend a Special Detainer action.

---

[153] *See, e.g.,* Unif. Residential Landlord And Tenant Act § 3.102; 7B U.L.A. 475 (1985).

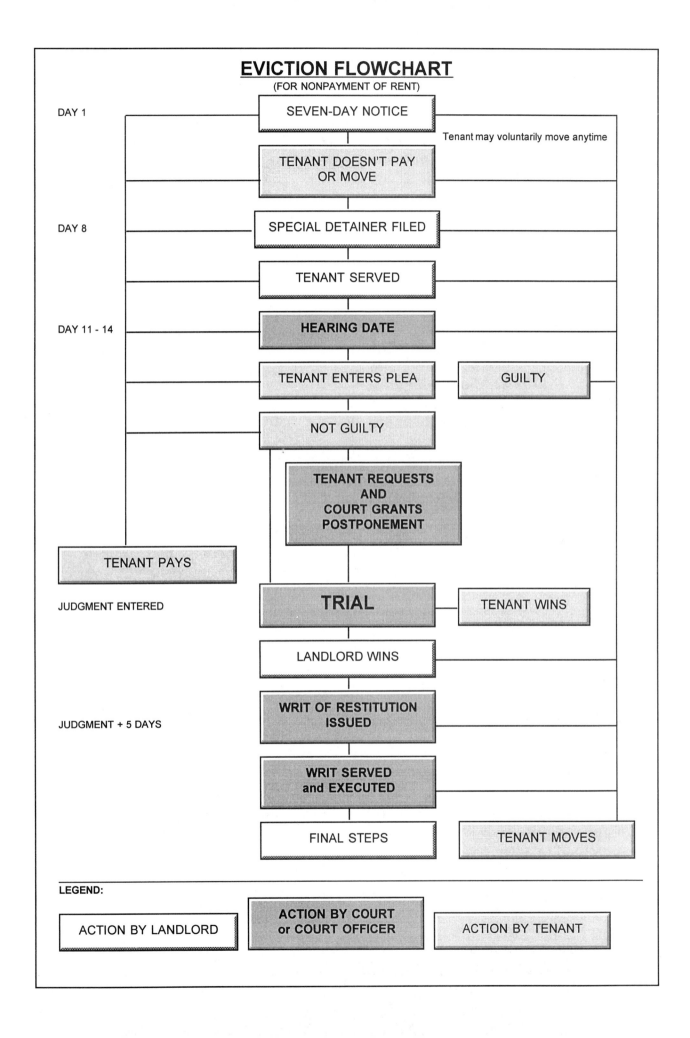

2. EVICTION PROCESS FOR NONPAYMENT OF RENT.

This flowchart (prior page; page 93) and the following discussion are similar, but not identical to the prior flowchart and discussion in Chapter 6, Section D(1) (which charts the eviction process for other types of noncompliance with the rental agreement). This flowchart discusses the various procedures and steps that a landlord **must** take to successfully evict a tenant from the rental unit for nonpayment of rent. If the landlord fails to follow these procedures, the tenant may have sufficient grounds to defeat the landlord's eviction proceedings.

SEVEN-DAY NOTICE

TIME FRAME: Day 1

Step 1: The landlord must serve the tenant with a ***Seven-Day Notice to Pay or Quit*** (a.k.a. ***Seven-Day Notice***). For a Seven-Day Notice to be legally sufficient, it must give notice of: (1) the nonpayment of rent; and (2) the landlord's intention to terminate the rental agreement if rent is not paid within the seven-day period.[154] For an example of what a Seven-Day Notice looks like, *see* page 34.

```
+-------------------------------------------+
|                                           |
|                                           |
|   +-----------------------------------+   |
|   |        SEVEN-DAY NOTICE           |   |
|   +-----------------------------------+   |
|                                           |
|                                           |
+-------------------------------------------+
```

Service of the Seven-Day Notice. The Seven-Day Notice may be served on the first day that rent is past due. The landlord may serve the Seven-Day Notice in person or by certified mail. The landlord may also have the sheriff or a private process server serve it.

TENANT PAYS

TIME FRAME: Anytime, up to entry of judgment on the trial date.

The tenant can stop the eviction process by paying all amounts due, including all past rent, late fees, attorneys' fees and court costs. The landlord <u>must</u> accept tender of said

```
+-------------------------------------------+
|                                           |
|   +-----------------------------------+   |
|   |           TENANT PAYS             |   |
|   +-----------------------------------+   |
|                                           |
+-------------------------------------------+
```

payment by tenant.[155] <u>After</u> entry of judgment in the landlord's favor, however, the tenant is not entitled to reinstate the rental agreement and the landlord is not obligated to accept payment.

---

[154] A.R.S. § 33-1368(B) (West Supp. 1993).

[155] A.R.S. § 33-1368(B) (West Supp. 1993).

TENANT MOVES

TIME FRAME: Anytime prior to execution of Writ of Restitution.

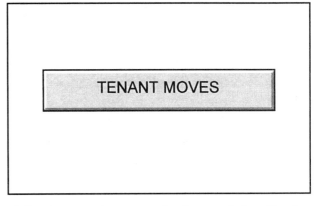

Naturally, anytime prior to actual "forcible" eviction by the sheriff, the tenant may elect to voluntarily move. When this happens, the landlord may still have a legal cause of action against the tenant for past due rent, money damages for breach of the lease, damages to the rental unit, etc. As a practical matter, however, if the amount that the tenant owes is small, most landlords will not go to the time and trouble of chasing a tenant down and filing a lawsuit to collect a nominal sum.

IMPORTANT NOTE: You should also be aware of the distinction between: (1) a tenant voluntarily moving out; and (2) a tenant offering to surrender possession <u>and</u> the landlord accepting surrender of possession of the premises. The tenant's conduct of voluntarily moving out <u>does not</u> automatically equate to an acceptance of surrender of possession of the premises by the landlord. Why is this important? A Special Detainer action is a lawsuit to recover possession of rental property. As long as the landlord does not have possession, the Special Detainer action may go forward. But if the tenant voluntarily surrenders possession of the rental unit <u>and</u> <u>the landlord accepts</u> the surrender of possession before the hearing date, the court will dismiss the Special Detainer action. Why is that important? Because the landlord loses the opportunity to get a judgment against you for past rent. Moreover, acceptance of surrender by the landlord may be (and usually is) deemed a waiver of the landlord's right to pursue the tenant for <u>all</u> damages (i.e., past due rent, damages to the unit, etc.). If you are being <u>lawfully</u> evicted (i.e., <u>you</u> breached the rental agreement), it is **very important** that you try to get the landlord to accept surrender of the premises. This may significantly reduce, or completely eliminate, your liability to the landlord. Naturally, you may voluntarily move out anytime you wish, but the landlord is not required to accept surrender of possession of the premises. "Acceptance" of surrender turns on the <u>landlord's</u> intent. For example, a tenant may abandon the premises and deposit the keys in the landlord's mail slot, but this conduct does not "force" the landlord to accept surrender of the premises.

LANDLORD FILES SPECIAL DETAINER ACTION
TIME FRAME: Day 8

SPECIAL DETAINER FILED

The landlord must wait seven days (calendar days, not business days) <u>after</u> serving the Seven-Day Notice before s/he may file the Special Detainer action.[156] Therefore, the eighth day after service of the Seven-Day Notice is the earliest day that the landlord may file the lawsuit. *The day that the Seven-Day Notice is served is not counted.* Example: if the Seven-Day Notice is served on the second day of the month, the earliest date that the Special Detainer action may be filed is the ninth day of the month.

The Act provides that after a Special Detainer action has been filed, the tenant may reinstate the rental agreement only by paying past due rent, late fees, attorneys' fees and court costs.[157] If the tenant tenders a partial payment with the understanding that the lawsuit will be terminated and s/he will be given more time to come up with the balance due, the tenant should <u>make sure that this "agreement" is in writing</u>. Otherwise, the landlord's "understanding" may be different than that of the tenant's and the lawsuit will go forward.

TENANT MUST BE SERVED
TIME FRAME: Hearing date, minus two (2) business days.

TENANT SERVED

The **summons** and **complaint** must be served on the tenant. The complaint is the legal document that the landlord must file with the court to institute the Special Detainer action. Service of the summons and complaint is known as **service of process**. Service of process must be made by a person authorized by law to deliver legal papers. Typically, this is the sheriff or a private **process server**. Service must be completed at least two business days (not calendar days) before the entry of the tenant's plea on the hearing date/trial date. The plea and/or trial date is entered on the summons by the clerk of the court at the time the complaint is filed and the summons issued.

---

[156] A.R.S. § 33-1368(B) (West Supp. 1993).

[157] A.R.S. § 33-1368(B) (West Supp. 1993).

HEARING DATE
TIME FRAME: Day 11 - 14

This date is entered on the summons by the clerk of the court at the time the complaint is filed and the summons issued. This date cannot be less than three (3) business days nor more than six (6) business days from the date the summons was issued (i.e., the date the landlord filed the Special Detainer action).[158]

> HEARING DATE

TENANT ENTERS PLEA

Entry of the tenant's plea occurs on the hearing date. Tenant enters his/her plea -- guilty or not guilty.

> TENANT ENTERS PLEA

> TENANT REQUESTS
> AND
> COURT GRANTS
> POSTPONEMENT

TENANT REQUESTS AND COURT GRANTS POSTPONEMENT

A tenant may request a postponement of the trial, but s/he must show "good cause" for the postponement. If the court grants the postponement, the postponement may be no longer than three (3) business days in justice court or five (5) business days in superior court.[159] If the tenant does not request a postponement or if the court denies the request, trial of the case may immediately follow entry of the tenant's plea, which is the normal practice in justice court, or may be scheduled for a few days later, which is the normal practice in superior court.

---

[158] A.R.S. § 33-1377(B) (West Supp. 1993).

[159] A.R.S. § 33-1377(C) (West Supp. 1993).

TRIAL

TIME FRAME: Day 11-14, or if postponement granted, Day 14-19

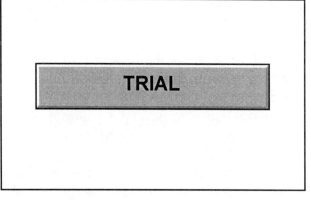

The only issue the court will examine in a Special Detainer action is which party is entitled to immediate possession of the premises. Essentially, this boils down to a question of whether the rental agreement was properly terminated (i.e., Was there a material noncompliance, a noncompliance that materially affects health and safety, or a material and irreparable noncompliance?). Unfortunately, there are very few defenses available to the tenant (i.e., improper notice, breach by landlord, etc). *See* Note 2, at the end of this Flowchart.

Judgment is typically entered for the prevailing party at the conclusion of the trial. If the tenant wins (i.e., s/he shows that there was "just cause" for the noncompliance, that the breach was curable and s/he cured the breach, etc.), the court will enter judgment in the tenant's favor, the tenant will be entitled to retain possession of the unit and the tenant will be entitled to judgment against the landlord for his/her attorneys' fees and costs. If the landlord wins, the court will enter judgment in the landlord's favor, including attorneys' fees and costs, and the judgment will restore the landlord's legal right of possession to the rental unit.

If the landlord fails to appear at the trial, the judge will dismiss the Special Detainer action. If the tenant fails to appear at the trial, the landlord must still prove to the judge that s/he is entitled to judgment in his/her favor. If the landlord presents sufficient evidence to prove his/her case, the judge will enter judgment in the landlord's favor. This process is known as obtaining a judgment by default (i.e., in the tenant's absence). If judgment is obtained by default and the tenant was personally served with the summons and complaint (as opposed to service by ***posting***),[160] the judgment <u>may</u> also include a specific monetary amount, representing past due rent (but not including damages to the unit, which must be pursued in a separate action). Actual eviction, however, may not be initiated until a Writ of Restitution is issued by the court.

---

[160] The Justice Court Administrator for Maricopa County has issued instructions to the justice courts that money judgments against tenants may not be granted unless the tenant is personally served – posting service of process on the door and mailing the tenant a copy of the forcible detainer complaint is sufficient to obtain a determination of possession only – posting and mailing is not sufficient to obtain a money judgment. *See* Letter from Peter M. Gorski, Justice Court Administrator for Maricopa County, to Litigants and Process Servers, dated July 11, 1991 (on file with author).

> **WRIT OF RESTITUTION ISSUED**

WRIT OF RESTITUTION ISSUED
TIME FRAME: Judgment + 5 days

The Writ of Restitution will not issue until five business days (not calendar days) after entry of judgment. Issuance of the writ is not automatic; the landlord must request the court to issue the Writ of Restitution. Upon receiving the writ, the landlord takes the writ to the sheriff or constable, who will then serve the writ.

WRIT SERVED and EXECUTED

Service and execution of the writ may be a two-step process. The precise time of service/execution will depend on the present backlog -- it may be one day or it may be three weeks. Actual eviction must be conducted by the sheriff or constable (not the landlord; not a process server). Eviction may not be initi-

> **WRIT SERVED and EXECUTED**

ated until a Writ of Restitution is issued by the court and delivered to the sheriff or constable (the sheriff serves and executes the writ in superior court cases; the constable serves and executes the writ in justice court cases) along with a payment of the fee. The sheriff/constable has the legal authority to forcibly remove the tenant, but the responsibility for removing the tenant's personal property falls on the landlord. Typically, the procedure is as follows: the sheriff/constable goes to the tenant's home, tells the tenant that s/he must get out within twenty-four (24) hours or the sheriff/constable will forcibly remove the tenant and his/her belongings. If the tenant does not move out within the time specified, the sheriff/constable will forcibly remove the tenant. The landlord is responsible for moving and storage of the tenant's personal property. To reclaim the personal property, the tenant must pay the charge for moving and storage of the property, but not any other amounts that are due.[161] If the tenant does not claim the property within sixty (60) days, the property may be sold at public auction.[162] Once the tenant and his/her property is removed and the premises re-keyed, the landlord is lawfully in possession of the premises. If the tenant subsequently attempts to reenter the premises, the tenant has committed criminal trespass upon the landlord's property. If the tenant does, in fact, reenter the rental unit, the tenant has committed criminal trespass, breaking and entering, criminal damage and burglary.

---

[161] A.R.S. § 33-1368(E) (West Supp. 1993).

[162] A.R.S. § 33-1368(E) (West Supp. 1993).

FINAL STEPS

These steps do not appear individually on the flowchart, but they are critical.

Inspection.
Just prior to vacating the unit, the tenant should conduct an inspection of the rental unit. The tenant should use the same property inspection form that s/he completed when s/he moved in. The tenant should take copious notes and photographs, if necessary. This evidence may be crucial if the landlord attempts to pursue the tenant for damage to the rental unit that s/he did not cause.

Security deposit.
Within fourteen (14) calendar days, the landlord must send the tenant a statement disclosing the disposition of their deposit (*see* Chapter 3, Section B(5)). Although the tenant has been evicted, s/he may still be entitled to a refund of "some portion" of the security deposit. Therefore, the tenant should provide the landlord with an address where the funds may be sent. Otherwise, the landlord may be justified in holding the tenant's funds for longer than the statutory fourteen days. The address can be any address that the tenant would like the refund check sent to.

Lawsuit for damages.
After eviction, the landlord may file a lawsuit against the tenant for: (1) past due rent (if personal service was not obtained in the Special Detainer action), (2) rent that accrued after entry of the Special Detainer judgment through the last date that s/he occupied the rental unit, (3) damages to the rental unit, and (4) any other amounts to which the landlord is entitled under the law.

ADDITIONAL IMPORTANT NOTES.

1. Assuming that the tenant does not voluntarily vacate during the eviction process, the entire process, from the date the Written Notice is served until the date the tenant is "forcibly evicted" by the sheriff or constable, cannot take less than twenty-five (25) days and could take as long as sixty days, depending on how tenacious the landlord is.

2. The tenant has very few defenses available in a Special Detainer action. Most defenses are procedural. The tenant may raise the following defenses:

a. The rent was not yet due when the tenant was served with the Seven-Day Notice, the Notice was improperly served or the Notice itself was defective (i.e., lacks required information).

b. The Special Detainer complaint was filed before the seven-day period (after service of the Seven-Day Notice) expired.

c. The Special Detainer action was filed in the wrong court. *See* Chapter 6, Section D.

d. The summons and complaint were improperly served.

e. The tenant no longer lives in the rental unit and the landlord has accepted surrender of possession.

f. The Special Detainer action is an unlawful retaliation against the tenant (i.e., retaliation for reporting building code violations, etc.).

g. Nonpayment of rent was justified because of some type of breach of the rental agreement by the landlord (i.e., failure to repair, failure to provide heat/cooling, etc.).

h. The rent has been paid, or part of the rent was paid and accepted after service of the Seven-Day Notice.

i. The landlord inconsistently enforces the terms in the rental agreement (i.e., s/he allows some tenants to be late with the rent, but not others). If the tenant can demonstrate to the court that s/he is the victim of "selective enforcement," the landlord's action may be dismissed.[163]

j. The language of the rental agreement provides (or suggests) that the landlord **must** accept partial rent payments, but the landlord has refused to accept a partial payment from you. See Chapter 3, Section B(3)(c).

3. Depending on the situation, if the tenant has breached the agreement, s/he may wish to consider offering the landlord some amount of money (e.g., $100, $200, $300, or more, depending on the particular facts) in exchange for a complete release of liability. This has the distinct advantage of limiting the tenant's liability (not to mention that s/he will not have to lose any sleep over whether or not the landlord will be "chasing him/her down" to garnish his/her bank accounts and/or wages). In addition, the tenant's credit will not be adversely affected. And most importantly, the tenant may be able to use this landlord as a reference. Thus, there are many advantages for payment of this nominal sum.

4. The "Eviction Flowchart" and the foregoing discussion are intended to illustrate the critical stages of a Special Detainer action brought by a landlord against a tenant, however, these steps are not exhaustive. You should consult with your attorney before appearing in court to defend a Special Detainer action.

---

[163] *See, e.g.,* UNIF. RESIDENTIAL LANDLORD AND TENANT ACT, § 3.102; 7B U.L.A. 475 (1985).

APPENDIX A

CHECKLISTS

Okay, you have read this entire book, or at least the parts that you feel apply to you. Your head is undoubtedly spinning with all the things I told you to do. The following three checklists are designed to help you remember some of the most important ideas that were presented.

CHECKLIST 1 -   What to do when you have finished reading this book and are ready to rent a unit.

CHECKLIST 2 -   Review your rental agreement.

CHECKLIST 3 -   Deposits - Everything you need to know.

<u>CHECKLIST NUMBER 1</u>

What to do when you have finished reading this book and are ready to rent a unit

a. Follow the Legal Advice to Tenants (*See* Chapter 3)

- Get a lawyer.
- Get the right lawyer.
- Have your lawyer review your rental agreement <u>before</u> you sign it.
- Be sure you have enough insurance.
- Discuss asset protection with your lawyer.

b. Review the rental agreement (*See* Chapter 4, Section B)

See Checklist 2

c. If you are presently being evicted, refer to Chapter 7, Section D(1) or Section D(2), depending on your particular facts.

d. When looking for a rental unit, keep the following tips in mind:

- Notice the curb appeal of the individual unit and the complex (if applicable)
- Ask about pets before seeing the unit
- See the unit before filling out the application
- Ask about parking before filling out the application
    - If you have a commercial vehicle, check whether local law will allow you to park on the property -- do not merely ask the landlord.
    - If you plan on doing a lot of vehicle repairs and/or maintenance, you should find out the landlord's policy on this issue before completing the application
- Provide complete and accurate information on the application
- Look at your answers *from the landlord's point of view.*
- Remember, everything you do and say is part of the application
- If you are applying for the position of "on-site manager," ask the landlord to include language in the rental agreement that will make the Act apply. *See* Chapter 4, Section A(1).

CHECKLIST NUMBER 2

Review your rental agreement

a. What must be in your rental agreement
   - Disclosure of manager and owner or owner's agent.
   - Deliver a signed copy of the written rental agreement.
   - The written rental agreement must be complete.
   - Nonrefundable deposits must be stated in writing.
   - Rental agreements longer than one-year must be written.

b. What cannot be in your rental agreement
   - The landlord cannot require the tenant to:
     - waive the tenant's rights;
     - agree to pay attorneys' fees; or
     - agree to limit the landlord's liability.
   - The landlord cannot collect a security deposit equal to more than one and one-half month's rent.

c. What should be in your rental agreement
   - The rental agreement should be written.
   - The written rental agreement should be comprehensive.
   - The rental agreement should provide for abandonment.
   - The rental agreement should provide for payment of expenses incurred to bring a Special Detainer action.
   - The rental agreement should provide that the landlord may accept partial payments without waiving any rights.
   - The rental agreement should provide how partial payments are applied to amounts due.

d. What to LOOK OUT for in your rental agreement
   - Abandonment clause.
   - Language requiring tenant to pay attorneys' fees and litigation expenses.
   - Language agreeing to payment of "other" expenses.

CHECKLIST NUMBER 3

Deposits - Everything you need to know

- The landlord cannot collect a deposit equal to more than one and one-half month's rent.[1] Example: if rent is $500 per month, s/he cannot collect a security deposit of more than $750.

- In addition to a security deposit, a "reasonable" cleaning or redecorating deposit may be collected by the landlord.[2]

- Nonrefundable cleaning and redecorating deposits must be clearly stated in writing and a copy of must be given to the tenant.[3] Normally, this is addressed in the rental agreement, but if your landlord does not have a written rental agreement (shame on you for letting him/her get away with that), s/he must nevertheless have some written document that clearly states which deposits are nonrefundable. If the landlord has not disclosed in writing that a cleaning and/or redecorating deposit is nonrefundable and then fails to return said deposit to the tenant, the tenant may recover the deposit together with damages in an amount equal to **twice** the amount wrongfully withheld.[4]

- The Act does not require landlords to pay tenants interest on tenants' deposits.

- After the tenant vacates the rental unit, the landlord must either: (1) refund 100% of the tenant's deposits that s/he is holding or (2) refund the amount due the tenant, if any, and provide a written notice that itemizes deductions from the tenant's deposits. The Act requires the landlord to do either 1 or 2, above, within fourteen (14) calendar days after: (1) termination of tenancy, (2) delivery of possession of the rental unit by the tenant to the landlord, and (3) demand for return of his/her deposit(s) by the tenant. If the landlord does not comply by either failing to return the security deposit or failing to deliver a written itemization, the tenant may recover the property and money due him/her together with damages in an amount equal to **twice** the amount wrongfully withheld.[5] Consequently, whenever you vacate a rental unit, you should be in the habit of *personally* turning the keys over to the landlord and, at the same time, providing the landlord with a written demand for return of your deposits. A short, hand-written note is sufficient:

> Dear Mr. Landlord:
>
> On [date], I, Terry Tenant, delivered possession of the rental property located at 101 N. Rental Avenue, Phoenix, Arizona, to Larry Landlord. I hereby request that my refundable deposit(s) be refunded to me.
>
> NOTE: KEEP A COPY   Terry Tenant   May 2, 1994

[1] A.R.S. § 33-1321(A) (West 1990).

[2] A.R.S. § 33-1310(13) (West 1990) ("'Security' does not include a reasonable charge for redecorating or cleaning.").

[3] A.R.S. § 33-1321(B) (West 1990).

[4] A.R.S. § 33-1321(D) (West 1990).

[5] A.R.S. § 33-1321(D) (West 1990).

The foregoing summarizes virtually all that you need to know about security deposits. Nevertheless, you should read the portion of the Act that specifically addresses deposits (reprinted below).

Security deposits

A. A landlord shall not demand or receive security, however denominated, including, but not limited to, prepaid rent in an amount or value in excess of one and one-half month's rent. This subsection does not prohibit a tenant from voluntarily paying more than one and one-half month's rent in advance.

B. Cleaning and redecorating deposits, if nonrefundable, must be so stated in writing by the landlord.

C. Upon termination of the tenancy, property or money held by the landlord as prepaid rent and security may be applied to the payment of accrued rent and the amount of damages which the landlord has suffered by reason of the tenant's noncompliance with § 33-1341 [tenant's obligations for maintaining the dwelling unit] all as itemized by the landlord in a written notice delivered to the tenant together with the amount due within fourteen days after termination of the tenancy and delivery of possession and demand by the tenant.

D. If the landlord fails to comply with subsections B and C of this section the tenant may recover the property and money due him together with damages in an amount equal to twice the amount wrongfully withheld.[6]

---

[6] A.R.S. § 33-1321(A)-(D) (West 1990).

APPENDIX B

FORMS

This appendix contains blank forms for you to copy and use. Also included are sample completed forms, to clarify the type of information that should be inserted into each blank space. If you are unsure how to properly complete **any** blank form (i.e., those included here or forms from another source), you should consult your attorney.

FORM 1 - PROPERTY INSPECTION CHECKLIST
Cross Reference: Chapter 4, Section C(3).

FORM 2 - NOTICE TO TERMINATE TENANCY (by tenant)
Cross Reference: Chapter 4, Section C(5).
Chapter 7, Section A.

FORM 3 - TEN-DAY NOTICE OF TERMINATION OF RENTAL AGREEMENT FOR NONCOMPLIANCE WITH RENTAL AGREEMENT MATERIALLY AFFECTING HEALTH AND SAFETY
Cross Reference: Chapter 4, Section C(11).
Chapter 6, Section C(2).

FORM 4 - FOURTEEN-DAY NOTICE OF TERMINATION OF RENTAL AGREE-MENT FOR MATERIAL NONCOMPLIANCE WITH RENTAL AGREEMENT
Cross Reference: Chapter 4, Section C(10).
Chapter 6, Section C(1).

FORM 5 - NOTICE OF TERMINATION OR RENT REDUCTION BECAUSE OF DAMAGE DUE TO FIRE OR CASUALTY
Cross Reference: Chapter 6, Section C(4).

FORM 6 - NOTICE OF TENANT'S INTENT TO EFFECT REPAIRS
Cross Reference: Chapter 6, Section C(1).

FORM 7 - NOTICE OF WRONGFUL FAILURE TO PROVIDE ESSENTIAL SERVICES
Cross Reference: Chapter 6, Section C(3).

Other than the Rental Agreement, the Property Inspection Checklist is the most important form to the tenant. If you do not properly complete this form, you may be charged for defects or damage that existed *before* you moved in. The Property Inspection Checklist is discussed in Chapter Four, Section C(3).

PROPERTY INSPECTION CHECKLIST

The premises located at: 111 North Maple Street, #2, Phoenix, Arizona, are clean, safe, in good repair and without defects, with only the following exceptions noted:

Exterior: <u>Northwest bedroom window cracked; south side of building needs paint (existing paint is peeling).</u>

(i.e., condition of the exterior structure, etc.)

Living room* : <u>2" circular hole in carpet (burn mark); stain on carpet, near door.</u>

Family room* : <u>1" x 2" oval hole in south hall; outlet cover missing.</u>

Kitchen: <u>Cabinet above stove scratched; oven dented near bottom; faucet drips; one piece of floor tile broken (near refrigerator).</u>

(i.e., appliances, cabinets, walls, floor, ceiling, etc.)

Laundry room** : <u>None.</u>

Hall: <u>None.</u>

Hall bathroom** : <u>Towel rack bent; light cover missing; bathtub porcelain chipped (near drain).</u>

Bedroom 1* : <u>Door marred; 1" hole in carpet, near window; drapes torn.</u>

Bedroom 2* : <u>Light fixture doesn't work.</u>

Master Bedroom** : <u>Carpet stain near closet; hole in wall behind door.</u>

When completed and signed, this form will be attached to your Rental Agreement. Costs to repair defects not noted on this checklist are the tenant(s)'s responsibility and will be deducted from the security deposit if not repaired prior to vacating the premises. Make a thorough inspection of the premises & note all defects!

Terry Tenant   January 1, 1994   *Larry Landlord   January 1, 1994*
(Tenants)   (Landlord/Owner)
* i.e., floor, carpet, walls, ceilings, doors, hardware, windows.   ** i.e., fixtures, walls, ceilings, floor, outlets, door, windows.

PROPERTY INSPECTION CHECKLIST

The premises located at: _____, _____, Arizona, are clean, safe, in good repair and without defects, with only the following exceptions noted:

Exterior: _____
_____
(i.e., condition of the exterior structure, etc.)

Living room* : _____
_____

Family room* : _____
_____

Kitchen: _____
_____
(i.e., appliances, cabinets, walls, floor, ceiling, etc.)

Laundry room** : _____
_____

Hall: _____
_____

Hall bathroom** : _____
_____

Bedroom 1* : _____
_____

Bedroom 2* : _____
_____

Master Bedroom** : _____
_____

When completed and signed, this form will be attached to your Rental Agreement. Costs to repair defects not noted on this checklist are the tenant(s)'s responsibility and will be deducted from the security deposit if not repaired prior to vacating the premises. MAKE A THOROUGH INSPECTION OF THE PREMISES & NOTE ALL DEFECTS!

Date _____   Date _____

_____   _____
(Tenants)   (Landlord/Owner)

* i.e., floor, carpet, walls, ceilings, doors, hardware, windows.   ** i.e., fixtures, walls, ceilings, floor, outlets, door, windows.

When terminating tenancy, make sure that you give the landlord "adequate notice" and that you provide the landlord with a **written** notice.   *See* Chapter Seven, Sections A(2) and A(4).

NOTICE TO TERMINATE TENANCY
(Voluntary termination by tenant)

Larry Landlord
101 North Slum Lord Avenue   Date: August 30, 1994
Phoenix, Arizona 85999

Notice to Landlord:

Pursuant to the notice requirement of my (our) written rental agreement or, in the absence of a written rental agreement, pursuant to A.R.S. § 33-1375, I (we) hereby submit my (our) written notice to terminate tenancy. On <u>September 30, 1994</u>, I (we) will vacate the rental unit located at:
      (date)

<u>111 North Maple Street, #2, Phoenix, Arizona 85000</u>
(address)

I (we) understand that any refundable deposits must be sent to me (us) within fourteen days from the date I (we) vacate. Please send all refundable deposits to my (our) forwarding address.

FORWARDING ADDRESS:
<u>222 North Oak Street, #1, Tucson, Arizona 85000</u>

<u>Terry Tenant</u>   <u>*Terry Tenant*</u>
    (Print Name)   (Tenants' Signature)
<u>Tina Tenant</u>   <u>*Tina Tenant*</u>
    (Print Name)   (Tenants' Signature)

This notice delivered this date <u>August 30, 1994</u> via:

☐ Certified mail
☐ Regular first class mail
■ Hand delivered

Acknowledgment of hand delivery and receipt hereof:

<u>*Larry Landlord*</u>   <u>*August 30, 1994*</u>
(signature of landlord)   (date)

NOTICE TO TERMINATE TENANCY
(Voluntary termination by tenant)

_____   Date: _____

_____

_____, _____ _____

Notice to Landlord:

Pursuant to the notice requirement of my (our) written rental agreement or, in the absence of a written rental agreement, pursuant to A.R.S. § 33-1375, I (we) hereby submit my (our) written notice to terminate tenancy. On _____, I (we) will vacate the rental unit located at: (date)

_____

(address)

I (we) understand that any refundable deposits must be sent to me (us) within fourteen days from the date I (we) vacate. Please send all refundable deposits to my (our) forwarding address.

FORWARDING ADDRESS:

_____

_____

_____   _____
(Print Name)   (Tenants' Signature)

_____   _____
(Print Name)   (Tenants' Signature)

This notice delivered this date _____ via:

☐ Certified mail
☐ Regular first class mail
☐ Hand delivered

Acknowledgment of hand delivery and receipt hereof:

_____   _____

(signature of landlord)   (date)

Consult Chapter Six, Section C(2) for the proper use of this form.

**TEN-DAY NOTICE OF TERMINATION OF RENTAL AGREEMENT
FOR NONCOMPLIANCE WITH RENTAL AGREEMENT
MATERIALLY AFFECTING HEALTH AND SAFETY**

Larry Landlord
101 North Slum Lord Avenue   Date: September 1, 1994
Phoenix, Arizona 85999

Notice to Landlord:

You are in violation of your Rental Agreement and the Arizona Residential Landlord and Tenant Act, Article 3, Section 33-1324 (Landlord Obligations, Landlord to maintain fit premises). The specific acts constituting the violation are:

1 - Failure to repair sliding glass door, broken by Landlord's maintenance man.
2 - Failure to have refuse removed from premises.
3 - Failure to repair unsafe wiring in kitchen.

You are hereby notified, pursuant to A.R.S. § 33-1361(A), that this noncompliance materially affects health and safety and that the Rental Agreement will terminate upon a date not less than ten (10) days after receipt of this notice if this noncompliance is not remedied within FIVE (5) DAYS.

The Rental Agreement will terminate on: September 11, 1994
If the noncompliance is not remedied by: September 6, 1994

Terry Tenant

This notice delivered this date Sept. 1, '94 via:
□ Certified mail
□ Regular first class mail
☒ Hand delivered

Acknowledgment of hand delivery and receipt hereof:
Larry Landlord   *September 1, 1994*
(signature of landlord)   (date)

TEN-DAY NOTICE OF TERMINATION OF RENTAL AGREEMENT
FOR NONCOMPLIANCE WITH RENTAL AGREEMENT
MATERIALLY AFFECTING HEALTH AND SAFETY

_____

_____   Date: _____

_____, _____ _____

Notice to Landlord,

You are in violation of the Rental Agreement and the Arizona Residential Landlord and Tenant Act, Article 2, Section 33-1324 (Landlord Obligations, Landlord to maintain fit premises). The specific acts constituting the violation are:

_____

_____

_____

_____

You are hereby notified, pursuant to A.R.S. § 33-1361(A), that this noncompliance materially affects health and safety and that the Rental Agreement will terminate upon a date not less than ten (10) days after receipt of this notice if this noncompliance is not remedied within FIVE (5) DAYS.

The Rental Agreement will terminate on: _____
If the noncompliance is not remedied by: _____

_____
(signature of tenant)

This notice delivered this date _____ via:

☐ Certified mail
☐ Regular first class mail
☐ Hand delivered

Acknowledgment of hand delivery and receipt hereof:

_____ _____
(signature of landlord)   (date)

Consult Chapter Six, Section C(1) for the proper use of this form.

FOURTEEN-DAY NOTICE OF
TERMINATION OF RENTAL AGREEMENT
FOR MATERIAL NONCOMPLIANCE WITH RENTAL AGREEMENT

Larry Landlord
101 North Slum Lord Avenue   Date: September 1, 1994
Phoenix, Arizona 85999

Notice to Landlord:

      You are in violation of the Rental Agreement and the Arizona Residential Landlord and Tenant Act, Article 2, Section 33-1324 (Landlord Obligations, Landlord to maintain fit premises). The specific acts constituting the violation are:

      1 - Failure to repair toilet in hall bathroom; toilet leaks, requiring it to be shut-off at the wall valve, to prevent flooding of the rental unit.
      2 - Failure to repair/replace defective dead-bolt lock on rear exterior door.

      You are hereby notified, pursuant to A.R.S. § 33-1361(A), that the above constitutes a material noncompliance and that the Rental Agreement will terminate upon a date not less than fourteen (14) days after receipt of this notice if this noncompliance is not remedied WITHIN TEN (10) DAYS.

The Rental Agreement will terminate on: September 15, 1994
If the noncompliance is not remedied by: September 11, 1994

Terry Tenant

This notice delivered this date Sept. 1, '94 via:
☐ Certified mail
☐ Regular first class mail
☒ Hand delivered

      Acknowledgment of hand delivery and receipt hereof:

Larry Landlord   *September 1, 1994*
(signature of tenant)   (date)

FOURTEEN-DAY NOTICE OF
TERMINATION OF RENTAL AGREEMENT
FOR MATERIAL NONCOMPLIANCE WITH RENTAL AGREEMENT

_____

_____   Date: _____

_____, _____ _____

Notice to Landlord,

      You are in violation of the Rental Agreement and the Arizona Residential Landlord and Tenant Act, Article 2, Section 33-1324 (Landlord Obligations, Landlord to maintain fit premises). The specific acts constituting the violation are:

_____

_____

_____

      You are hereby notified, pursuant to A.R.S. § 33-1361(A), that the above constitutes a <u>material noncompliance</u> and that the Rental Agreement will terminate upon a date not less than fourteen (14) days after receipt of this notice if this noncompliance is not remedied WITHIN TEN (10) DAYS.

The Rental Agreement will terminate on: _____
If the noncompliance is not remedied by: _____

_____
(signature of tenant)

This notice delivered this date _____ via:

☐ Certified mail
☐ Regular first class mail
☐ Hand delivered

Acknowledgment of hand delivery and receipt hereof:

_____   _____
(signature of landlord)   (date)

Consult Chapter Six, Section C(4) for the proper use of this form.

NOTICE OF TERMINATION OR RENT REDUCTION
BECAUSE OF FIRE OR CASUALTY DAMAGE

Larry Landlord
101 North Slum Lord Avenue   Date: September 1, 1994
Phoenix, Arizona 85999

Notice to Landlord:

You are hereby notified, pursuant to A.R.S. § 33-1366, that the leased premises have been damaged or destroyed by fire or casualty to an extent that enjoyment of the dwelling unit is substantially impaired.

☒   As a consequence thereof, I have vacated the premises on   August 20, 1994   and, pursuant to A.R.S. § 33-1366(A)(1), the rental agreement has terminated on that date.

☐   As a consequence thereof, I have vacated the portion of the leased premises rendered unusable by the fire or casualty and have reduced my rent in proportion to the diminution in the fair rental value of the premises.   Current rent is $_____; because of the damage, fair rental value has been reduced by ____%; therefore, rent shall be reduced to $_____ until the premises are repaired.

                                                     Terry Tenant

This notice delivered this date Sept. 1, '94 via:
☐ Certified mail
☐ Regular first class mail
☒ Hand delivered

                    Acknowledgment of hand delivery and receipt hereof:
_____ *Larry Landlord* _____   _____ *September 1, 1994* _____
        (signature of tenant)   (date)

NOTICE OF TERMINATION OR RENT REDUCTION
BECAUSE OF DAMAGE DUE TO FIRE OR CASUALTY

_____

_____   Date: _____

_____, _____ _____

Notice to Landlord:

      You are hereby notified, pursuant to A.R.S. § 33-1366, that the leased premises have been damaged or destroyed by fire or casualty to an extent that enjoyment of the dwelling unit is substantially impaired.

☐   As a consequence thereof, I have vacated the premises on _____ and, pursuant to A.R.S. § 33-1366(A)(1), the rental agreement has terminated on that date.

☐   As a consequence thereof, I have vacated the portion of the leased premises rendered unusable by the fire or casualty and have reduced my rent in proportion to the diminution in the fair rental value of the premises. My (our) current rent is $_____. As a result of the damage or casualty, fair rental value has been reduced by _____%. Therefore, rent shall be reduced to $_____ until the premises are repaired. This does not effect a waiver of my (our) right to terminate the rental agreement and vacate the premises if the repairs are not timely commenced and completed.

      _____
                  (signature of tenant)

This notice delivered this date _____ via:

☐ Certified mail
☐ Regular first class mail
☐ Hand delivered

      Acknowledgment of hand delivery and receipt hereof:

      _____   _____
          (signature of landlord)   (date)

Consult Chapter Six, Section C(1) for the proper use of this form.

NOTICE OF TENANT'S INTENT TO EFFECT REPAIRS

Larry Landlord
101 North Slum Lord Avenue　　　　　　　　　Date: _September 1, 1994_
Phoenix, Arizona 85999

Notice to Landlord:

You are in violation of the Rental Agreement and the Arizona Residential Landlord and Tenant Act, Article 3, Section 33-1324 (Landlord Obligations, Landlord to maintain fit premises). The specific acts constituting the violation are:

1 - Failure to repair toilet in hall bathroom; toilet leaks, requiring it to be
shut-off at the wall valve, to prevent flooding of the rental unit.
2 - Failure to repair/replace defective dead-bolt lock on rear exterior door.

You are hereby notified, pursuant to A.R.S. § 33-1363(A), if above defect(s) is not remedied by the landlord within:

☒ Ten (10) days,
☐ _____ days, because of the emergency nature of the defect,

that tenant shall cause the same to be repaired by a licensed contractor and deduct the cost thereof from next month's rent, not to exceed the greater of $150.00 or one-half month's rent. Tenant will provide landlord with a lien release from the contractor. Tenant asserts that the defect(s) was not caused by Tenant, a member of Tenant's family or Tenant's guests.

Landlord has until September 11, 1994 to take corrective action.

Terry Tenant

This notice delivered this date Sept. 1, '94 via:
☐ Certified mail
☐ Regular first class mail
☒ Hand delivered

Acknowledgment of hand delivery and receipt hereof:
Larry Landlord　　　　　_September 1, 1994_
(signature of landlord)　　　　　(date)

NOTICE OF TENANT'S INTENT TO EFFECT REPAIRS

_____

_____   Date: _____

_____ , _____ _____

Notice to Landlord:

      You are in violation of the Rental Agreement and the Arizona Residential Landlord and Tenant Act, Article 2, Section 33-1324 (Landlord Obligations, Landlord to maintain fit premises). The specific acts constituting the violation are:

_____

_____

_____

      You are hereby notified, pursuant to A.R.S. § 33-1363(A), that if the above defect(s) is (are) not remedied by the landlord within:

        □ Ten (10) days,

        □ _____ days, because of the emergency nature of the defect,

then the tenant shall cause the same to be repaired by a licensed contractor and deduct the cost thereof from next month's rent, not to exceed the greater of $150.00 or one-half month's rent. Tenant will provide landlord with a lien release from the contractor. Tenant asserts that the defect(s) was not caused by Tenant, a member of Tenant's family or Tenant's guests.

      Landlord has until _____ to take corrective action.

This notice delivered this date _____ via:

□ Certified mail

□ Regular first class mail

□ Hand delivered

_____
(signature of tenant)

Acknowledgment of hand delivery and receipt hereof:

_____   _____
(signature of landlord)   (date)

Consult Chapter Six, Section C(3) for the proper use of this form.

NOTICE OF WRONGFUL FAILURE TO PROVIDE ESSENTIAL SERVICES

Larry Landlord
101 North Slum Lord Avenue   Date: August 1, 1994
Phoenix, Arizona 85999

Notice to Landlord:

You are in violation of your Rental Agreement and the Arizona Residential Landlord and Tenant Act, Article 4, Section 33-1364 (Wrongful failure to supply heat, air conditioning, cooling, water, hot water or essential services). The specific acts constituting the violation are:

1 - Failure to supply air condition (unit ceased to function on September 1, 1994).
2 - Failure to supply water (water company employee stated you failed to pay water bill).
3 - Failure to supply essential services (garbage collection has been cancelled).

You are hereby notified, pursuant to A.R.S. § 33-1364, that if these matters are not remedied by August 2, 1994, Tenant will take the following action:

□ Tenant shall procure reasonable amounts of water, hot water, heat and essential services during the
period
of landlord's noncompliance and deduct their actual reasonable cost from the rent.

□ Tenant shall seek to recover damages based on the diminution in the fair rental value of the premises.

☒ Tenant shall procure reasonable substitute housing during the period of landlord's noncompliance and
shall
seek to recover the excess cost of the substitute housing, not to exceed the statutory amount. Tenant shall not pay rent during the period of noncompliance.

Terry Tenant

This notice delivered this date Aug. 1, '94 via:
□ Certified mail
□ Regular first class mail
☒ Hand delivered

Acknowledgment of hand delivery and receipt hereof:
_____*Larry Landlord*_____   _____*August 1, 1994*_____
(signature of landlord)   (date)

NOTICE of Wrongful Failure to Provide Essential Services

_____

_____   Date: _____

_____, _____ _____

Notice to Landlord:

You are in violation of your Rental Agreement and the Arizona Residential Landlord and Tenant Act, Article 4, Section 33-1364 (Wrongful failure to supply hear, air conditioning, cooling, water, hot water or essential services). The specific acts constituting the violation are:

1 - _____

2 - _____

You are hereby notified, pursuant to A.R.S. § 33-1364, that if these matters are not remedied by _____, Tenant will take the following action:

☐   Tenant shall procure reasonable amounts of water, hot water, heat and essential services during the period of landlord's noncompliance and deduct their actual reasonable cost from the rent.

☐   Tenant shall seek to recover damages based on the diminution in the fair rental value of the premises.

☐   Tenant shall procure reasonable substitute housing during the period of landlord's noncompliance and shall seek to recover the excess cost of the substitute housing, not to exceed the statutory amount. Tenant shall not pay rent during the period of noncompliance.

This notice delivered this date _____ via:

    _____
    (signature of tenant)

☐ Certified mail
☐ Regular first class mail
☐ Hand delivered

Acknowledgment of hand delivery and receipt hereof:

_____ _____
(signature of landlord)   (date)

APPENDIX C

STATUTES

- ARIZONA RESIDENTIAL LANDLORD AND TENANT ACT

- LANDLORD AND TENANT STATUTES

- FORCIBLE ENTRY AND DETAINER STATUTES

ARIZONA RESIDENTIAL LANDLORD AND TENANT ACT
ARIZONA REVISED STATUTES, TITLE 33, CHAPTER 10
(effective September 30, 1992; unchanged in 1993)

ARTICLE 1. GENERAL PROVISIONS

Section
33-1301. Short title.
33-1302. Purposes.
33-1303. Supplementary principles of law applicable.
33-1304. Applicability of chapter.
33-1305. Administration of remedies; enforcement.
33-1306. Settlement of disputed claim or right.
33-1307. Territorial application.
33-1308. Exclusions from application of chapter.
33-1309. Jurisdiction and service of process.
33-1310. General definitions.
33-1311. Obligation of good faith.
33-1312. Unconscionability.
33-1313. Notice.
33-1314. Terms and conditions of rental agreement.
33-1315. Prohibited provisions in rental agreements.
33-1316. Separation of rents and obligations to maintain property forbidden.
33-1317. Discrimination by landlord or lessor against tenant with children prohibited; classification; exceptions; civil remedy; applicability.

ARTICLE 2. LANDLORD OBLIGATIONS

33-1321. Security deposits.
33-1322. Disclosure and tender of written rental agreement.
33-1323. Landlord to supply possession of dwelling unit.
33-1324. Landlord to maintain fit premises.
33-1325. Limitation of liability.
33-1329. Regulation of rents; authority.

ARTICLE 3. TENANT OBLIGATIONS

33-1341. Tenant to maintain dwelling unit.
33-1342. Rules and regulations.
33-1343. Access.
33-1344. Tenant to use and occupy as a dwelling unit.

ARTICLE 4. REMEDIES

33-1361. Noncompliance by the landlord.
33-1362. Failure to deliver possession.
33-1363. Self-help for minor defects.
33-1364. Wrongful failure to supply heat, air conditioning, cooling, water, hot water or essential services.
33-1365. Landlord's noncompliance as defense to action for possession or rent.
33-1366. Fire or casualty damage.
33-1367. Tenant's remedies for landlord's unlawful ouster, exclusion or diminution of services.
33-1368. Noncompliance with rental agreement by tenant; failure to pay rent; utility discontinuation.
33-1369. Failure to maintain.
33-1370. Abandonment; notice; remedies; personal property; definition.
33-1371. Waiver of landlord's right to terminate.
33-1372. Landlord liens; distraint for rent.
33-1373. Remedy after termination.
33-1374. Recovery of possession limited.
33-1375. Periodic tenancy; hold-over remedies.
33-1376. Landlord and tenant remedies for abuse of access.
33-1377. Special detainer actions; service; trial postponement.

ARTICLE 5. RETALIATORY ACTION

33-1381. Retaliatory conduct prohibited.

ARTICLE 1. GENERAL PROVISIONS

§ 33-1301. Short title

This chapter shall be known and may be cited as the Arizona Residential Landlord and Tenant Act.

§ 33-1302. Purposes

Underlying purposes and policies of this chapter are:

1. To simplify, clarify, modernize and revise the law governing the rental of dwelling units and the rights and obligations of landlord and tenant.

2. To encourage landlord and tenant to maintain and improve the quality of housing.

§ 33-1303. Supplementary principles of law applicable

Unless displaced by the provisions of this chapter, the principles of law and equity, including the law relating to capacity to contract, mutuality of obligations, principal and agent, real property, public health, safety and fire prevention, estoppel, fraud, misrepresentation, duress, coercion, mistake, bankruptcy or other validating or invalidating cause supplement its provisions.

§ 33-1304. Applicability of chapter

This chapter shall apply to the rental of dwelling units. Any conflict between the provisions of chapter 3 and chapter 7 of this title with the provisions of this chapter shall be governed by the provisions of this chapter.

§ 33-1305. Administration of remedies; enforcement

A. The remedies provided by this chapter shall be so administered that the aggrieved party may recover appropriate damages. The aggrieved party has a duty to mitigate damages.

B. Any right or obligation declared by this chapter is enforceable by action unless the provision declaring it specifies a different and limited effect.

§ 33-1306. Settlement of disputed claim or right

A claim or right arising under this chapter or on a rental agreement, if disputed in good faith, may be settled by agreement.

§ 33-1307. Territorial application

This chapter applies to, regulates, and determines rights, obligations and remedies under a rental agreement, wherever made, for a dwelling unit located within this state.

§ 33-1308. Exclusions from application of chapter

Unless created to avoid the application of this chapter, the following arrangements are not covered by this chapter:

1. Residence at an institution, public or private, if incidental to detention or the provision of medical, educational, counseling or religious services.

2. Occupancy under a contract of sale of a dwelling unit or the property of which it is a part, if the occupant is the purchaser or a person who succeeds to his interest.

3. Occupancy by a member of a fraternal or social organization in the portion of a structure operated for the benefit of the organization.

4. Transient occupancy in a hotel, motel or recreational lodging.

5. Occupancy by an employee of a landlord as a manager or custodian whose right to occupancy is conditional upon employment in and about the premises.

6. Occupancy by an owner of a condominium unit or a holder of a proprietary lease in a cooperative.

7. Occupancy in or operation of public housing as authorized, provided, or conducted under or pursuant to title 36, chapter 12,[1] or under or pursuant to any federal law or regulation.

[1] Section 36-1001 *et seq.*

§ 33-1309. Jurisdiction and service of process

A. The appropriate court of this state may exercise jurisdiction over any landlord with respect to any conduct in this state governed by this chapter or with respect to any claim arising from a transaction subject to this chapter. In addition to any other method provided by rule or by statute, personal jurisdiction over a landlord may be acquired in a civil action or proceeding instituted in the appropriate court by the service of process in the manner provided by this section.

B. If a landlord is not a resident of this state or is a corporation not authorized to do business in this state and engages in any conduct in this state governed by this chapter, or engages in a transaction subject to this chapter, he may designate an agent upon whom service of process may be made in this state. The agent shall be a resident of this state or a corporation authorized to do business in this state. The designation shall be in writing and filed with the secretary of state. If no designation is made and filed or if process cannot be served in this state upon the designated agent, process may be served upon the secretary of state, but the plaintiff or petitioner shall forthwith mail a copy of the process and pleading by registered or certified mail to the defendant or respondent at his last reasonably ascertained address. In the event there is no last reasonably ascertainable address and if the defendant or respondent has not complied with § 33-1322, subsections A and B, then service upon the secretary of state shall be sufficient service of process without the mailing of copies to the defendant or respondent. Service of process shall be deemed complete and the time shall begin to run for the purposes of this section at the time of service upon the secretary of state. The defendant shall appear and answer within thirty days after completion thereof in the manner and under the same penalty as if he had been personally served with the summons. An affidavit of compliance with this section shall be filed with the clerk of the court on or before the return day of the process, if any, or within any further time the court allows. Where applicable, the affidavit shall contain a statement that defendant or respondent has not complied with § 33-1322, subsections A and B.

§ 33-1310. General definitions

Subject to additional definitions contained in subsequent articles of this chapter which apply to specific articles thereof, and unless the context otherwise requires, in this chapter:

1. "Action" includes recoupment, counterclaim, setoff, suit in equity and any other proceeding in which rights are determined, including an action for possession.

2. "Building and housing codes" include any law, ordinance or governmental regulation concerning fitness for habitation, or the construction, maintenance, operation, occupancy, use or appearance of any premises, or dwelling unit.

3. "Dwelling unit" means a structure or the part of a structure that is used as a home, residence, or sleeping place by one person who maintains a household or by two or more persons who maintain a common household. "Dwelling unit" excludes real property used to accommodate a mobile home, unless the mobile home is rented or leased by the landlord.

4. "Good faith" means honesty in fact in the conduct or transaction concerned.

5. "Landlord" means the owner, lessor or sublessor of the dwelling unit or the building of which it is a part, and it also means a manager of the premises who fails to disclose as required by § 33-1322.

6. "Organization" includes a corporation, government, governmental subdivision or agency, business trust, estate, trust, partnership or association, two or more persons having a joint or common interest and any other legal or commercial entity which is a landlord, owner, manager or constructive agent pursuant to § 33-1322.

7. "Owner" means one or more persons, jointly or severally, in whom is vested all or part of the legal title to property or all or part of the beneficial ownership and a right to present use and enjoyment of the premises. The term includes a mortgagee in possession.

8. "Person" means an individual or organization.

9. "Premises" means a dwelling unit and the structure of which it is a part and existing facilities and appurtenances therein, including furniture and utilities where applicable, and grounds, areas and existing facilities held out for the use of tenants generally or whose use is promised to the tenant.

10. "Rent" means payments to be made to the landlord in full consideration for the rented premises.

11. "Rental agreement" means all agreements, written, oral or implied by law, and valid rules and regulations adopted under § 33-1342 embodying the terms and conditions concerning the use and occupancy of a dwelling unit and premises.

12. "Roomer" means a person occupying a dwelling unit that lacks a major bathroom or kitchen facility, in a structure where one or more major facilities are used in common by occupants of the dwelling unit and other dwelling units. Major facility in the case of a bathroom means toilet, or either a bath or

shower, and in the case of a kitchen means refrigerator, stove or sink.

13. "Security" means money or property given to assure payment or performance under a rental agreement. "Security" does not include a reasonable charge for redecorating or cleaning.

14. "Single family residence" means a structure maintained and used as a single dwelling unit. Notwithstanding that a dwelling unit shares one or more walls with another dwelling unit, it is a single family residence if it has direct access to a street or thoroughfare and shares neither heating facilities, hot water equipment nor any other essential facility or service with any other dwelling unit.

15. "Tenant" means a person entitled under a rental agreement to occupy a dwelling unit to the exclusion of others.

§ 33-1311. Obligation of good faith

Every duty under this chapter and every act which must be performed as a condition precedent to the exercise of a right or remedy under this chapter imposes an obligation of good faith in its performance or enforcement.

§ 33-1312. Unconscionability

A. If the court, as a matter of law, finds either of the following:

1. A rental agreement or any provision thereof was unconscionable when made, the court may refuse to enforce the agreement, enforce the remainder of the agreement without the unconscionable provision, or limit the application of any unconscionable provision to avoid an unconscionable result.

2. A settlement in which a party waives or agrees to forego a claim or right under this chapter or under a rental agreement was unconscionable at the time it was made, the court may refuse to enforce the settlement, enforce the remainder of the settlement without the unconscionable provision, or limit the application of any unconscionable provision to avoid any unconscionable result.

B. If unconscionability is put into issue by a party or by the court upon its own motion the parties shall be afforded a reasonable opportunity to present evidence as to the setting, purpose and effect of the rental agreement or settlement to aid the court in making the determination.

§ 33-1313. Notice

A. A person has notice of a fact if he has actual knowledge of it, has received a notice or notification of it or from all the facts and circumstances known to him at the time in question he has reason to know that it exists. A person "knows" or "has knowledge" of a fact if he has actual knowledge of it.

B. A person "notifies" or "gives" a notice or notification to another by taking steps reasonably calculated to inform the other in ordinary course whether or not the other actually comes to know of it. A person "receives" a notice or notification when it comes to his attention, or in the case of the landlord, it is delivered in hand or mailed by registered or certified mail to the place of business of the landlord through which the rental agreement was made or at any place held out by him as the place for receipt of the communication or delivered to any individual who is designated as an agent by § 33-1322 or, in the case of the tenant, it is delivered in hand to the tenant or mailed by registered or certified mail to him at the place held out by him as the place for receipt of the communication or, in the absence of such designation, to his last known place of residence. If notice is mailed by registered or certified mail, the tenant or landlord is deemed to have received such notice on the date the notice is actually received by him or five days after the date the notice is mailed, whichever occurs first.

C. "Notice," knowledge or a notice or notification received by an organization is effective for a particular transaction from the time it is brought to the attention of the individual conducting the transaction and in any event from the time it would have been brought to his attention if the organization had exercised reasonable diligence.

§ 33-1314. Terms and conditions of rental agreement

A. The landlord and tenant may include in a rental agreement terms and conditions not prohibited by this chapter or other rule of law including rent, term of the agreement and other provisions governing the rights and obligations of the parties.

B. In absence of a rental agreement, the tenant shall pay as rent the fair rental value for the use and occupancy of the dwelling unit.

C. Rent shall be payable without demand or notice at the time and place agreed upon by the parties. Unless otherwise agreed, rent is payable at the dwelling unit and periodic rent is payable at the beginning of any term of one month or less and otherwise in equal monthly installments at the beginning of each month. Unless otherwise agreed, rent shall be uniformly apportionable from day-to-day.

D. Unless the rental agreement fixes a definite term, the tenancy shall be week-to-week in case of a roomer who pays weekly rent, and in all other cases month-to-month.

§ 33-1315. Prohibited provisions in rental agreements

A. A rental agreement shall not provide that the tenant does any of the following:

1. Agrees to waive or to forego rights or remedies under this chapter.

2. Agrees to pay the landlord's attorney's fees, except an agreement in writing may provide that attorney's fees may be awarded to the prevailing party in the event of court action and except that a prevailing party in a contested forcible detainer action is eligible to be awarded attorney fees pursuant to § 12-341.01 regardless of whether the rental agreement provides for such an award.

3. Agrees to the exculpation or limitation of any liability of the landlord arising under law or to indemnify the landlord for that liability or the costs connected therewith.

B. A provision prohibited by subsection A of this section included in a rental agreement is unenforceable. If a landlord deliberately uses a rental agreement containing provisions known by him to be prohibited, the tenant may recover actual damages sustained by him and not more than two months' periodic rent.

§ 33-1316. Separation of rents and obligations to maintain property forbidden

A rental agreement, assignment, conveyance, trust deed or security instrument may not permit the receipt of rent free of the obligation to comply with § 33-1324, subsection A.

§ 33-1317. Discrimination by landlord or lessor against tenant with children prohibited; classification; exceptions; civil remedy; applicability

A. A person who knowingly refuses to rent to any other person a place to be used for a dwelling for the reason that the other person has a child or children, or who advertises in connection with the rental a restriction against children, either by the display of a sign, placard, written or printed notice, or by publication thereof in a newspaper of general circulation, is guilty of a petty offense.

B. No person shall rent or lease his property to another in violation of a valid restrictive covenant against the sale of such property to persons who have a child or children living with them.

C. No person shall rent or lease his property to persons who have a child or children living with them when his property meets the definition of housing for older persons as defined in section 41-1491.04.

D. A person who knowingly rents or leases his property in violation of the provisions of subsection B or C is guilty of a petty offense.

E. A person whose rights under this section have been violated may bring a civil action against a person who violates this section for all of the following:

1. Injunctive or declaratory relief to correct the violation.

2. Actual damages sustained by the tenant or prospective tenant.

3. A civil penalty of three times the monthly rent of the housing accommodation involved in the violation if the violation is determined to be intentional.

4. Court costs and reasonable attorney fees.

F. Nothing in this section shall prohibit a person from refusing to rent a dwelling by reason of reasonable occupancy standards which apply to persons of all ages, which are based upon size of dwelling unit or laws relating to health and safety and which reasonable occupancy standards have been promulgated and published prior to the event in issue.

G. Subsection B of this section applies only to dwellings occupied or intended to be occupied by no more than four families living independently of each other and in which the owner maintains and occupies one of the living quarters as the owner's residence.

ARTICLE 2. LANDLORD OBLIGATIONS

§ 33-1321. Security deposits

A. A landlord shall not demand or receive security, however denominated, including, but not limited to, prepaid rent in an amount or value in excess of one and one-half month's rent. This subsection does not prohibit a tenant from voluntarily paying more than one and one-half month's rent in advance.

B. Cleaning and redecorating deposits, if nonrefundable, must be so stated in writing by the landlord.

C. Upon termination of the tenancy, property or money held by the landlord as prepaid rent and security may be applied to the payment of accrued rent and the amount of damages which the landlord has suffered by reason of the tenant's noncompliance with § 33-1341 all as itemized by the landlord in a written notice delivered to the tenant together with the amount due within fourteen days after termination of the tenancy and delivery of possession and demand by the tenant.

D. If the landlord fails to comply with subsections B and C of this section the tenant may recover the property and money due him together with damages in an amount equal to twice the amount wrongfully withheld.

E. This section does not preclude the landlord or tenant from recovering other damages to which he may be entitled under this chapter.

F. The holder of the landlord's interest in the premises at the time of the termination of the tenancy is bound by this section.

§ 33-1322. Disclosure and tender of written rental agreement

A. The landlord or any person authorized to enter into a rental agreement on his behalf shall disclose to the tenant in writing at or before the commencement of the tenancy the name and address of each of the following:

1. The person authorized to manage the premises.

2. An owner of the premises or a person authorized to act for and on behalf of the owner for the purpose of service of process and for the purpose of receiving and receipting for notices and demands.

B. The information required to be furnished by this section shall be kept current and refurnished to tenant upon tenant's request. This section extends to and is enforceable against any successor landlord, owner or manager.

C. A person who fails to comply with subsections A and B becomes an agent of each person who is a landlord for the following purposes:

1. Service of process and receiving and receipting for notices and demands.

2. Performing the obligations of the landlord under this chapter and under the rental agreement and expending or making available for the purpose all rent collected from the premises.

D. If there is a written rental agreement, the landlord must tender and deliver a signed copy of the rental agreement to the tenant and the tenant must sign and deliver to the landlord one fully executed copy of such rental agreement within a reasonable time after the agreement is executed. A written rental agreement shall have all blank spaces completed. Noncompliance with this subsection shall be deemed a material noncompliance by the landlord or the tenant, as the case may be, of the rental agreement.

§ 33-1323. Landlord to supply possession of dwelling unit

At the commencement of the term the landlord shall deliver possession of the premises to the tenant in compliance with the rental agreement and § 33-1324. The landlord may bring an action for possession against any person wrongfully in possession and may recover the damages provided in § 33-1375, subsection C.

§ 33-1324. Landlord to maintain fit premises

A. The landlord shall:

1. Comply with the requirements of applicable building codes materially affecting health and safety.

2. Make all repairs and do whatever is necessary to put and keep the premises in a fit and habitable condition.

3. Keep all common areas of the premises in a clean and safe condition.

4. Maintain in good and safe working order and condition all electrical, plumbing, sanitary, heating, ventilating, air-conditioning and other facilities and appliances, including elevators, supplied or required to be supplied by him.

5. Provide and maintain appropriate receptacles and conveniences for the removal of ashes, garbage, rubbish and other waste incidental to the occupancy of the dwelling unit and arrange for their removal.

6. Supply running water and reasonable amounts of hot water at all times, reasonable heat and reasonable air-conditioning or cooling where such units are installed and offered, when required by seasonal weather conditions, except where the building that includes the dwelling unit is not required by law to be equipped for that purpose or the dwelling unit is so constructed that heat, air--conditioning, cooling or hot water is generated by an installation within the exclusive control of the tenant and supplied by a direct public utility connection.

B. If the duty imposed by subsection A, paragraph 1 is greater than any duty imposed by any other paragraph of this section, the landlord's duty shall be determined by reference to such paragraph.

C. The landlord and tenant of a single family residence may agree in writing, supported by adequate consideration, that the tenant perform the landlord's duties specified in subsection A, paragraphs 5 and 6, and also specified repairs, maintenance tasks, alterations and remodeling, but only if the transaction is entered into in good faith, not for the purpose of evading the obligations of the landlord and the work is not necessary to cure noncompliance with subsection A, paragraphs 1 and 2.

D. The landlord and tenant of any dwelling unit other than a single family residence may agree that the tenant is to perform specified repairs, maintenance tasks, alterations or remodeling only if:

1. The agreement of the parties is entered into in good faith and not for the purpose of evading the obligations of the landlord and is set forth in a separate writing signed by the parties and supported by adequate consideration.

2. The work is not necessary to cure non-compliance with subsection A, paragraphs 1 and 2.

3. The agreement does not diminish or affect the obligation of the landlord to other tenants in the premises.

E. If the landlord purchases utility services from a public service corporation for distribution through a system owned or operated by the landlord and imposes separately stated utility or similar charges on the tenants, the aggregate amount of the separately stated charges shall not exceed the actual cost paid by the landlord to the public service corporation for the utility services. The tenant is not required to pay any other separately stated charges for provision of the utility services.

§ 33-1325. Limitation of liability

A. Unless otherwise agreed, a landlord, who conveys premises that include a dwelling unit subject to a rental agreement in a good faith sale to a bona fide purchaser, is relieved of liability under the rental agreement and this chapter as to events occurring subsequent to written notice to the tenant of the conveyance. He remains liable to the tenant for any property and money to which the tenant is entitled under § 33-1321.

B. Unless otherwise agreed, a manager of premises that include a dwelling unit is relieved of liability under the rental agreement and this chapter as to events occurring after written notice to the tenant of the termination of his management.

§ 33-1329. Regulation of rents; authority

A. Notwithstanding any other provisions of law to the contrary the state legislature determines that the imposition of rent control on private residential housing units by cities, including charter cities, and towns is of statewide concern. Therefore, the power to control rents on private residential property is preempted by the state. Cities, including charter cities, or towns shall not have the power to control rents.

B. The provisions of subsection A shall not apply to residential property which is owned, financed, insured or subsidized by any state agency, or by any city, including charter city, or town.

ARTICLE 3. TENANT OBLIGATIONS

§ 33-1341. Tenant to maintain dwelling unit
The tenant shall:

1. Comply with all obligations primarily imposed upon tenants by applicable provisions of building codes materially affecting health and safety.

2. Keep that part of the premises that he occupies and uses as clean and safe as the condition of the premises permit.

3. Dispose from his dwelling unit all ashes, rubbish, garbage and other waste in a clean and safe manner.

4. Keep all plumbing fixtures in the dwelling unit or used by the tenant as clean as their condition permits.

5. Use in a reasonable manner all electrical, plumbing, sanitary, heating, ventilating, air-conditioning and other facilities and appliances including elevators in the premises.

6. Not deliberately or negligently destroy, deface, damage, impair or remove any part of the premises or knowingly permit any person to do so.

7. Conduct himself and require other persons on the premises with his consent to conduct themselves in a manner that will not disturb his neighbors' peaceful enjoyment of the premises.

§ 33-1342. Rules and regulations

A. A landlord, from time to time, may adopt rules or regulations, however described, concerning the tenant's use and occupancy of the premises. Such rules or regulations are enforceable against the tenant only if:

1. Their purpose is to promote the convenience, safety or welfare of the tenants in the premises, preserve the landlord's property from abusive use or make a fair distribution of services and facilities held out for the tenants generally.

2. They are reasonably related to the purpose for which adopted.

3. They apply to all tenants in the premises in a fair manner.

4. They are sufficiently explicit in prohibition, direction or limitation of the tenant's conduct to fairly inform him of what he must or must not do to comply.

5. They are not for the purpose of evading the obligations of the landlord.

6. The tenant has notice of them at the time he enters into the rental agreement.

B. A rule or regulation adopted after the tenant enters into the rental agreement is enforceable against the tenant if reasonable notice of its adoption is given to the tenant and it does not work a substantial modification of his rental agreement.

§ 33-1343. Access

A. The tenant shall not unreasonably withhold consent to the landlord to enter into the dwelling unit in order to inspect the premises, make necessary or agreed repairs, decorations, alterations or improvements, supply necessary or agreed services or exhibit the dwelling unit to prospective or actual purchasers, mortgagees, tenants, workmen or contractors.

B. The landlord may enter the dwelling unit without consent of the tenant in case of emergency.

C. The landlord shall not abuse the right to access or use it to harass the tenant. Except in case of emergency or if it is impracticable to do so, the landlord shall give the tenant at least two days' notice of his intent to enter and enter only at reasonable times.

D. The landlord has no other right of access except by court order and as permitted by §§ 33-1369 and 33-1370, or if the tenant has abandoned or surrendered the premises.

§ 33-1344. Tenant to use and occupy as a dwelling unit

Unless otherwise agreed, the tenant shall occupy his dwelling unit only as a dwelling unit.

ARTICLE 4. REMEDIES

§ 33-1361. Noncompliance by the landlord

A. Except as provided in this chapter, if there is a material noncompliance by the landlord with the rental agreement, the tenant may deliver a written notice to the landlord specifying the acts and omissions constituting the breach and that the rental agreement will terminate upon a date not less than fourteen days after receipt of the notice if the breach is not remedied in ten days. If there is a noncompliance by the landlord with § 33-1324 materially affecting health and safety, the tenant may deliver a written notice to the landlord specifying the acts and omissions constituting the breach and that the rental agreement will terminate upon a date not less than ten days after receipt of the notice if the breach is not remedied in five days. The rental agreement shall terminate and the dwelling unit shall be vacated as provided in the notice subject to the following:

1. If the breach is remediable by repairs or the payment of damages or otherwise and the

landlord adequately remedies the breach prior to the date specified in the notice, the rental agreement will not terminate.

2. The tenant may not terminate for a condition caused by the deliberate or negligent act or omission of the tenant, a member of his family or other person on the premises with his consent.

B. Except as provided in this chapter, the tenant may recover damages and obtain injunctive relief for any noncompliance by the landlord with the rental agreement or § 33-1324.

C. The remedy provided in subsection B of this section is in addition to any right of the tenant arising under subsection A of this section.

D. If the rental agreement is terminated, the landlord shall return all security recoverable by the tenant under § 33-1321.

§ 33-1362. Failure to deliver possession

A. If the landlord fails to deliver physical possession of the dwelling unit to the tenant as provided in § 33-1323, rent abates until possession is delivered and the tenant may do either of the following:

1. Upon at least five days' written notice to the landlord terminate the rental agreement and upon termination the landlord shall return all prepaid rent and security.

2. Demand performance of the rental agreement by the landlord and, if the tenant elects, maintain an action for possession of the dwelling unit against the landlord or any person wrongfully in possession and recover the damages sustained by him.

B. If the landlord fails to deliver constructive possession to the tenant because of noncompliance with § 33-1324, rent shall not abate. Tenant may proceed with the remedies provided for in § 33-1361.

C. If a person's failure to deliver possession is willful and not in good faith, an aggrieved person may recover from that person an amount not more than two months' periodic rent or twice the actual damages sustained by him, whichever is greater.

§ 33-1363. Self-help for minor defects

A. If the landlord fails to comply with § 33-1324, and the reasonable cost of compliance is less than one hundred fifty dollars, or an amount equal to one-half of the monthly rent, whichever amount is greater, the tenant may

recover damages for the breach under § 33-1361, subsection B, or may notify the landlord of his intention to correct the condition at the landlord's expense. After being notified by the tenant in writing, if the landlord fails to comply within ten days or as promptly thereafter as conditions require in case of emergency, the tenant may cause the work to be done by a licensed contractor and, after submitting to the landlord an itemized statement and a waiver of lien, deduct from his rent the actual and reasonable cost of the work, not exceeding the amount specified in this subsection.

B. A tenant may not repair at the landlord's expense if the condition was caused by the deliberate or negligent act or omission of the tenant, a member of his family or other person on the premises with his consent.

§ 33-1364. Wrongful failure to supply heat, air conditioning, cooling, water, hot water or essential services

A. If contrary to the rental agreement or § 33-1324 the landlord deliberately or negligently fails to supply running water, hot water or heat, air-conditioning or cooling, where such units are installed and offered, or essential services, the tenant may give reasonable notice to the landlord specifying the breach and may do one of the following:

1. Procure reasonable amounts of hot water, running water, heat and essential services during the period of the landlord's noncompliance and deduct their actual reasonable cost from the rent.

2. Recover damages based upon the diminution in the fair rental value of the dwelling unit.

3. Procure reasonable substitute housing during the period of the landlord's noncompliance, in which case the tenant is excused from paying rent for the period of the landlord's noncompliance. In the event the periodic cost of such substitute housing exceeds the amount of the periodic rent, upon delivery by tenant of proof of payment for such substitute housing, tenant may recover from landlord such excess costs up to an amount not to exceed twenty-five per cent of the periodic rent which has been excused pursuant to this paragraph.

B. In addition to the remedy provided in paragraph 3 of subsection A, in the event the landlord's noncompliance is deliberate, the tenant may recover the actual and reasonable cost or fair and reasonable value of the substitute housing not in excess of an amount equal to the periodic rent.

C. If the tenant proceeds under this section, he may not proceed under § 33-1361 or § 33-1363 as to that breach, except as to damages which occur prior to the tenant proceeding under subsection A or B of this section.

D. The rights under this section do not arise until the tenant has given notice to the landlord and such rights do not include the right to repair. Such rights do not arise if the condition was caused by the deliberate or negligent act or omission of the tenant, a member of his family or other person on the premises with his consent.

§ 33-1365. Landlord's noncompliance as defense to action for possession or rent

A. In an action for possession based upon nonpayment of the rent or in an action for rent where the tenant is in possession, the tenant may counterclaim for any amount which he may recover under the rental agreement or this chapter. In that event after notice and hearing the court from time to time may order the tenant to pay into court all or part of the undisputed rent accrued and all periodic rent thereafter accruing and shall determine the amount due to each party. The party to whom a net amount is owed shall be paid first from the money paid into court and the balance, if any, by the other party. However, if no rent remains due after application of this section, or if the tenant is adjudged to have acted in good faith and satisfies a judgment for rent entered for the landlord, judgment shall be entered for the tenant in the action for possession.

B. In an action for rent where the tenant is not in possession, the tenant may counterclaim as provided in subsection A but the tenant is not required to pay any rent into court.

§ 33-1366. Fire or casualty damage

A. If the dwelling unit or premises are damaged or destroyed by fire or casualty to an extent that enjoyment of the dwelling unit is substantially impaired, the tenant may do either of the following:

1. Immediately vacate the premises and notify the landlord in writing within fourteen days thereafter of his intention to terminate the rental agreement, in which case the rental agreement terminates as of the date of vacating.

2. If continued occupancy is lawful, vacate any part of the dwelling unit rendered unusable by the fire or casualty, in which case the tenant's liability for rent is reduced in proportion to the diminution in the fair rental value of the dwelling unit.

B. If the rental agreement is terminated the landlord shall return all security recoverable under § 33-1321. Accounting for rent in the event of termination or apportionment is to occur as of the date the tenant vacates all or part of the dwelling unit.

§ 33-1367. Tenant's remedies for landlord's unlawful ouster, exclusion or diminution of services

If the landlord unlawfully removes or excludes the tenant from the premises or wilfully diminishes services to the tenant by interrupting or causing the interruption of electric, gas, water or other essential service to the tenant, the tenant may recover possession or terminate the rental agreement and, in either case, recover an amount not more than two months' periodic rent or twice the actual damages sustained by him, whichever is greater. If the rental agreement is terminated the landlord shall return all security recoverable under § 33-1321.

§ 33-1368. Noncompliance with rental agreement by tenant; failure to pay rent; utility discontinuation

A. Except as provided in this chapter, if there is a material noncompliance by the tenant with the rental agreement, the landlord may deliver a written notice to the tenant specifying the acts and omissions constituting the breach and that the rental agreement will terminate upon a date not less than fourteen days after receipt of the notice if the breach is not remedied in ten days. If there is a noncompliance by the tenant with § 33-1341 materially affecting health and safety, the landlord may deliver a written notice to the tenant specifying the acts and omissions constituting the breach and that the rental agreement will terminate upon a date not less than ten days after receipt of the notice if the breach is not remedied in five days. However, if the breach is remediable by repair or the payment of damages or otherwise, and the tenant adequately remedies the breach prior to the date specified in the notice, the rental agreement will not terminate. If there is an additional act of these types of noncompliance of the same or similar nature within a period of six months from the previous remedy of noncompliance, the landlord may institute a special detainer action pursuant to § 33-1377 thirty days after delivery of a written notice advising the tenant that a second noncompliance of the same or similar nature has occurred. If there is a breach that is both material and irreparable, such as an illegal discharge of a weapon on the premises or infliction of serious bodily harm, threatening or intimidating as defined in § 13-1202 or assault as defined in § 13-1203 of the landlord, his agent or another tenant or involving imminent serious property damage, the landlord may deliver a written notice for immediate termination of the rental agreement and shall proceed under § 33-1377.

B. If rent is unpaid when due and the tenant fails to pay rent within seven days after written notice by the landlord of nonpayment and his intention to terminate the rental agreement if the rent is not paid within that period of time, the landlord may terminate the rental agreement by filing a special detainer action pursuant to § 33-1377. Prior to the filing of a special detainer action the rental agreement shall be reinstated if the tenant tenders all past due and unpaid periodic rent and a reasonable late fee set forth in a written rental agreement. After a special detainer action is filed the rental agreement is reinstated only if the tenant pays all past due rent, reasonable late fees set forth in a written rental agreement, attorney fees and court costs.

C. The landlord may recover all reasonable damages, resulting from noncompliance by the tenant with the rental agreement or § 33-1341 or occupancy of the dwelling unit, court costs, reasonable attorney fees and all quantifiable damage caused by the tenant to the premises.

D. The landlord may discontinue utility services provided by the landlord on the day following the day that a writ of restitution or execution is executed pursuant to § 12-1181. Disconnection shall be performed only by a person authorized by the utility whose service is being discontinued. Nothing in this section shall supersede standard tariff and operational procedures that apply to any public service corporation, municipal corporation or special districts providing utility services in this state.

E. The landlord shall hold the tenant's personal property for a period of sixty days beginning on the first day after a writ of restitution or writ of execution is executed as prescribed in § 12-1181. The landlord shall use reasonable care in moving and holding the tenant's property and may store the tenant's property in an unoccupied dwelling unit owned by the landlord or off the premises if an unoccupied dwelling unit is not available. The landlord shall prepare an inventory and promptly notify the tenant of the location and cost of storage of the personal property by sending a notice by certified mail, return receipt requested, addressed to the tenant's last known address and to any of the tenant's alternative addresses known to the landlord. To reclaim the personal property, the tenant shall pay the landlord only for the cost of removal and storage for the time the property is held by the landlord. If the landlord holds the property for the sixty day period and the tenant does not make a reasonable effort to recover it, the landlord, upon the expiration of sixty days as provided in this subsection, may administer the personal property as provided in § 33-1370, subsection E. The landlord shall hold personal property after a writ of restitution or writ of execution is executed for not more than sixty days after such an execution.

F. The reference to number of days in this section means calendar days.

§ 33-1369. Failure to maintain

If there is noncompliance by the tenant with § 33-1341 materially affecting health and safety that can be remedied by repair, replacement of a damaged item or cleaning and the tenant fails to comply as promptly as conditions require in case of emergency or within fourteen days after written notice by the landlord specifying the breach and requesting that the tenant remedy it within that period of time, the landlord may enter the dwelling unit and cause the work to be done in a workmanlike manner and submit an itemized bill for the actual and reasonable cost or the fair and reasonable value thereof as rent on the next date when periodic rent is due, or if the rental agreement has terminated, for immediate payment.

§ 33-1370. Abandonment; notice; remedies; personal property; definition

A. If a dwelling unit is abandoned after the time prescribed in subsection H of this section, the landlord shall send the tenant a notice of abandonment by certified mail, return receipt requested, addressed to the tenant's last known address and to any of the tenant's alternate addresses known to the landlord. The landlord shall also post a notice of abandonment on the door to the dwelling unit or any other conspicuous place on the property for five days.

B. Five days after notice of abandonment has been both posted and mailed, the landlord may retake the dwelling unit and rerent the dwelling unit at a fair rental value if no personal property remains in the dwelling unit. After the landlord retakes the dwelling unit, money held by the landlord as a security deposit is forfeited and shall be applied to the payment of any accrued rent and other reasonable costs incurred by the landlord by reason of the tenant's abandonment.

C. If the tenant abandons the dwelling unit, the landlord shall make reasonable efforts to rent it at a fair rental. If the landlord rents the dwelling unit for a term beginning prior to the expiration of the rental agreement, it is deemed to be terminated as of the date the new tenancy begins. If the landlord fails to use reasonable efforts to rent the dwelling unit at a fair rental or if the landlord accepts the abandonment as a surrender, the rental agreement is deemed to be terminated by the landlord as of the date the landlord has notice of the abandonment. If the tenancy is from month to month or week to week, the term of the rental agreement for this purpose shall be deemed to be a month or a week, as the case may be.

D. After the landlord has retaken possession of the dwelling unit, the landlord may remove all personal property left by the tenant in the dwelling unit. The landlord shall notify the tenant of the location of the personal property in the same manner prescribed in subsection A.

E. The landlord shall hold the tenant's personal property for a period of sixty days beginning on the first rental due date occurring after the landlord's declaration of abandonment. The landlord shall use reasonable care in holding the tenant's personal property. If the landlord holds the property for this sixty day period and the tenant makes no reasonable effort to recover it, the landlord may sell the property, retain the proceeds and apply them toward the tenant's outstanding rent. If provided by a written rental agreement, the landlord may destroy or otherwise dispose of some or all of the property if the landlord reasonably determines that the value of the property is so low that the cost of moving, storage and conducting a public sale exceeds the amount that would be realized from the sale.

F. For a period of twelve months after the sale the landlord shall:

  1. Keep adequate records of the outstanding and unpaid rent and the sale of the tenant's personal property.

  2. Hold any excess proceeds for the benefit of the tenant.

G. If the tenant notifies the landlord in writing on or before the date the landlord sells or otherwise disposes of the personal property that the tenant intends to remove the personal property from the dwelling unit or the place of safekeeping, the tenant has five days to reclaim the personal property. To reclaim the personal property the tenant must only pay the landlord for the cost of removal and storage for the period the tenant's personal property remained in the landlord's safekeeping.

H. In this section "abandonment" means the absence of the tenant from the dwelling unit, without notice to the landlord for at least seven days, if rent for the dwelling unit is outstanding and unpaid for ten days and there is no reasonable evidence other than the presence of the tenant's personal property that the tenant is occupying the residence.

§ 33-1371. Acceptance of partial payments.

Acceptance of rent, or any portion thereof, with knowledge of a default by tenant or acceptance of performance by the tenant that varied from the terms of the rental agreement or rules or regulations subsequently adopted by the landlord constitutes a waiver of his right to terminate the rental agreement for that breach, unless otherwise agreed after the breach has occurred. Nothing in this section shall prohibit a landlord from accepting a partial payment of rent, without waiving any right to proceed against a tenant, where the tenant agrees in a contemporaneous writing to the terms and conditions of the partial payment with regard to continuation of the tenancy.

§ 33-1372. Landlord liens; distraint for rent

A. A lien or security interest on behalf of the landlord in the tenant's household goods is not enforceable unless perfected before the effective date of this chapter.

B. Distraint for rent is abolished.

§ 33-1373. Remedy after termination

If the rental agreement is terminated, the landlord may have a claim for possession and for rent and a separate claim for actual damages for breach of the rental agreement.

§ 33-1374. Recovery of possession limited

A landlord may not recover or take possession of the dwelling unit by action or otherwise, including willful diminution of services to the tenant by interrupting or causing the interruption of electric, gas, water or other essential service to the tenant, except in case of abandonment, surrender or as permitted in this chapter.

§ 33-1375. Periodic tenancy; hold-over remedies

A. The landlord or the tenant may terminate a week-to-week tenancy by a written notice given to the other at least ten days prior to the termination date specified in the notice.

B. The landlord or the tenant may terminate a month-to-month tenancy by a written notice given to the other at least thirty days prior to the periodic rental date specified in the notice.

C. If the tenant remains in possession without the landlord's consent after expiration of the term of the rental agreement or its termination, the landlord may bring an action for possession and if the tenant's holdover is willful and not in good faith the landlord, in addition, may recover an amount equal to not more than two months' periodic rent or twice the actual damages sustained by him, whichever is greater. If the landlord consents to the tenant's continued occupancy, § 33-1314, subsection D, applies.

§ 33-1376. Landlord and tenant remedies for abuse of access

A. If the tenant refuses to allow lawful access, the landlord may obtain injunctive relief to compel access, or terminate the rental agreement. In either case, the landlord may recover actual damages.

B. If the landlord makes an unlawful entry or a lawful entry in an unreasonable manner or makes repeated demands for entry otherwise lawful but which have the effect of unreasonably harassing the tenant, the tenant may obtain injunctive relief to prevent the recurrence of the conduct or terminate the rental agreement. In either case, the tenant may recover actual damages not less than an amount equal to one month's rent.

§ 33-1377. Special detainer actions; service; trial postponement

A. Special detainer actions shall be instituted for remedies prescribed in § 33-1368. Except as provided in this section, the procedure and appeal rights prescribed in title 12, chapter 8, article 4[1] apply to special detainer actions.

[1] Section 12-1171 *et seq.*

B. The summons shall be issued on the day the complaint is filed and shall command the person against whom the complaint is made to appear and answer the complaint at the time and place named which shall be not more than six nor less than three days from the date of the summons. The tenant is deemed to have received the summons three days after the summons is mailed if personal service is attempted and within one day of issuance of the summons a copy of the summons is conspicuously posted on the main entrance of the tenant's residence and on the same day the summons is sent by certified mail, return receipt requested, to the tenant's last known address. The summons in a special detainer action shall be served at least two days before the return day and the return day made on the day assigned for trial.

C. For good cause shown supported by an affidavit, the trial may be postponed for not more than three days in a justice court or five days in the superior court.

D. In addition to determining the right to actual possession, the court may assess damages, attorney fees and costs as prescribed by law.

E. If a complaint is filed alleging a material and irreparable breach pursuant to § 33-1368, subsection A, the summons shall be issued as provided in subsection B of this section, except that the trial date and return date shall be set no later than the third day following the filing of the complaint. If after the hearing the court finds that the material and irreparable breach did occur, the court shall order restitution in favor of the plaintiff not less than twelve nor more than twenty-four hours later.

F. If the defendant is found guilty, the court shall give judgment for the plaintiff for restitution of the premises, for late charges stated in the rental agreement, for costs and, at the plaintiff's option, for all rent found to be due and unpaid at the date of judgment, and shall grant a writ of restitution.

G. If the defendant is found not guilty, judgment shall be given for the defendant against the plaintiff for costs, and if it appears that the plaintiff has acquired possession of the premises since commencement of the action, a writ of restitution shall issue in favor of the defendant.

ARTICLE 5. RETALIATORY ACTION

§ 33-1381. Retaliatory conduct prohibited
A. Except as provided in this section, a landlord may not retaliate by increasing rent or decreasing services or by bringing or threatening to bring an action for possession after any of the following:

1. The tenant has complained to a governmental agency charged with responsibility for enforcement of a building or housing code of a violation applicable to the premises materially affecting health and safety.

2. The tenant has complained to the landlord of a violation under § 33-1324.

3. The tenant has organized or become a member of a tenants' union or similar organization.

4. The tenant has complained to a governmental agency charged with the responsibility for enforcement of the wage-price stabilization act.

B. If the landlord acts in violation of subsection A of this section, the tenant is entitled to the remedies provided in § 33-1367 and has a defense in action against him for possession. In an action by or against the tenant, evidence of a complaint within six months prior to the alleged act of retaliation creates a presumption that the landlord's conduct was in retaliation. The presumption does not arise

if the tenant made the complaint after notice of termination of the rental agreement. "Presumption", in this subsection, means that the trier of fact must find the existence of the fact presumed unless and until evidence is introduced which would support a finding of its nonexistence.

C. Notwithstanding subsections A and B of this section, a landlord may bring an action for possession if either of the following occurs:

1. The violation of the applicable building or housing code was caused primarily by lack of reasonable care by the tenant or other person in his household or upon the premises with his consent.

2. The tenant is in default in rent.

The maintenance of the action does not release the landlord from liability under § 33-1361, subsection B.

LANDLORD AND TENANT
ARIZONA REVISED STATUTES, TITLE 33, CHAPTER 3

ARTICLE 1. OBLIGATIONS AND LIABILITIES OF LANDLORD

Section

33-301. Posting of lien law and rates by innkeepers.
33-302. Maintenance of fireproof safe by innkeeper for deposit of valuables by guests; limitations on liability of innkeeper for loss of property of guests.
33-303. Discrimination by landlord or lessor against tenant with children prohibited; penalty; exceptions.

ARTICLE 2. OBLIGATIONS AND LIABILITIES OF TENANT

Section

33-321. Maintenance of premises.
33-322. Damages to premises; classification.
33-323. Liability of person in possession of land for rent due thereon.
33-324. Denial of landlord's title by lessee in possession prohibited.

ARTICLE 3. TERMINATION OF TENANCIES

Section

33-341. Termination of tenancies.
33-342. Effect of lessee holding over.
33-343. Premises rendered untenantable without fault of lessee; nonliability of tenant for rent; right to quit premises.

ARTICLE 4. REMEDIES OF LANDLORD

Section

33-361. Violation of lease by tenant; right of landlord to re-enter; summary action for recovery of premises; appeal; lien for unpaid rent; enforcement.
33-362. Landlord's lien for rent.

ARTICLE 5. APPLICABILITY OF CHAPTER

Section

33-381. Limitation

ARTICLE 1. OBLIGATIONS AND LIABILITIES OF LANDLORD

§ 33-301. Posting of lien law and rates by innkeepers

Every keeper of a hotel, inn, boarding, lodging or apartment house, or auto camp, shall post in a conspicuous place in the office or public room, and in every bedroom of the establishment, a printed copy of §§ 33-951 and 33-952, with a printed statement of charges by the day, week or month for meals, lodging or other items furnished.

§ 33-302. Maintenance of fireproof safe by innkeeper for deposit of valuables by guests; limitations on liability of innkeeper for loss of property of guests

A. An innkeeper who maintains a fireproof safe and gives notice by posting in a conspicuous place in the office or in the room of each guest that money, jewelry, documents and other articles of small size and unusual value may be deposited in the safe, is not liable for loss of or injury to any such article not deposited in the safe, which is not the result of his own act.

B. An innkeeper may refuse to receive for deposit from a guest articles exceeding a total value of five hundred dollars, and unless otherwise agreed to in writing shall not be liable in an amount in excess of five hundred dollars for loss of or damage to property deposited by a guest in such safe unless the loss or damage is the result of the fault or negligence of the innkeeper.

C. The innkeeper shall not be liable for loss of or damage to merchandise samples or merchandise for sale displayed by a guest unless the guest gives prior written notice to the innkeeper of having and displaying the merchandise or merchandise samples, and the innkeeper acknowledges receipt of such notice, but in no event shall liability for such loss or damage exceed five hundred dollars unless it results from the fault or negligence of the innkeeper.

D. The liability of an innkeeper to a guest shall be limited to one hundred dollars for property delivered to the innkeeper to be kept in a storeroom or baggage room and to seventy-five dollars for property deposited in a parcel or checkroom.

E. For the purpose of this section the term "inn" includes hotel, boarding house, lodging house, apartment house, motel and auto camp.

§ 33-303. Discrimination by landlord or lessor against tenant with children prohibited; penalty; exceptions

A. A person who knowingly refuses to rent to any other person a place to be used for a dwelling for the reason that the other person has a child or children, or who advertises in connection with the rental a restriction against children, either by the display of a sign, placard, written or printed notice, or by publication thereof in a newspaper of general circulation, is guilty of a petty offense.

B. No person shall rent or lease his property to another in violation of a valid restrictive covenant against the sale of such property to persons who have a child or children living with them nor shall a person rent or lease his property to persons who have a child or children living with them when his property lies within a subdivision which subdivision is presently designed, advertised and used as an exclusive adult subdivision. A person who knowingly rents or leases his property in violation of the provisions of this subsection is guilty of a petty offense.

ARTICLE 2. OBLIGATIONS AND LIABILITIES OF TENANT

§ 33-321. Maintenance of premises

A tenant shall exercise diligence to maintain the premises in as good condition as when he took possession, ordinary wear and tear excepted.

§ 33-322. Damage to premises; classification

Removal or intentional and material alteration or damage of any part of a building, the furnishings thereof, or any permanent fixture, by or at the instance of the tenant, without written permission of the landlord or his agent, is a class 2 misdemeanor.

§ 33-323. Liability of person in possession of land for rent due thereon

Every person in possession of land out of which rent is due is liable for the amount or proportion of rent due from the lands in his possession, although it is only a part of the land originally demised, without depriving the landlord of other legal remedies for recovery of rent.

§ 33-324. Denial of landlord's title by lessee in possession prohibited

When a person enters into possession of real property under a lease, he may not, while in possession, deny the title of his landlord in an action brought upon the lease by the landlord or a person claiming under him.

ARTICLE 3. TERMINATION OF TENANCIES

§ 33-341. Termination of tenancies

A. A tenancy from year to year terminates at the end of each year unless written permission is given to remain for a longer period. The permission shall specify the time the tenant may remain, and upon termination of such time the tenancy expires.

B. A lease from month to month may be terminated by the landlord giving at least ten days notice thereof. In case of nonpayment of rent notice is not required.

C. A tenant from month to month shall give ten days notice, and a tenant on a semimonthly basis shall give five days notice, of his intention to terminate possession of the premises. Failure to give the notice renders the tenant liable for the rent for the ensuing ten days.

D. When a tenancy is for a certain period under verbal or written agreement, and the time expires, the tenant shall surrender possession. Notice to quit or demand of possession is not then necessary.

E. A tenant who holds possession of property against the will of the landlord, except as provided in this section, shall not be considered a tenant at sufferance or at will.

§ 33-342. Effect of lessee holding over

When a lessee holds over and retains possession after expiration of the term of the lease without express contract with the owner, the holding over shall not operate to renew the lease for the term of the former lease, but thereafter the tenancy is from month to month.

§ 33-343. Premises rendered untenantable without fault of lessee; nonliability of tenant for rent; right to quit premises

The lessee of a building which, without fault or neglect on the part of the lessee, is destroyed or so injured by the elements or any other cause as to be untenantable or unfit for occupancy, is not liable thereafter to pay rent to the lessor or owner unless expressly provided by written agreement, and the lessee may thereupon quit and surrender possession of the premises.

ARTICLE 4. REMEDIES OF LANDLORD

33-361. Violation of lease by tenant; right of landlord to re-enter; summary action for recovery of premises; appeal; lien for unpaid rent; enforcement

A. When a tenant neglects or refuses to pay rent when due and in arrears for five days, or when tenant violates any provision of the lease, the landlord or person to whom the rent is due, or his agent, may re-enter and take possession, or, without formal demand or re-entry, commence an action for recovery of possession of the premises.

B. The action shall be commenced, conducted and governed as provided for actions for forcible entry or detainer, and shall be tried not less than five nor more than thirty days after its commencement.

C. If judgment is given for the plaintiff, the defendant, in order to perfect an appeal, shall file a bond with the court in an amount fixed and approved by the court payable to the clerk of the superior court, conditioned that appellant will prosecute the appeal to effect and will pay the rental value of the premises pending the appeal and all damages, costs, and rent adjudged against him.

D. If the tenant refuses or fails to pay rent owing and due, the landlord shall have a lien upon and may seize as much personal property of the tenant located on the premises and not exempted by law as is necessary to secure payment of the rent. If the rent is not paid and satisfied within sixty days after seizure as provided for in this section, the landlord may sell the seized personal property in the manner provided by § 33-1023.

E. When premises are sublet or the lease assigned, the landlord shall have a like lien against the sublessee or assignee as he has against the tenant and may enforce it in the same manner.

§ 33-362. **Landlord's lien for rent**
A. The landlord shall have a lien on all property of his tenant not exempt by law, placed upon or used on the leased premises, until the rent is paid. The lien shall not secure the payment of rent accruing after the death or bankruptcy of the lessee, or after an assignment for the benefit of the lessee's creditors.
B. The landlord may seize for rent any personal property of his tenant found on the premises, but the property of any other person, although found on the premises, shall not be liable therefor. If the tenant fails to allow the landlord to take possession of such property, the landlord may reduce the property to possession by an action to recover possession, and may hold or sell the property for the payment of the rent.

C. The landlord shall have a lien for rent upon crops grown or growing upon the leased premises, whether the rent is payable in money, articles of property or products of the premises, and also for the faithful performance of the terms of the lease, and the lien shall continue for a period of six months after expiration of the term of the lease.
D. When premises are sublet, or when the lease is assigned, the landlord shall have the same lien against the sublessee or assignee as he has against the tenant and may enforce the lien in like manner.

ARTICLE 5. APPLICABILITY OF CHAPTER

§ 33-381. **Limitation**
This chapter shall apply to all landlord-tenant relationships except for landlord-tenant relationships arising out of the rental of dwelling units which shall be governed by chapter 10 or 11[1] of this title.

[1] Section 33-1301 *et seq.* or 33-1401 *et seq.*

SPECIAL ACTIONS AND PROCEEDINGS RELATING TO PROPERTY

ARIZONA REVISED STATUTES, TITLE 12, CHAPTER 8

ARTICLE 4. FORCIBLE ENTRY AND DETAINER

Section
12-1171. Acts which constitute forcible entry or detainer.
12-1172. Definition of forcible entry.
12-1173. Definition of forcible detainer; substitution of parties.
12-1173.01. Additional definition of forcible detainer.
12-1174. Immateriality of time possession obtained by tenant.
12-1175. Complaint and answer; service and return.
12-1176. Demand for jury; trial procedure.
12-1177. Trial and issue; postponement of trial.
12-1178. Judgment; writ of restitution; limitation on issuance.
12-1179. Appeal to superior court; notice; bond.
12-1180. Stay of proceedings on judgment; record on appeal.
12-1181. Trial and judgment on appeal; writ of restitution.
12-1182. Appeal to supreme court; stay and bond.
12-1183. Proceedings no bar to certain actions.

§ 12-1171. Acts which constitute forcible entry or detainer

A person is guilty of forcible entry and detainer, or of forcible detainer, as the case may be, if he:

1. Makes an entry into any lands, tenements or other real property, except in cases where entry is given by law.

2. Makes such an entry by force.

3. Wilfully and without force holds over any lands, tenements or other real property after termination of the time for which such lands, tenements or other real property were let to him or to the person under whom he claims, after demand made in writing for the possession thereof by the person entitled to such possession.

§ 12-1172. Definition of forcible entry

A "forcible entry," or an entry where entry is not given by law within the meaning of this article, is:

1. An entry without the consent of the person having the actual possession.

2. As to a landlord, an entry upon the possession of his tenant at will or by sufferance, whether with or without the tenant's consent.

§ 12-1173. Definition of forcible detainer; substitution of parties

There is a forcible detainer if:

1. A tenant at will or by sufferance or a tenant from month to month or a lesser period whose tenancy has been terminated retains possession after his tenancy has been terminated or after he receives written demand of possession by the landlord.

2. The tenant of a person who has made a forcible entry refuses for five days after written demand to give possession to the person upon whose possession the forcible entry was made.

3. A person who has made a forcible entry upon the possession of one who acquired such pos-session by forcible entry refuses for five days after written demand to give possession to the person upon whose possession the first forcible entry was made.

4. A person who has made a forcible entry upon the possession of a tenant for a term refuses to deliver possession to the landlord for five days after written demand, after the term expires. If the term expires while a writ of forcible entry applied for by the tenant is pending, the landlord may, at his own cost and for his own benefit, prosecute it in the name of the tenant.

§ 12-1173.01. Additional definition of forcible detainer

A. In addition to other persons enumerated in this article, a person in any of the following cases who retains possession of any land, tenements or other real property after he received written demand of possession may be removed through an action for forcible detainer filed with the clerk of the superior court in accordance with this article:

1. If the property has been sold through the foreclosure of a mortgage, deed of trust or contract for conveyance of real property pursuant to title 33, chapter 6, article 2.[1]

2. If the property has been sold through a trustee's sale under a deed of trust pursuant to title 33, chapter 6.1.[2]

3. If the property has been forfeited through a contract for conveyance of real property pursuant to title 33, chapter 6, article 3.[3]

4. If the property has been sold by virtue of an execution and the title has been duly transferred.

5. If the property has been sold by the owner and the title has been duly transferred.

B. The remedies provided by this section do not affect the rights of persons in possession under a lease or other possessory right which is superior to the interest sold, forfeited or executed upon.

C. The remedies provided by this section are in addition to and do not preclude any other remedy granted by law.

[1] Section 33-721 *et seq.*
[2] Section 33-801 *et seq.*
[3] Section 33-741 *et seq.*

§ 12-1174. Immateriality of time possession obtained by tenant

It is not material whether a tenant received possession from his landlord or became his tenant after obtaining possession.

§ 12-1175. Complaint and answer; service and return

A. When a party aggrieved files a complaint of forcible entry or forcible detainer, in writing and under oath, with the clerk of the superior court or a justice of the peace, summons shall issue no later than the next judicial day.

B. The complaint shall contain a description of the premises of which possession is claimed in sufficient detail to identify them and shall also state the facts which entitle the plaintiff to possession and authorize the action.

C. The summons shall be served at least two days before the return day, and return made thereof on the day assigned for trial.

§ 12-1176. Demand for jury; trial procedure

A. The clerk or justice of the peace shall at the time of issuing the summons, if requested by the plaintiff, issue a venire to the sheriff or constable of the county commanding him to summon a jury of eight persons, if the proceeding is in the superior court, and six persons, if in the justice court, qualified jurors of the county, to appear on the day set for trial to serve as jurors in the action. The venire shall be served and returned on the day assigned for trial. The trial date shall be no more than five judicial days after the aggrieved party files the complaint.

B. If the plaintiff does not request a jury, the defendant may do so when he appears, and the jury shall be summoned in the manner set forth in subsection A.

C. If any jurors fail to attend, or are excused after being challenged, the jury shall be completed by causing other qualified jurors to be summoned immediately.

D. The action shall be docketed and tried as other civil actions.

§ 12-1177. Trial and issue; postponement of trial

A. On the trial of an action of forcible entry or forcible detainer, the only issue shall be the right of actual possession and the merits of title shall not be inquired into.

B. If a jury is demanded, it shall return a verdict of guilty or not guilty of the charge as stated in the complaint. If a jury is not demanded the action shall be tried by the court.

C. For good cause shown, supported by affidavit, the trial may be postponed for a time not to exceed three calendar days in a justice court or ten calendar days in a superior court.

§ 12-1178. Judgment; writ of restitution; limitation on issuance

A. If the defendant is found guilty, the court shall give judgment for the plaintiff for restitution of the premises, for late charges stated in the rental agreement and for costs and, at the plaintiff's option, for all rent found to be due and unpaid at the date of the judgment, and shall grant a writ of restitution.

B. If the defendant is found not guilty, judgment shall be given for the defendant against the plaintiff for costs, and if it appears that the plaintiff has acquired possession of the premises since commencement of the action, a writ of restitution shall issue in favor of the defendant.

C. No writ of restitution shall issue until the expiration of five days after the rendition of judgment. The writ of restitution shall be enforced as promptly and expeditiously as possible.

§ 12-1179. Appeal to superior court; notice; bond

A. Either party may appeal from a justice court to the superior court of the county in which the judgment is given by giving notice as in other civil actions within five days after rendition of the judgment pursuant to this section.

B. A party seeking to appeal a judgment shall file with the notice of appeal a bond for costs on appeal, which shall be in an amount set by the justice of the peace sufficient to cover the costs on appeal. The bond shall be payable to the clerk of the superior court. If a party is unable to file a bond for costs on appeal, the party shall file with the justice court a notice of appeal along with an affidavit stating that he is unable to give bond for costs on appeal and the reasons therefor. Within five court days after the filing of the affidavit, any other party may file, in the justice court, objections to the affidavit. The justice of the peace shall hold a hearing on the affidavit and objections within five court days thereafter. If the justice court sustains the objections, the appellant shall file, within five court days thereafter, a bond for costs on appeal as provided for in this section or in such lesser amount as ordered by the justice court.

C. A party seeking to appeal a judgment may stay the execution of either the judgment for possession or any judgment for money damages by filing a supersedeas bond. The justice court shall hold a hearing on the motion within five court days after the parties advise the justice court of their failure to stipulate on the amount of the bond. The stay is effective when the supersedeas bond or bonds are filed.

D. The party seeking to stay the execution of the judgment for possession shall file a supersedeas bond in the amount of rent accruing from the date of the judgment until the next periodic rental date, together with costs and attorney's fees, if any. The tenant shall pay to the clerk of the superior court, on or before each periodic rental date during the pendency of the appeal, the amount of rent due under the terms of the lease or rental agreement. Such amounts shall be made payable by the superior court to the owner, landlord or agent as they accrue to satisfy the amount of periodic rent due under the lease or rental agreement. In all cases where the rent due under the terms of the lease or rental agreement is paid through the office of the clerk of the superior court as set forth in this subsection, the order of the court may include a one-time handling fee in the amount of ten dollars to be paid by the party seeking to stay the execution of the judgment for possession. In no event shall the amounts paid per month exceed the amount of monthly rent charged by the owner for the premises. Where habitability as provided for in § 33-1324 and § 33-1364 has been raised as an affirmative defense by the tenant to the nonpayment of rent or when the tenant has filed a counterclaim asserting a habitability issue, the superior court will retain all money paid under this subsection pending a final judgment.

E. If during the pendency of the appeal the party seeking to stay the execution of the judgment for possession fails to pay the rent on the periodic rental due date, the party in whose favor a judgment for possession was issued may move the superior court to lift the stay of execution of the judgment for possession. The superior court shall hear the motion to lift the stay of the execution of the judgment for possession and release accrued monies, if any, within five court days from the failure of the party to pay the periodic rent due under the terms of the lease or rental agreement.

F. The party seeking to stay the execution of the judgment for money damages shall file a supersedeas bond in the amount of the judgment, together with costs and attorney's fees, if any. The amount of the bond shall be fixed by the court and payable to the clerk of the superior court.

§ 12-1180. Stay of proceedings on judgment; record on appeal

When the appeal bond is filed and approved, the justice of the peace shall stay further proceedings on the judgment and immediately prepare a transcript of all entries on his docket in the action and transmit it, together with all the original papers, to the clerk of the superior court of the county in which the trail was had.

§ 12-1181. Trial and judgment on appeal; writ of restitution

A. On trial of the action in the superior court, appellee, if out of possession and the right of possession is adjudged to him, shall be entitled to damages for withholding possession of the premises during pendency of the appeal and the court shall also render judgment in favor of appellee and against appellant and the sureties on his bond for damages proved and costs.

B. The writ of restitution or execution shall be issued by the clerk of the superior court and shall be executed by the sheriff or constable as in other actions.

§ 12-1182. Appeal to supreme court; stay and bond

A. In a forcible entry or forcible detainer action originally commenced in the superior court, an appeal may be taken to the supreme court as in other civil actions.

B. The appeal, if taken by the party in possession of the premises, shall not stay execution of the judgment unless the superior court so orders, and appellant shall file a bond in an amount fixed and approved by the court, conditioned that appellant will prosecute the appeal to effect and will pay the rental value of the premises pending the appeal and all damages, costs, and rent adjudged against him by the superior court or the supreme court.

§ 12-1183. Proceedings no bar to certain actions

The proceedings under a forcible entry or forcible detainer shall not bar an action for trespass, damages, waste, rent or mesne profits.

APPENDIX D

LEGAL SERVICES ORGANIZATIONS

Community Legal Services 305 South 2nd Avenue P.O. Box 21538 Phoenix, AZ 85036 258-3434	Community Legal Services 101 East 1st Avenue Suite 103 Mesa, AZ 85210 833-1442	Community Legal Services 722 East Beale Street P.O. Box 509 Kingman, AZ 86402 753-1177
Community Legal Services 8355 West Peoria Peoria, AZ 85345 937-2733	Community Legal Services 51 West Second Street Yuma, AZ 85364 782-7511	Community Legal Services 401 North Mount Vernon Prescott, AZ 86301 445-9240
Urban Indian Law Project 2601 North 3rd Street Suite 301 Phoenix, AZ 85004 263-0021	Farmworker Program 9201 West Van Buren Street Tolleson, AZ 85353 936-1443	Volunteer Lawyers Program 305 South 2nd Avenue P.O. Box 21538 Phoenix, AZ 85036 258-3434
Navajo Legal Aid and Defender Office P.O. Box 2575 Window Rock, AZ 86515 871-6370	Pinal & Gila Counties Legal Aid Society 343 West Central Avenue Coolidge, AZ 85228 723-5410 (1-800-293-2412)	Pinal & Gila Counties Legal Aid Society 718 B. Sullivan Street Miami, AZ 85539 473-2412 (1-800-293-2411)
Pinal & Gila Counties Legal Aid Society Cor. of Apache & Tonto Ave. P.O. Box 58 San Carlos, AZ 85550 475-2804	Southern Arizona Legal Aid, Inc. 64 East Broadway Boulevard Tucson, AZ 85701 623-9465	Southern Arizona Legal Aid, Inc. 1065 F. Avenue P.O. Box GG Douglas, AZ 85608 364-7973
Southern Arizona Legal Aid, Inc. 1201 East Cooley Suite E Show Low, AZ 85901 537-8383	Southern Arizona Legal Aid, Inc. 114 West 5th Street Safford, AZ 85546-2322 428-4213	Southern Arizona Legal Aid, Inc. 180 West Loam Street, #4 Nogales, AZ 85621 287-9441
Volunteer Lawyers Program 64 East Broadway Boulevard Tucson, AZ 85701 623-9465	Four Rivers Indian Legal Services P.O. Box 68 Sucaton, AZ 85247 562-3369	Salt River Indian Community Route 1, Box 215-X Scottsdale, AZ 85256 949-5512

Pasqua-Yaqui Office 64 East Broadway Boulevard Tucson, AZ 85701 623-9461	DNA-People's Legal Services, Inc. P.O. Box 306 Window Rock, AZ 86515 871-4151	DNA-People's Legal Services, Inc. P.O. Box 767 Chinle, AZ 86503 674-5242
DNA-People's Legal Services, Inc. P.O. Box 765 Tuba City, AZ 86045 283-5265	Coconino County Legal Aid 19 East Phoenix Avenue Flagstaff, AZ 86001 774-0653	Papago Legal Services P.O. Box 246 Sells, AZ 85634 383-2420
Fort Apache Legal Aid P.O. Box 1030 Whiteriver, AZ 85941 338-4845	Hopi Legal Services (A project of DNA-People's Legal Services) P.O. Box 558 Keams Canyon, AZ 86034 738-2251	Arizona Statewide Legal Services Project 305 South Second Avenue Suite F P.O. Box 311 Phoenix, AZ 85001 252-3432
Specialty Groups Advocates for the Disabled 1314 North 3rd Street Suite 116 Phoenix, AZ 85004 256-9673	Arizona Center for Law in the Public Interest 3724 North 3rd Street Suite 300 Phoenix, AZ 85012 274-6287	Arizona Center for Law in the Public Interest 3208 East Fort Lowell, #106 Tucson, AZ 85716 329-9547
Arizona Senior Citizens Law Project 1818 South 16th Street Phoenix, AZ 85034 252-6710	Friendly House 802 South First Avenue Phoenix, AZ 85003 257-1870	Arizona Center for Immigration 2 North Central Avenue Suite 1600 Phoenix, AZ 85004-2393 253-3657
Arizona Center for Immigration P.O. Box 1152 Phoenix, AZ 85001 253-3657 (mailing address)	Tucson Ecumenical Council Legal Aid (TECLA) P.O. Box 3007 Tucson, AZ 85702 623-5739	

GLOSSARY

A

Abandonment - As defined in the Act, "means the absence of the tenant from the dwelling unit, without notice to the landlord for at least seven days, if rent for the dwelling unit is outstanding and unpaid for ten days and there is no reasonable evidence other than the presence of the tenant's personal property that the tenant is occupying the residence. *See* A.R.S. § 33-1370(H) (West 1990).

Act - Refers to the Arizona Residential Landlord and Tenant Act. The Act is contained in Chapter 10 of Title 33 of the Arizona Revised Statutes, A.R.S. §§ 33-1301 to -1381 (West 1990 & Supp. 1993).

Action - As defined in the Act, "includes recoupment, counterclaim, setoff, suit in equity and any other proceeding in which rights are determined, including an action for possession." *See* A.R.S. § 33-1310(1) (West 1990).

Adequate notice - Defined in the rental agreement of, if not addressed in the rental agreement, by statute. In short it is the amount of notice required (by the rental agreement or statute) necessary to be given by a party before certain action is taken (i.e., increase in rent, vacating rental unit, terminating the rental agreement). *See* page 73.

Answer - A pleading filed by a defendant in response to a complaint or by cross-defendant in response to a cross-claim.

Arizona Reports - A legal publication containing written opinions of Arizona courts.

A.R.S. § ##-#### - Refers to Arizona Revised Statutes Annotated, which is properly cited as: ARIZ. REV. STAT. ANN. § ##-#### (West 1990), but for brevity is cited herein as A.R.S. § ##-####, where "##-####" is the specific statute title and section number.

Asset protection - A plan or strategy that shields some, most or all of your assets from liability. Asset protection is briefly discussed in Chapter 3, Section C.

Asset search - A search of public records and records that are not readily available to the public, for the purpose of discovering the location and/or extent of assets and holdings of a person or entity. An asset search is typically ordered from some type of investigative service. The cost ranges from $50 to $250 (more if you want to expand the search to include other counties and/or states).

B

Building and housing codes - As defined in the Act, "include any law, ordinance or governmental regulation concerning fitness for habitation, or the construction, maintenance, operation, occupancy, use or appearance of any premises, or dwelling unit." *See* A.R.S. § 33-1310(2) (West 1990).

C

Case - A general term for an action, cause, suit, or controversy at law or in equity. A judicial proceeding for the determination of a controversy between parties, wherein rights are enforced or protected, or wrongs are prevented or redressed.

Citations - Reference to legal authorities and precedents, such as constitutions, statutes, reported cases and treatises. Used in arguments to courts, in legal text-books, law review articles, legal briefs, or the like, to establish or fortify the proposition(s) advanced.

Cite - See Citation.

Cleaning deposit - Money belonging to the tenant and held by the landlord to pay for cleaning of the rental unit in the event the tenant does not leave it clean when the tenant vacates the unit at the end of the tenancy.

Complaint - A pleading filed by a plaintiff to initiate a lawsuit (i.e., the document filed by the landlord to initiate a Special Detainer action). *See Answer* for related reference.

Counterclaim - A pleading filed by a defendant against the plaintiff, asserting a cause of action against the plaintiff that may or may not be related to the factual situation giving rise to the plaintiff's cause of action against the defendant. The counterclaim is filed with the answer.

D

Deposits - See *security*, *cleaning deposit*, or *redecorating deposit*.

Distraint for rent - Seizure; the act of distraining or making a distress. Normally referring to a landlord seizing the property of a tenant for failure of the tenant to pay rent when due. Distraint for rent is not permissible under the Act.

Dwelling unit - As defined in the Act, "means a structure or the part of a structure that is used as a home, residence, or sleeping place by one person who maintains a household or by two or more persons who maintain a common household. 'Dwelling unit' excludes real property used to accommodate a mobile home, unless the mobile home is rented or leased by the landlord." *See* A.R.S. § 33-1310(3) (West 1990).

E, F, G

Et seq. - An abbreviation for *et sequentes* or *et sequentia*; means, "and the following." Thus a reference to A.R.S. § 33-1301, *et seq.*, means Section 33-1301 and the following sections.

Eviction - Dispossession by process of law; the act of depriving a person of the possession of land or rental property which he has held or leased. *See Special Detainer action*.

Exclusions - As used in A.R.S. § 33-1308, means particular circumstances under which the rental of residential rental property is not subject to the Act. As used in connection with an insurance policy, refers to certain conditions or circumstances that are not covered by the policy.

Execution - See *Writ of Execution*.

Forcible detainer - Term for court action to evict a commercial tenant and certain types of residential tenants, when said tenancy is not subject to the Act. Properly called a Special Detainer action when used in connection with an eviction from residential real property. *See Special Detainer action*.

Garnishment - See *Writ of Garnishment*.

Good faith - As defined in the Act, "means honesty in fact in the conduct or transaction concerned." *See* A.R.S. § 33-1310(4) (West 1990).

H

Housing codes - Building and housing codes, as defined in the Act, "include any law, ordinance or governmental regulation concerning fitness for habitation, or the construction, maintenance, operation, occupancy, use or appearance of any premises, or dwelling unit." *See* A.R.S. § 33-1310(2) (West 1990).

I, J, K

Judgment - The official and authentic decision of a court of justice upon the respective rights and claims of the parties to an action or suit therein litigated and submitted to its determination.

Judgment creditor - One who has obtained a money judgment against his debtor (or defendant), under which he may enforce execution.

L

Landlord - As defined in the Act, "means the owner, lessor or sublessor of the dwelling unit or the building of which it is a part, and it also means a manager of the premises who fails to disclose as required by § 33-1322." *See* A.R.S. § 33-1310(5) (West 1990).

Lease - Any agreement that gives rise to a relationship of landlord and tenant (in the case of real property). *See* **rental agreement**.

Litigation - A lawsuit; legal action, including all proceedings therein. A contest in a court of law for the purpose of enforcing a right or seeking a remedy.

M, N

Noncompliance - As used in the Act, refers to a failure of the landlord or the tenant to comply with the terms and conditions of the rental agreement, rules and regulations, and/or the Act. *See* A.R.S. §§ 33-1361 (1990), -1368 (West Supp. 1993).

Nonrefundable deposit - A deposit given by a tenant to the landlord, normally at the commencement of the tenancy, that both parties understand will be retained by the landlord at the end of the tenancy. Pursuant to A.R.S. § 33-1321(B), nonrefundable cleaning and redecorating deposits <u>must</u> be stated in writing.

Notice
- *See* **Seven-Day Notice to Pay or Quit**.
- *See* **Ten-Day Notice of Termination of Rental Agreement for Noncompliance with Rental Agreement Materially Affecting Health and Safety**.
- *See* **Fourteen-Day Notice of Termination of Rental Agreement for Material Noncompliance with Rental Agreement**.

Notice of Complaint/Violation - Written notice given by landlord to tenant to inform tenant of: (1) complaints against the tenant by other tenants, neighbors, etc. and/or (2) violation of some term or condition of the rental agreement or rules and regulations. This notice may form the basis for subsequent eviction if the problem reoccurs.

Notice of Immediate Termination of Rental Agreement for Material and Irreparable Breach - Written notice given by landlord to tenant, pursuant to A.R.S. § 33-1368(A), to immediately terminate a tenant's rental agreement if a breach occurs that is both material and irreparable, such as a discharge of a weapon on the premises or infliction of serious bodily harm on the landlord, his agent or another tenant or involving imminent serious property damage.

Notice Reinstating Time of the Essence - Written notice given by landlord to tenant to inform the tenant that, although the landlord may have waived certain violations and noncompliance in the past, the landlord will require strict compliance with the terms and conditions of the rental agreement and/or the rules and regulations.

Notice to Terminate Tenancy - Written notice given by tenant to landlord to inform the landlord that the tenant wishes to terminate his/her tenancy.

O

Opinion - When used in connection with a judge's decision in a case, means the written opinion of the judge outlining the facts and law pertinent to the case and (normally) the judge's reason(s) for deciding the case the way s/he did.

Organization - As defined in the Act, "includes a corporation, government, governmental subdivision or agency, business trust, estate, trust, partnership or association, two or more persons having a joint or common interest and any other legal or commercial entity which is a landlord, owner, manager or constructive agent pursuant to § 33-1322." *See* A.R.S. § 33-1310(6) (West 1990).

Owner - As defined in the Act, "means one or more persons, jointly or severally, in whom is vested all or part of the legal title to property or all or part of the beneficial ownership and a right to present use and enjoyment of the premises. The term includes a mortgagee in possession." *See* A.R.S. § 33-1310(7) (West 1990).

P

Pacific Reporter, Second Series - A legal publication that contains written opinions of courts from Alaska, Arizona, California, Colorado, Hawaii, Idaho, Kansas, Montana, Nevada, New Mexico, Oklahoma, Oregon, Utah, Washington and Wyoming.

Pay or Quit - *See* ***Seven-Day Notice to Pay or Quit***.

Person - As defined in the Act, "means an individual or organization." *See* A.R.S. § 33-1310(8) (West 1990).

Posting - A form of service of process consisting of displaying the documents in a prominent place (i.e., upon the door) when other forms of service are unavailing.

Precedent - An adjudged case or decision of a court, considered as furnishing an example or authority for an identical or similar case afterwards arising or a similar question of law. A rule of law established for the first time by a court for a particular type of case and thereafter referred to in deciding similar cases.

Pre-empted - Pre-emption is a doctrine adopted by the United States Supreme Court holding that certain matters are of such a national, as opposed to local, character that federal laws pre-empt or take precedence over state laws. As such, a state may not pass a law that is inconsistent with a federal law.

Premises - As defined in the Act, "means a dwelling unit and the structure of which it is a part and existing facilities and appurtenances therein, including furniture and utilities where applicable, and grounds, areas and existing facilities held out for the use of tenants generally or whose use is promised to the tenant." *See* A.R.S. § 33-1310(9) (West 1990).

Process server - One authorized by the court to deliver *service of process*.

Promulgated - To publish or proclaim formally (i.e., a law, decree of court, etc.) or to put into operation.

Public housing - Is more specifically defined in Chapter 12 of Title 36 of the Arizona Revised Statutes Annotated, A.R.S. §§ 36-1401 to -1501 (West 1990 & Supp. 1993), but generally refers to housing that is owned and operated by the government for low-income families.

Q, R

Redecorating deposit - Money paid by the tenant to the landlord at the commencement of the tenancy (or thereafter) to pay for redecorating of the rental unit (i.e., new paint, new carpet, new drapes, etc.) at the end of the tenancy, to prepare the unit for occupancy by the next tenant.

Rent - As defined in the Act, "means payments to be made to the landlord in full consideration for the rented premises." *See* A.R.S. § 33-1310(10) (West 1990).

Rental agreement - As defined in the Act, "means all agreements, written, oral or implied by law, and valid rules and regulations adopted under § 33-1342 embodying the terms and conditions concerning the use and occupancy of a dwelling unit and premises." *See* A.R.S. § 33-1310(11) (West 1990).

Roomer - As defined in the Act, "means a person occupying a dwelling unit that lacks a major bathroom or kitchen facility, in a structure where one or more major facilities are used in common by occupants of the dwelling unit and other dwelling units. Major facility in the case of a bathroom means toilet, or either a bath or shower, and in the case of a kitchen means refrigerator, stove or sink." *See* A.R.S. § 33-1310(12) (West 1990).

Rules and regulations - Guidelines established by the landlord that govern the use and occupancy of the leased premises. *See* A.R.S. § 33-1342 (West 1990).

S

Section 8 Housing - The federal housing assistance program that provides rent subsidies for low-income families. *See* Tax Exemption of Obligations of Public Housing Agencies and Related Amendments, 24 C.F.R. §§ 811.101 to -.211 (1991).

Security - As defined in the Act, "means money or property given to assure payment or performance under a rental agreement. 'Security' does not include a reasonable charge for redecorating or cleaning." *See* A.R.S. § 33-1310(13) (West 1990). Generally means money or property held by the landlord as security for unpaid rent or damages to the rental unit.

Security deposit - *See* **Security**.

Service of Process - Delivery of summons, complaint, writ, etc.; signifies delivery to or leaving them with the party to whom or with whom they ought to be delivered or left. The mode of delivery (i.e., personal service, service by mail, service by publication, etc.) may be prescribed by statute or by rule of procedure.

Seven-Day Notice to Pay or Quit - Written notice given by the landlord to the tenant, pursuant to A.R.S. § 33-1368(B), informing the tenant that if s/he does not pay rent that is due within seven days, the landlord may terminate the rental agreement and file a Special Detainer action.

Single family residence - As defined in the Act, "means a structure maintained and used as a single dwelling unit. Notwithstanding that a dwelling unit shares one or more walls with another dwelling unit, it is a single family residence if it has direct access to a street or thoroughfare and shares neither heating facilities, hot water equipment nor any other essential facility or service with any other dwelling unit." *See* A.R.S. § 33-1310(14) (West 1990).

Special Detainer action - Legal process, brought pursuant to A.R.S. § 33-1377, to evict a tenant from residential rental property.

Statute - An act of the legislature declaring, commanding or prohibiting something; a particular law enacted and established by the will of the legislative department of government.

T

Tenant - As defined in the Act, "means a person entitled under a rental agreement to occupy a dwelling unit to the exclusion of others." *See* A.R.S. § 33-1310(15) (West 1990).

U, V, W, X, Y, Z

With prejudice - As applied to a judgment of dismissal, means that the dismissal has the same conclusive effect as does an adjudication of the case on the merits; the action cannot be refiled against the same adversary, based on the same facts.

Writ of Execution - An order of the court empowering the Sheriff to seize property of a judgment debtor to satisfy a money judgment.

Writ of Garnishment - An order of the court whereby a person's property, money or credits, that are in the possession or control of another party, are applied to payment of a debt to a judgment creditor.

Writ of Restitution - When used herein, refers to an order of the court, after judgment is entered in the landlord's favor in a Special Detainer action, restoring the right to possess residential real property to the landlord.

1 - 14

7-Day Notice to Pay or Quit - Written notice given by the landlord to the tenant, pursuant to A.R.S. § 33-1368(B), informing the tenant that if s/he does not pay rent that is due within seven days, the landlord may terminate the rental agreement and file a Special Detainer action.

Ten-Day Notice of Termination of Rental Agreement for Noncompliance with Rental Agreement Materially Affecting Health and Safety - Written notice given by the landlord to the tenant, pursuant to A.R.S. § 33-1368(A), informing the tenant that there is a noncompliance with the rental agreement that materially affects health and safety and that if not remedied by the tenant within five days of the notice, the rental agreement will terminate in ten days.

Fourteen-Day Notice of Termination of Rental Agreement for Material Non-compliance with Rental Agreement - Written notice given by the landlord to the tenant, pursuant to A.R.S. § 33-1368(A), informing the tenant that there is a material noncompliance with the rental agreement and that if not remedied by the tenant within ten days of the notice, the rental agreement will terminate in fourteen days.

INDEX

- Words that appear in *highlighted text* (i.e., bold and italics) in the main section of the Tenant's Handbook are found in this Index, followed by a list of pages where the term may be found. The page number in bold print indicates the page where the term is discussed at length.

- **(QRS)** - QRS followed by a roman numeral (i.e., QRS-XVII), indicates that the term appears in the Quick Reference Section.

- **(form)** - A page number followed by - (form) - indicates the location of a form that pertains to that term.

A B C D

Abandonment. . . . . **23-24**, 55.

Act . . . . QRS-III, 2, 7, **12**, **15**-20, 22-25, 27, 33, 36, 53, 60, 61, 63, 64, 66, 76, 77, 80, 82, 96.

Adequate notice. . . . . .43, 72, **73**.

Agreement to Tender and Accept Partial Rent Payment - *See* Partial Rent Payments.

Application . . . . QRS-III, 29, **39**, 40(form), 41-48, 56, Checklist 1.

Arizona Residential Landlord and Tenant Act - *See* Act.

Arizona Reports . . . . **3**.

Arizona Revised Statutes Annotated.**3**, 15, 18.

Asset protection . . . . **8**-10, 103.

Case (i.e., lawsuit) . . . . **2-4**, 35, 48.

Checklists.1, 6, 26, 29, 30, 31(form), **32**, 102.

Children . . . . QRS-III, 42, **46**-48.

Citations (citations to legal authority) . . . . **2-4**.

Cleaning deposit - *See* Deposits.

Combined Real Property and Personal Property Inspection Checklist . . . . **32**.

Comments . . . . **5**.

Commercial vehicles . . . . **59**.

Common tenant problems . . . . Chapter 5, **51**.

Complaint (i.e., form of pleading in a lawsuit) . . . . 83, **87**-89, 92, **96**-98, 101. (*see also* Notice of Complaint/Violation)

Conventions. . . . . **2**.

Damages to rental unit . . . . **75**, 86, 87, 89, 91, 95, 98, 100.

Deposits . . . . QRS-V, 3, 15, 19, 21, **26**, 27, 29, 32, 33, 75, 76, 91, 100, **Checklist 3**.

Nonrefundable deposits. . . . . . **19**, 26, 27, 75.

Discrimination . . . . . . QRS-III, 42, 46, **47**, 48.

Disposition of Deposit(s) - *See* Deposits or Forms.

E

Errors . . . . **5**.

Eviction . . . QRS-VII, VIII, IX, 23, 25, 36, 41, 46, 47, 52, 53, 55, **76**, 77, 81-83, 85-92, 94-101.

Exclusions
    Exclusions from insurance coverage . . . **9**.
    Exclusions from the Act . . . . . 15, **16**-18.

Execution - *See* Writ of execution.

F

Flowchart . . . . **84**, **93**.

Forcible detainer - *See* Special Detainer action

Forms:

    Combined Real Property and Personal Property Inspection Checklist . . . . 32.

    Disposition of Deposit(s). . . . 32, 33(form).

    Fourteen-Day Notice of Termination of Rental Agreement for Material Noncompliance with Rental Agreement . . . . 36, 60-62(form), 114(form).

    Notice of Complaint/Violation. . . 29 (form).

    Notice of Immediate Termination of Rental Agreement for Material and Irreparable Breach . . . . 36.

    Notice of Termination or Rent Reduction Because of Fire or Casualty Damage . . . . **68**, 69(form), 116(form).

    Notice of Wrongful Failure to Supply Essential Services . . . .53-55, 60, **66**, 68(form), 120(form).

    Notice to Terminate Tenancy (by tenant) . . . . 32, 110.

    Parking Violation . . . . 35.

    Property Inspection Checklist. 29-31(form).

    Seven-Day Notice to Pay or Quit . . . . 33-34(form).

    Tenant Application. . . . . . 39-47, 40(form).

    Tenant Information Sheet. 44-47, 45(form).

    Ten-Day Notice of Termination of Rental Agreement for Noncompliance with Rental Agreement Materially Affecting Health and Safety . . . . 64-66(form), 112(form).

Footnotes. . . . . **2**.

Fourteen-Day Notice of Termination of Rental Agreement for Material Noncompliance with Rental Agreement - *See* Forms: Fourteen-Day Notice of Termination of Rental Agreement for Material Noncompliance with Rental Agreement.

G H I

Garnishment - *See* Writ of garnishment.

Getting Tenants - *See* Chapter 5.

Inspection form - *See* Forms.

J K L M

Judgment 8, 9, 25, 52, 86, 89-91, 94, 95, 98-100.

Justice court . . . . . 25, 82, 83, 88, 90, 97, 99.

Late fees . . . . . . QRS-VII, 25, 51, **52**, 94, 96.

Lease - *See* Rental Agreement.

Legal advise to tenants. . . . . 6-13.

Litigation. . . . . **6**-8, 18, 25, 51.

Material and Irreparable Breach - *See* Forms: Notice of Immediate Termination of Rental Agreement for Material and Irreparable Breach.

Material Noncompliance with Rental Agreement . . . . 19, 36, 53, 55, 59, **60**-62(form), 76, **77**, 78, 85-92.

N

Neighbor conflicts . . . . **56**.

Noncompliance with Rental Agreement Materially Affecting Health and Safety
. 36, 53, 60, **64**-66(form), 76, **78**-80, 85-92.

Nonrefundable deposits - *See* Deposits.

Notice
    See also Adequate notice

    Notice of Complaint/Violation - *See* Forms: Notice of Complaint/Violation.

    Notice of Immediate Termination of Rental Agreement for Material and Irreparable Breach - *See* Forms: Notice of Immediate Termination of Rental Agreement for Material and Irreparable Breach.

    Notice of Termination of Rental Agreement for Material Noncompliance with Rental Agreement, Fourteen-Day - *See* Forms: Fourteen-Day Notice of Termination of Rental Agreement for Material Noncompliance with Rental Agreement.

    Notice of Termination of Rental Agreement for Noncompliance with Rental Agreement Materially Affecting Health and Safety, Ten-Day - *See* Forms: Ten-Day Notice of Termination of Rental Agreement for Noncompliance with Rental Agreement Materially Affecting Health and Safety.

    Notice to Pay or Quit, Seven-Day - *See* Forms: Seven-Day Notice to Pay or Quit.

    Notice to Terminate Tenancy - *See* Forms: Notice to Terminate Tenancy.

O P

On-Site Manager . . . QRS-III, **17**, Checklist 1.

Pacific Reporter, Second Series . . . . **3**.

Parking . . . . . . 29, **56**-59, 78, 80, Checklist 1.

Parking Violation - *See* Forms: Parking Violation.

Partial rent payments . . . . . . 22, 23, 96, 101.

Pay or Quit - *See* Seven-Day Notice to Pay or Quit.

Pets . . . . **47**, Checklist 1.

Pre-emption . . . . QRS-III, **14**, 15, 18.

Private process server - *See* Process server.

Process server . . . . **87**, 90, 94, **96**, 99.

Prohibited provisions in a rental agreement . .
. . . . **17**, **20**, 21.

Property Inspection Checklist - *See* Forms: Property Inspection Checklist.

Q R

Real estate brokers/agents . . . . **37-38**.

Redecorating deposit - *See* Deposits.

Rental Agreement . . . . QRS-IV, 1, 2, 7, 8, 12, 15, 17, **18**-26, 29, 30, 33, 34, 36, 44, 49, 51-56, 59-63, 65, 66, 68, 69, 71-74, 76-80, 83, 85, 86, 89, 92, 94-96, 98, 101.

Residential dwelling . . . . 15.

Restitution - *See* Writ of Restitution.

S

Scope
    Scope of the Act . . . . QRS-III, **14**.
        (*see also* Exclusions)
    Scope of this book . . . . **2**.

Security deposit - *See* Deposits.

Seven-Day Notice to Pay or Quit . . . . . QRS-VIII, IX, 1, 29, **33** 34(form), **94** 96, 100, 101.

Special Detainer action
. . . 2, 12, 19, 20, 24, 33, 34, 52, **76**, 77, 79, 80, 82, 83, 85-89, 91, 92, 95-98, 100, 101.

Suggestions. . . . .**5**.

T

Tenant Application . . . . QRS-III, 29, **39**, 40(form), 41-48, 56, Checklist 1.

Tenant Information Sheet - See Forms: Tenant Information Sheet.

Ten-Day Notice of Termination of Rental Agreement for Noncompliance with Rental Agreement Materially Affecting Health and Safety - *See* Forms: Ten-Day Notice of Termination of Rental Agreement for Noncompliance with Rental Agreement Materially Affecting Health and Safety.

Term of Tenancy. . . . . **49**.

U V W X Y Z

Vehicles - *See* Parking or Commercial vehicles

Violation - *See* Notice of Complaint/Violation.

Writ of execution. 9.

Writ of garnishment . . . . 10, 92, 100.

Writ of restitution 76, 80-82, 89, 90, 95, 98, 99.

1 - 14

7-Day Notice to Pay or Quit - *See* Seven-Day Notice to Pay or Quit *and* Forms.

10-Day Notice of Termination of Rental Agreement for Noncompliance with Rental Agreement Materially Affecting Health and Safety - *See* Forms: Ten-Day Notice of Termination of Rental Agreement for Noncompliance with Rental Agreement Materially Affecting Health and Safety.

14-Day Notice of Termination of Rental Agreement for Material Noncompliance with Rental Agreement - *See* Forms: Fourteen-Day Notice of Termination of Rental Agreement for Material Noncompliance with Rental Agreement.

REGISTRATION FORM

If you purchased the *Tenant's Survival Guide* by calling the Order Desk, then you are already registered to receive notice when the laws change and the *Tenant's Survival Guide* is updated in accordance therewith.

If you purchased this book at a bookstore or by any means other than the *Tenant's Survival Guide* Order Desk, then you are not registered and will not receive notice when the laws change and the *Tenant's Survival Guide* is updated in accordance therewith. If you wish to be registered, simply complete the form below (or a copy of the form below) and mail it to the publisher.

REGISTRATION FORM

NAME _____

ADDRESS _____
_____
_____

Phone # _____

Point of Purchase:

☐ Bookstore (name of store) _____
☐ Mail order
☐ Other _____

Mail to: Consumer Law Books Publishing House
c/o Golden West Publishers
4113 North Longview
Phoenix, Arizona 85014

REORDER

To order additional copies of the *Tenant's Survival Guide*, call the Order Desk:

(602) 255-0100